Development in
Theory and Practice

Development in Theory and Practice

BRIDGING THE GAP

Jan Knippers Black
MONTEREY INSTITUTE
OF INTERNATIONAL STUDIES

Westview Press
BOULDER • SAN FRANCISCO • OXFORD

The photo of Jan Knippers Black on the back cover was taken by Martin C. Needler; all other photos were taken by the author.

Copyright © 1991 by Westview Press, Inc.

Published in 1991 in the United States of America by Westview Press, Inc., 5500 Central Avenue, Boulder, Colorado 80301, and in the United Kingdom by Westview Press, 36 Lonsdale Road, Summertown, Oxford OX2 7EW

Library of Congress Cataloging-in-Publication Data
Black, Jan Knippers, 1940–
  Development in theory and practice : bridging the gap / Jan
Knippers Black.
    p.   cm.
  Includes bibliographical references and index.
  ISBN 0-8133-1124-1—ISBN 0-8133-1125-X (pbk.)
  1. Economic development.   2. Economic assistance, American—
Developing countries.   3. Developing countries—Economic policy.
I. Title.
HD75.B54   1991
338.9′009172′4—dc20   90-20968
                                                                          CIP

Printed and bound in the United States of America

The paper used in this publication meets the requirements
of the American National Standard for Permanence of Paper
for Printed Library Materials Z39.48-1984.

10   9   8   7   6   5   4   3   2   1

To my mentors at American University,
including Ted Couloumbis, John Finan, Glynn Wood,
Larman Wilson, and particularly Brady Tyson
and the late Harold E. Davis

The law condemns the man or woman who steals the goose from off the common, but lets the greater villain loose who steals the common from the goose.
—Old English folk saying

Contents

Tables and Illustrations

Acknowledgments

The author acknowledges with gratitude the assistance of the Fulbright-Hays Program and the Mellon Foundation in funding portions of the research for this book. Special thanks are due also to Professor Jorge Nef of the University of Guelph, Ontario, for his critical comments on the manuscript; to my patient and helpful editor at Westview, Barbara Ellington; to my diligent typists, Frances Romero and Ronna Kalish; and to my husband, Professor Martin C. Needler, who first suggested the paradox format for organizing my thoughts. Errors and irreverences are, of course, my own.

Jan Knippers Black

Development in
Theory and Practice

Introduction:
In Pursuit of
Appropriate Theory

1 Talleyrand, asked for a definition of nonintervention, said it was a term used in politics that meant intervention. The problem with using a term common in public affairs is that such terms are adopted and adapted in accordance with particular needs and may in fact be employed by different spokesmen or at different times to convey contradictory meanings.

Development is such a term. It has no precise meaning, no generally accepted definition. Metaphors aside, society is not an organism with a genetically programmed innate potential. We cannot say of a society, as a gardener might of a flower, that it has become what it should be.[1] Like other terms that have acquired a positive connotation, *development* is user-friendly: It means whatever one wants or needs it to mean.

Why, then, should we bother to study it? For academics, the answer is simple. A term or concept in such common and yet multifarious use may be liberating. It gives us license to poach—to bring intellectual and scholarly traditions to bear on a broad range of issue and policy problem areas without becoming trapped by disciplinary, jurisdictional, cultural, or geographic boundaries.

There are more compelling reasons, however, for studying development. One is that, for better or worse, a lot of things are being done in its name that any well-informed person should know about. Another is that given the ambiguity and generally positive connotation attached to the term, useful things can be done in the name of development. Finally, the very open-endedness of the study of development gives us an incentive to elaborate our visions of what might be—a wagon to hitch to a star.

For the most part, however, it has not been the study of development and underdevelopment that has led to a mushrooming of official development assistance programs; rather, the latter has given rise to the former. In fact, the study of development has flourished in recent years, but its very currency has in some ways made the study of it more difficult. The more public attention in the wealthier countries has been focused on the ravages of poverty and the maldistribution of the world's bounty, the more elaborate, abstract, and jargonized have become our rationales for what we do or fail to do about it. And the more the literature has proliferated, the more strained has become communication among those who approach it from different perspectives, disciplines, and professions. Let us deal briefly with each of these obstacles.

USEFUL FALLACIES

It should not be surprising that along with a wealth of insight and information, the flourishing of development studies has also brought forth misinformation, disinformation, and new conceptual vehicles for ethnocentricity and prejudice. In the first place, there has been a serious disjuncture among field practitioners, theoreticians, and policymakers. In the design of theories and policies, informational vacuums tend to be filled by prejudice. In the second place, policymakers routinely invoke widely shared moral ideals to justify the pursuit of cruder interests. And finally, nationalities and classes clearly favored by global inequality seek relief from impotence or guilt through the resolution of cognitive dissonance. That resolution is likely to take one or more of the following general forms: (1) there is no problem; (2) there is a problem, but it is not *our* problem; (3) there is a problem, but it is not our fault; (4) there is a problem, but we are solving it; or (5) there is no solution. These circumstances of ignorance, interest, and psychological need have nurtured a number of useful fallacies.

Assuming Progress

India's progress since independence in increasing life expectancy has been truly remarkable; the figure has risen from an average of twenty-seven years in 1947 to fifty-seven years in 1988. Population has doubled during that period, with food production, overall, keeping pace—a consequence largely of the so-called green revolution. Food and other amenities, however, have not been efficiently distributed. In fact, there has been increasing inequality and pauperization in the rural areas. Whereas in 1947, 25 percent of the rural population was landless, by 1988 that proportion had risen to 40 percent. The landless were continually swelling the population of urban areas, placing severe strains on municipal governments. In Madras, slums or shantytowns accounted for 25 percent of the population in 1961, 33 percent in 1971, 40 percent in 1981, and 50 percent in 1988.[2]

For the developing countries as a whole, it is certainly clear that progress has been made in the period since World War II in some areas (e.g., life expectancy), but there has been slippage in others (e.g., self-sufficiency); and it is not clear that progress or development, by any definition, is inevitable. Immanuel Wallerstein, who has identified 75-to-100-year cycles of "expansion" and "contraction," or prosperity and depression, in the capitalist world economy over several centuries, has written that we are slipping into the downside of a cycle.[3]

At any rate, there does not appear to be any felicitous unidirectional locomotion, fueled by divinity or fate, that lets us off the hook. Nor is there convincing evidence that the thrust of policy to date on the part of rich countries and areas with respect to the less fortunate has been to the benefit of the latter. And while outcomes are not necessarily attributable to the intentions and efforts of policymakers and implementers, they are not wholly independent of them either.

Furthermore, although none would claim that there are easy ways for the "unpowerful" to influence policy, it remains true that "if enough people beat their heads against a brick wall, that wall will fall."[4] In short, there is no legitimate rationale for escape—through either complacency or despair—from concern about the planet and its passengers.

Patenting Modernism

In one version of a perhaps apocryphal story, a visitor to India asked Gandhi what he thought of Western civilization. Gandhi replied, "It would be a good idea."

Contrary to the ethnocentric and tempocentric impression sometimes conveyed by development literature, modernism was not invented by the West, much less by the United States. Nor is there anything particularly new about the essence or the major components of international development. One should not need a stroll through Egypt's Valley of the Kings or through the Mayan temples of Mexico's Yucatan Peninsula or along China's Great Wall to be reminded that the contribution of "the West" to modernity and its diffusion is a thin veneer, most likely soon to fall beneath another Asian layer.

Technology transfer is probably as old as trade, certainly as old as empire. Economic planning was presumably in effect in Egypt when the Pharaoh reacted to Joseph's dream by storing grain from the years of abundant harvest for the anticipated seven lean years; and the planning and social-welfare systems of the Incas were apparently in many respects superior to those of their contemporary Andean counterparts. The ambitions of larger or richer states with respect to their neighbors have always been coated with the rhetoric of higher cause—spiritual or material uplift. And as for unsolicited advice, we need no carbon 14 dating to judge it timeless.

For the affluent of the First World, as well as for the Westernized elite of the Third, a major obstacle to understanding the challenges facing less-affluent peoples has been a tone pervading official pronouncements, and even much of the academic literature, of self-congratulation on the one hand, condescension on the other.

The dichotomous use of the terms *modern* and *traditional* is generally more pernicious than a mere lack of definition. It may mean that we have lumped together under a single derogatory heading all cultures other than our own. As the opposite of modernism, tradition is the essence of the national self-determination and cultural identity that is everywhere under assault.

Furthermore, while there can be little doubt that the past several decades have seen an unprecedented diffusion of some of the values and life-styles of some of the most highly industrialized Western states and the near suffocation of many less-aggressive cultures, there is some doubt as to whether that diffusion is unavoidable and much doubt as to whether it is desirable or universally desired.

Any assessment of the achievements of the "West" must surely weigh in the balance its failures and self-destructive tendencies as well. Anthropologist Johannes Wilbert has pointed out, for example, that observance of the loving care with which some of the so-called "primitive" peoples of the Amazon Basin attempt to protect their ecological systems makes us look quite primitive by comparison.

Blaming the Victim

A director of the U.S. Agency for International Development in northeast Brazil, justifying the agency's efforts in 1963–1964 to undermine Brazil's regional development agency for the severely depressed Northeast, said, "They didn't see their problems as clearly as we felt we did."[5] All too often, U.S. officials in the post–World War II period have structured events in the Third World on the assumption that the problems in Africa, Asia, and Latin America lay in the quality of Africans, Asians, and Latin Americans. The blame for poverty and powerlessness has been placed squarely on the poor and powerless. It has followed, then, that the imposition of foreign models on their societies has been for their own good.

The tendency to blame the victim is by no means peculiar to the field of development. Means of explaining inequality so as to justify it were systematized in religion and philosophy long before such was undertaken by modern social science. Conservative Catholic thought, which has prevailed in Iberia and Latin America, at least until recently, held that existing social hierarchy was an expression of divine will (rather than, say, the outcome of a bloody conquest). Hindu rationalization was even more to the point: The higher castes were being rewarded in this life, as lower castes and outcastes were being punished, for their behavior in a previous incarnation.

The rationalization most common in the contemporary United States—an adaptation of the so-called Protestant Ethic—is even more devastatingly effective, more emboldening to the rich and demeaning and debilitating to the poor; it is that one's station is reflective of virtue or shame (e.g., of industriousness and thrift versus laziness and profligacy) in *this* life.

The business of explaining and promoting development probably has more than its share of the selfless and empathetic. Even so, traces of this ethic are sprinkled among the terms that have come into common usage. A number of perfectly good words have been devalued as a consequence of their use as euphemisms. Ideology, for example, has been used to designate the pursuit of self-interest by "have-nots." The pursuit of self-interest by "haves," on the other hand, has been labeled pragmatism.

Words like *secularism* and *rationalism,* used to distinguish modern societies from traditional ones, are often defined in circular fashion, thinly veiling the implication that they refer to the thought processes of clear-headed folks like us. Any attempt to define them in more precise terms runs the risk of making self-serving theories susceptible to empirical testing. Secularism in its most limited formulation connotes low receptivity to religious and ideological appeals, hardly a characteristic of the supposedly modern contemporary United States.

Rationalism is sometimes clarified by reference to such poles of Parsonian pattern variables as value instrumental action.[6] In theory, instrumentality should be an operationalizable concept, but even psychiatrists and clinical psychologists are hard put to determine whether the behavior of their patients is instrumental. And yet, we presume to know enough about the values and options available to a few billion people to determine whose behavior is instrumental and whose is not.

While there is an obvious correlation between national levels of wealth and industrialization and levels of formal education and literacy, formal education is not the only kind of education and illiteracy is not the same as ignorance, much less irrationality. Our assumption that non-Westernized folk are less rational than we are says more about our rationality problems than about theirs, and our assumption that the illiterate are ignorant is a projection of our own ignorance of them.

Certainly a glance at folklore challenges the view that the poor are ignorant of their own needs or of why they are not being met. The "Juan Bimbo" of Venezuelan rural folklore and the "roto" of Chilean shantytown humor are not subservient, grateful clients; they are shrewd operators who feign humility while trying to outsmart their patrons.

It may well be true, as Brazilian educator Paulo Freire has claimed, that "self-depreciation is a characteristic of the oppressed, which derives from their internalization of the opinion the oppressors hold of them."[7] But there is a very important shade of difference between self-esteem and sense of efficacy. The "fatalistic" conviction so often noted among the Third World peasantry that efforts to organize in pursuit of class interests would be dangerous and probably futile is empirically well grounded. It might be that a sense of efficacy on the part of the severely and systematically repressed would be beneficial to the society as a whole in the long run, but, as John Maynard Keynes said, "In the long run we're all dead"; and in the short run it could be quite suicidal.

Limiting the Options

In the late 1980s, U.S.-born Jesuit economist Peter Marchetti, who has been among the intellectual pathfinders of the Nicaraguan revolution, hosted an informal gathering in Managua for students and young Sandinista activists. The group's discussion generally centered on means of dealing with the country's dire economic problems. One of the guests, a middle-aged foreigner, tended to dominate the conversation with suggestions of expensive, highly centralized, high-tech approaches that the young Nicaraguans viewed as absurdly inappropriate. After he left, the local guests asked Marchetti why he had invited "that American businessman." Marchetti replied that that was no American businessman; that was a Soviet technical adviser.[8]

A Third World perspective that virtually equates First and Second World approaches to development, that views those approaches not as alternative ones but as the same inappropriate one, becomes increasingly widespread as the world shrinks and as the failures of large-scale development programs mount. Such a perspective must be disconcerting to many development theorists, policymakers, and practitioners of the overdeveloped world. The Cold War worldview, which has supplied the overriding rationale for most major programs and disbursements of foreign assistance by major First World donors, particularly the United States, has held that Third World countries have two options, and only two—dog eat dog or all eat dog—for organizing their societies and their economies. Those who would reject whatever is being marketed at a given moment as "private enterprise" are opting, by definition, for a "centrally planned economy," or "communism." At times, spokesmen of the Second World have appeared to be projecting the same message.

For most of the Third World in the postwar period, modernization has meant exposure to the influences, if not the dictates, of the First World. Such exposure has not, on balance, contributed to a narrowing of the gap either between rich and poor nations or between rich and poor within Third World nations. Per capita income in the poorest region of the world, Sub-Saharan Africa, dropped from $560 in 1980 to $450 (in 1980 dollars) in 1988. During the same period, per capita income in the industrialized countries increased from $11,000 to $13,000.[9] Moreover, in the 1980s the gap within was widening relentlessly in the First World's most recent colonial and neocolonial centers—Great Britain and the United States—and those two states exhibited other strong indicators as well of "de-development."[10] Staggering under unanticipated burdens of environmental contamination, resource depletion, inflation, unemployment, and, above all, debt, Third World nations may have little choice but to look to the First World for loans, credit, or "relief"; but they are no longer likely to look there for guidance.

Then what of the Second World?[11] Did it not promise a means more just and more readily sustainable of escaping underdevelopment? But alas, true socialism had no more of a reign in the Second World than did true liberalism in the First; as the twentieth century draws to a close, true socialism is utterly without a forum and the only true liberals to be found are bearing the socialist standard. As liberalism was to provide a platform for a previously excluded middle class, socialism was to be the vehicle for drawing the working class into political participation. As it turned out, the concept of a working-class state was not left devoid of all meaning; but as a new bureaucratic class assumed responsibility for major decisions, workers were left with control only of their own workplaces. The upshot, as a Polish sociologist expressed it to this author, was "a massive conspiracy by Poles as workers against Poles as consumers."[12]

Even if a Second World model remained intact, such a model, with its assumption that bigger is better and its stress on centralized decision-making and on production for its own sake, without regard for environmental constraints or for consumer preferences, would hardly be attractive to the contemporary Third World. And it is not intact. From the People's Republic of China through the Soviet Union and what used to be its East European bloc, "capitalist roaders" have the road all to themselves. Already, though, these newly overhauled vehicles must negotiate not only the bottlenecks of the model they are fleeing but also the washouts of the world system they would join. Most are mired in debt and sinking under inflation or austerity or both. The question now, as the Second World closes down, is whether its peoples will attach themselves to the First World or the Third.

The smugness of the First World's cold warriors at this turn of events is inappropriate to say the least. The winners, if there are such, of the Cold War, are not those countries that fought it but those that avoided its extremes, that were able to make the most of both free-market competition and government intervention in the public interest to generate dynamic economies underpinned by comprehensive social-welfare systems. Meanwhile, the worst of both worlds—of bureaucratic rigor mortis coupled with the utter unavailability or unaffordability of essential goods and services for large sectors of the population—is all too familiar in the Third World. But that is not to say that all options have been exhausted. There remain as many options as there are people with ideas and commitment to the common good.

SPEAKING IN TONGUES: THE COMMUNICATION PROBLEM

Despite the fact that no single discipline can lay exclusive claim to the study of development, the potential for escape from disciplinary shackles and reintegration of the social sciences afforded by the topic has not been fully exploited. Most studies falling under the rubric of development have found their points of departure in a single discipline and have failed to deal adequately with the interactions among cultural, social, economic, and political phenomena or have failed to take advantage of the insights that might be drawn from work in other disciplines. It seems, in fact, that the greater the volume of literature devoted to development, the more it gets pigeonholed into subcategories.

In addition to the gaps among disciplines, the gap that most needs to be bridged is that between theory and practice. Most of our theoretical approaches are pitched at a level too abstract—too global in purview, too dependent on aggregate data, in general too far removed from the workaday world of the would-be beneficiaries—to be much help to those who would actually design and/or implement projects in areas steeped in poverty. At the same time, there is an accumulated wealth of folk wisdom derived from on-the-job training that has yet to inform the theoretical literature. For the most part, theoreticians and practitioners appear to occupy different worlds and perhaps even speak different languages; at any rate, they are too infrequently found talking to each other.

There is also a breach between those who deal in the hardware of development (that is, the technology, appropriate or otherwise) and those who deal in the software (techniques of management and training); and there is a further breach between both of those categories and those who concern themselves, as scholars or practitioners, with the sociocultural, political, or environmental impacts of those technologies and techniques.

This is not to say that specialization is a negative development; it may be, in fact, a very necessary one. But with it comes an ever greater need for reintegration and cross-fertilization. This book does not pretend to satisfy that need; it does aspire, though, to call attention to it, to move the discourse in the indicated direction, and to make a modest contribution to the development of "appropriate" theory.

APPROPRIATE TECHNOLOGY
AND APPROPRIATE THEORY

Appropriate technology has sometimes been misconceived by advocates of Third World interests as necessarily referring to an older or lower order of technology. Such advocates have bristled at the idea of their countries being locked permanently into a lower order of productivity and their people subjected to unnecessary rigors in the accomplishment of potentially simple tasks. But the concept of appropriate technology does not apply to a particular level of technology; rather, it applies to a particular attitude about technology.

It rejects the "law of the instrument" approach to the selection of technology, whether the instrument be of high technology or low, in favor of selection based on a well-informed assessment of need and sustainability. Such an assessment would take into account shortage or surplus in the labor force; the particular roles and needs of the prospective employees or consumers; the availability of the resources needed for its operation; the impact of the new technology on community integrity and on the environment; and a host of other factors.

Perhaps the best indicator of the appropriateness of a particular technology or tool is its adoption, spontaneously, by a client or beneficiary community. The Kayapo Indian town of Gorotire, in the Brazilian Amazon, was selected by nonindigenous Brazilian investors in the 1980s to be the site of a gold mine. In the course of gaining access to the site and acceptance in the community, the visiting Brazilians recorded local dances on videotape and played back the tape to the villagers. As to the proceeds of the mine, the bargain struck, after extensive negotiation, was that the Brazilians would turn over to the Indians 10 percent of the returns for a designated period. After the mine began to produce, the Brazilians delivered 0.10 percent rather than 10 percent, telling local community leaders that they had misunderstood, or were misrepresenting, the outcome of their negotiations. When the Brazilians returned to Gorotire some time later for a subsequent bargaining session, they found that the session was being videotaped by the Kayapo.[13]

By the same token, the appropriateness of a theory with respect to development might be judged, to some degree, by its usefulness to those most in need—particularly organizers and members of low-income communities in the Third World and in pockets of poverty in the First and Second Worlds. Just as an inclination to appropriate technology does not imply rejection of high technology, the pursuit of appropriate theory does not imply the rejection of grand or macro theory but rather calls for the development of linkages that would facilitate cross-fertilization. A new body of midlevel theory might bring more of the findings of the various social sciences to bear on the work of planners and make implementers, or field agents, less vulnerable to blindsiding—to seeing their projects sabotaged by sponsoring agencies, local leaders, or supposed beneficiaries. Likewise, such theory might strengthen local leaders in their dealings with high-pressure donor agencies.

The social sciences, like the supposedly harder ones, have often succumbed to the law of the instrument. The availability of aggregate data and machines for crunching it has led us to portray human needs and governmental or societal performance in excessively compartmentalized ways. We may then take satisfaction in increases in aggregate income that in fact come at the expense of disaggregated community. We may fail to understand why target populations are less than enthusiastic about new opportunities extended by donor agencies or why benefits never seem to reach those sectors for whom they are allegedly intended.

Furthermore, those who deal in grand theory are understandably, perhaps necessarily, drawn to models that reduce actors to ideal types and predict behavior on the basis of a very limited number of factors. As anyone who has ever worked in development at the village level knows, the unexpected always happens. That is surely unavoidable; no model could possibly encompass all the factors. It makes a very great deal of difference, however, which factors are included and which excluded and how the predilections of actors are assessed. Economists in particular have tended to hold politics as a constant and to assume a profit-motivated "rationality." Greater familiarity by the theorists with the experience of the practitioners might lead to a more useful choice of factors and more realistic expectations of actors.

Have the theoreticians and planners alike failed to note that the greater the sums of money that have been spent on development in a particular locale, the less promising have been the prospects that any gains for the majority of supposed beneficiaries will be sustained? The fact that such sums in themselves generally denote inappropriate technology and inadequate planning only partially explains the frequency of spectacular failures. Nor do the inordinate overhead costs and the inevitable corruption that attach to big money projects provide sufficient explanation. Since the biggest investments in development kick in only when vested interests are perceived to be threatened, some skepticism as to the veracity of the stated goals of donor organizations might be in order. There would remain, of course, the very important questions as to whether donors', planners', and implementers' goals are in harmony and whether any of those goals are likely to be reflected in outcomes. And for the locale in question, even making benign and optimistic assumptions on other aspects of motive and outcome, there remain the legacies of dependency and debt.

Given all the factors likely to impede the development process, perhaps it is the occasional success that should most spark our curiosity. At any rate, if we are to push back the frontier of our ignorance and to find new patterns in the seeming chaos of development, we might start with a new order of questions, one that builds on what we know about interest and power relationships and organizational behavior, that idealizes neither supposed benefactors nor supposed beneficiaries—in short, one that addresses the real world, warts and all.

Such questions and, in general, the nature of interests and interactions among the many categories of protagonists in the development process will be dealt with in Part 3 of this volume. In the meantime, however, we will address ourselves also to a broader set of questions: What is meant by development? How is it explained? How is it measured? How is it planned, promoted, funded, and implemented by First World donors? By Third World governments? How is it sustained? And finally, what are its limits?

NOTES

1. As noted by Leonard Frank, "The Development Game," *Granta* 20, Winter 1986, pp. 229–243.
2. Data compiled by the Madras Institute of Development Studies, 1988.
3. Immanuel Wallerstein, ed., *World Inequality: Origins and Perspectives on the World System* (Montreal: Black Rose Books, 1975), pp. 12–28.
4. One of the columnist Ashleigh Brilliant's "pot-shots," or "unpoemed titles," syndicated 1975.

5. Peter D. Bell, "Brazilian-American Relations," *Brazil in the Sixties,* ed. Riordan Roett (Nashville: Vanderbilt University Press, 1972), chap. 3.

6. Talcott Parsons, *The Evolution of Societies,* ed. and with an introduction by Jackson Toby (Englewood Cliffs: Prentice Hall, 1977).

7. Cited in Coleman McCarthy, "Thinkers and Their Thoughts: Paulo Freire and Educating the Oppressed," *Washington Post,* July 31, 1972.

8. As told to the author by Peter Marchetti, Managua, January 1987.

9. Clive Crook, "The Third World: Survey," *Economist,* September 23, 1989 (special section, p. 3).

10. The Washington, D.C.–based Center on Budget and Policy Priorities reported that in 1990 the top 1 percent of the U.S. population would have almost the same after-tax income as the bottom 40 percent. The report also noted that the share of the national income going to middle-income Americans had fallen to the lowest level since the end of World War II.

11. First, Second, and Third World categories were first suggested in discussions at the United Nations in the early 1970s in reference to the production and consumption of petroleum. First World countries were those ranking high in energy consumption; Second World countries were those consuming less energy, but producing petroleum. Third World countries were neither high energy consumers nor petroleum producers. In common usage, however, First World has been taken to mean the relatively wealthy, industrialized capitalist states, and the Third World has referred to the poor, less-industrialized states. By implication or default, then, the Second World should be the so-called centrally planned economies.

12. Pawel Spiewak, sociologist and editor of *Republica* (Warsaw), June 1987.

13. The British Broadcasting Corporation aired a documentary feature on the Kayapo on June 3, 1987.

Part 1
Development in Theory: Meanings and Models

Defining Development
and Its Nemesis

2 Development, it has been noted, is a user-friendly term, having virtually as many potential meanings as potential users. If there is a commonality among its many uses, it might be in denoting enhancement, that is, increasing value or desirability; but that leads us once again back to subjectivity. The business of the land developer may be seen in very negative terms by community leaders or environmentalists. Likewise, the very limited concept of economic development now current among city and state governments in the United States and elsewhere—an elaborated version of the "cargo cult" designed to attract industry[1]—may be anathema to organized labor; pliable labor is assumed to be a prerequisite.

What so complicates the study of international, or Third World, development, however, is that the most commonly adopted meanings (and thus explanations and strategies) do not simply differ; from diagnosis to prescription, they are almost diametric opposites. Development is a standard borne by those who would promote the interests of the affluent and the powerful as well as by those who would serve the unaffluent and the unpowerful; by those who would expand the reach of the most-industrialized states and those who would shield the least-modernized from nefarious influences; by those who would stress the virtues of entrepreneurship and individualism and those who would nurture community and collective concerns; by those who would pursue strategies of top-down initiative and decision-making and those who advocate a bottom-up, or grass-roots, approach; and finally, by those who would exploit and maim Mother Nature for the benefit of either business or labor in today's world, as well as by those who concern themselves with a bountiful and livable environment for future generations.

The divergence of interpretations begins with the diagnosis of the central problem. In the late 1950s and early 1960s, when international development assistance was becoming a major enterprise and the academic community was laying out the rationales that were to support it, it was generally assumed that traditionalism was the problem and modernization was the solution. Dealing now with the flotsam of modernization, more-recent generations of theorists and practitioners are tempted to search for grounding in tradition.

IDENTIFYING THE PROBLEM

When much of the now-designated Third World was beginning to emerge from colonialism and poverty was becoming "underdevelopment," the problems seemed more than obvious to First World scholars. In some countries, the sharp skewing of land distribution resulted in poor land use as well as in concentration of profit and economic power. In others, the soil lacked nutrients, farming techniques had not changed since biblical times, and social and political organizations were highly fragmented. Subsistence farming and handcrafting of consumer goods generated no surplus for investment or for insurance against nature's tantrums. The most basic elements of infrastructure, such as roads, bridges, and dams, were primitive or nonexistent, and productivity was further stymied by the lack of health care and education. The solution seemed equally obvious: a transplantation of the clearly superior technologies (modes of production, e.g., industrialization), institutions, and ultimately habits and values, from West to non-West, or First World to Third.

By the late 1960s and to a far greater extent by the late 1980s, the thrust of late industrialization and other manifestations of the diffusion of "Western" culture had brought about dramatic changes. In demographics, one of the most consequential changes was urbanization. According to United Nations (UN) figures, the world's urban population, which had stood at 28.9 percent of the total in 1950, had risen to 41.1 percent by 1980 and was expected to reach 65.2 percent by 2025. Another change was the population explosion, which owed much to the diffusion of modern sanitation and medicine. In the late 1980s, world population was growing at the rate of about 88 million a year, and the UN Population Fund predicted a yearly increase of 90 million to 100 million in the 1990s.

In social organization there had been a considerable breakdown of extended family or tribal ties and a partial regrouping in such organizations as unions and parties. Social structure was also transformed, as the expansion of commerce and the growth of government itself generated middle classes, and industrialization gave rise to urban working classes.

In political organization, social and technological changes led generally to a weakening of regional caudillos or tribal leaders and to a greater concentration of power in the central government of the state. New patterns of trade, new modes of production, and increased productivity transformed the traditional market basket, resulting in the availability of a greater quantity and variety of consumer goods. And changes in attitude were manifest in rejection of communal ties and values and the embracing of consumerism.

WHAT PRICE "PROGRESS"?

There is no denying that the diffusion, or recycling, of the products and attendant social features of the vanguard of technology has brought many blessings to the Third World. But those are mixed blessings, to say the least, and the mix has often favored only a minority. Let's start with demographics. Although the provision of sanitation facilities and health-care services remains woefully inadequate in most countries, modern medicine has truly changed the face of the earth, bringing about dramatic improvement in infant- and maternal-mortality rates and thus in life expectancy. For the less-developed countries (LDCs) as a whole, life expectancy has risen over the past four decades from forty-one years to about sixty. One of the upshots, of course, of this modern miracle is what has come to be known as the population explosion. The explosion is often allotted the lion's share of the blame for the failure of development, or the failure of development to benefit the teeming masses of the Third World. (It is usually overlooked that rapid population growth was probably a precondition for the rapid economic growth that is seen by so many as the primary goal and manifestation of development.) The draconian measures for reducing the growth rate instituted briefly in India and over a longer term in China had many negative consequences, including exacerbation of the practice of female infanticide. Such measures are not likely to serve as models for other countries. Population growth drops somewhat with urbanization, but urbanization, with all its attendant problems, is hardly to be encouraged. The only benign formula we know of for dramatically reducing the growth rate is widely shared prosperity with greater opportunities, in particular, for women.

Urbanization has made possible the provision of such amenities as electricity and running water and such service institutions as hospitals and public schools. Indeed, as in health, gains in education, and particularly in literacy, have been impressive. The frantic pace of urbanization, however, and the sheer size of urban concentrations in some Third World countries, have placed a severe strain on municipal governments, resulting in extensive pockets of urban anarchy. And the population explosion has meant that on a global basis, while the absolute numbers of well-fed, literate persons rise, so do the numbers of the hungry and illiterate. The World Health Organization reported in 1989 that 1 in every 5 persons on earth—about 1 billion people—is suffering from malnutrition or disease. And the United Nations Children's Fund (UNICEF) estimated that 50 million infants will die of hunger and malnutrition in the 1990s.

Urbanization, along with technological advances, has facilitated the spread of the communications media, enhancing the distribution of information, but also of misinformation and of propaganda. It has also led to traffic congestion, pollution, and street crime. Progress in curing such respiratory diseases as tuberculosis has been offset by the development of new respiratory ailments resulting from the constant inhaling of gasoline fumes, particularly from diesel fuel, and other pollutants.

Changes in social organization have weakened the constraints imposed by family and community on individual behavior, dissolving patron-client networks, mitigating such practices as nepotism, and freeing the individual to choose his or her own locales, associates, and professions. But the same change process weakens also the socialization and security provided by extended families and traditional communities without necessarily generating enough jobs or social-welfare services to compensate for the loss. In fact, late industrialization, typically capital intensive, has scarcely begun to absorb the workforce so rapidly being pushed off the land or pulled by the attractions of the metropolis and swollen by the population explosion. Thus the new freedom may well be of the sort that means "nothing left to lose"—freedom to wander jobless, homeless, and hungry in alienated isolation. The streets of Bogotá, Bombay, and so many other cities have become cruel homes and schools for untold thousands of urchins, and this aspect of the Third World increasingly lurks beyond the gilded gates of the First World as well.

Socioeconomic changes have made possible new, more effective forms of political organization, resulting, in some cases, in the dissolution of feudal patterns; reinforced central governments have acquired greater capabilities for public service but also, given the expansion of military, paramilitary, and police forces, for surveillance and repression.

The new consumerism may have accelerated production and the creation of jobs. In fact, such attitudinal change may have been a necessary concomitant to the expansion of domestic markets, but it also increased demands for imports and contributed to burgeoning debt. Furthermore, it has generated an array of new problems. In India, for example, the new materialism is generally credited with the phenomenon of dowry abuse (see discussion in Chapter 6).

The spread of the new consumerism has not necessarily been reflected in the generation of a correspondingly large category of new consumers. The economic development strategy popular in the 1950s and 1960s that featured import-substitution industrialization was generally characterized by a simple transfer of technologies and product lines from First World to Third. Technologies thus were capital intensive and product lines catered to the middle and upper classes. The combination of production geared for the few and increasing demand by the many fed inflation and frustration and, in general, contributed to a climate of crisis.

Development planners might have met this crisis by increasing the range and volume of products to cater to the working classes and by taking other steps to accelerate the expansion of domestic markets, but the political and economic implications of such a commitment were generally frightening to elites. Thus, the most common reaction was that of dampening effective demand—in some cases so abruptly and by measures so harsh that military dictatorship seemed called for. Subsequently, planners, prodded by the International Monetary Fund (IMF) and other public and private creditors, turned again to an emphasis on production (often highly mechanized) for export, a strategy wherein the masses streaming into the cities were needed neither as workers nor as consumers. Meanwhile, land previously devoted to subsistence farming had been converted for export production.

Increasing landlessness is a particularly acute problem in much of the world, and development programs have done little to remedy it; in fact, such programs have sometimes made it worse. Richer farmers more readily have access to newly available products, technologies, and credit; and the enhanced value of the land tempts those richer farmers to buy out or push out their struggling tenants or neighbors. The alienation of the land—whether by force of arms or by market forces—has led, in many countries, to scarcity of basic foodstuffs and inflation of food prices. It has led to bloated urban labor forces and to ever-larger and more-desperate pools of migratory farm laborers. It has contributed to famine in Africa and to insurgency in Central America. Finally, it has contributed, in overdeveloped and underdeveloped states alike, to the ultimate, most profound kind of dependency, in which only a privileged or isolated few have the option of producing what they would consume or of consuming what they produce.

THE RECKONING

For many Third World countries modernization has brought spurts of rapid economic growth. For a number of them—especially the so-called

NICs (Newly Industrialized Countries)—it has brought about a major transformation in the nature of goods produced and exported, from unprocessed primary goods to processed ones, for example, or from primary goods to manufactured ones. A few countries that at midcentury were strictly dependent on wildly fluctuating markets for primary goods are competing now with the major powers in the marketing of state-of-the-art military hardware and other high-tech products. A few—but fewer still (Asia's "gang of four" [see Chapter 5], for example)—have even experienced rapid growth and economic transformation and at the same time achieved a more nearly egalitarian distribution.

For the great majority, however, modernization has been accompanied by chronic unemployment, chronic inflation, unpayable debts, denationalization of resources, environmental degradation, and a deepening of dependency. In the case of dependency, direct political ties between colony or client state and the metropole may have become attenuated and economic ties of investment, trade, and aid may have been diversified; but subsistence farming, almost everywhere under assault, threatens to go the way of subsistence hunting and fishing, and handicrafts have become virtually dependent on tourism for their survival. The world capitalist system has penetrated the steepest mountain ranges, the steamiest jungles, and the loneliest islands; and the community, in First World or Third, that does not depend for its livelihood on decisions made in faraway places by people unconcerned about its welfare is very rare indeed.

EMPOWERMENT:
AN ALTERNATE VISION

The mainstream of development professionals, pursuing the path of least resistance, continues to treat development—in practice if not always in rhetoric—as a top-down process. That implies control of decision-making by major donors in centers of established power; the diffusion of technology and other attributes of modernization from those centers to areas less fully integrated into the international economic system; the assumption of trickle-down of material benefits from those best positioned to profit from public or private investment to the neediest; and enhanced productivity as the goal and the evidence of development. Productivity, in turn, is measured in the currency values attached to goods and services.

The tendency to measure value, and thus development, in monetary terms is hardly surprising, given the fact that, at least in the most direct and immediate sense, money is what most of us work for. Nevertheless, as the United Nations First Development Decade (1961–

1971) gave way to the second, a growing number of theoreticians and practitioners of development were concluding that material product is the wrong goal and the wrong measure.[2] They refused to see socioeconomic change as developmental unless it proves to be nurturing, liberating, even energizing to the unaffluent and unpowerful. The focus, they said, should be on the animate rather than the inanimate—on human rather than material resources. The measure of enhanced value should be in the quality of life, including not only creature comforts and productive and creative capacity but also self-reliance and capacity to interact effectively with one's physical and social environment.

The bottom-up approach, designated in the 1980s in its most elaborated and ambitious form as empowerment, calls for attention to health and education, of course, but also to more effective locally based problem-solving techniques. Like some programs of the 1960s—generally meagerly funded ones—the approach encompasses the promotion of community development through self-help, but with greater emphasis on the process itself rather than on the completion of particular projects. Also, in the 1980s in particular, emphasis has been on the sustainability of the process enabling collective decision-making and collective action as well as any labor-saving or income-producing outcomes of such action.

The role of the development practitioner or change agent in such an approach is that of catalyst and information broker rather than of decision-maker or information giver, that of promoting self-reliance rather than dependency. It is not an easy role. Seeing promise in the recultivation of traditional ways, development specialists often feel that they are swimming upstream; the attractiveness to Third World peoples of modern ways and gadgets makes for a powerful current.

NOTES

1. For an explanation of the so-called cargo cult, as it emerged on isolated South Pacific islands, see Chapter 9, Paradox No. 16. In the modern elaborated version, localities, states, and nations seeing economic development as an exogenous force to be attracted build not only landing strips (airports) but also golf courses, convention centers, industrial parks, and the like. Strategies for attracting investment usually also include tax holidays or other fiscal incentives and various means of assuring that labor will be cheap and cooperative.

2. See Jorge Nef, "Development Processes: Contradictions Between Theory and Practice," *Worldscape* (Center for International Programs, University of Guelph, Ontario, Canada) 3, no. 1, Spring 1989, pp. 7–9; and Lester B. Pearson et al., *Partners in Development: Report of the Commission on International Development* (New York: Praeger, 1969).

SUGGESTED READINGS

Adelman, I., and C. T. Morris, *Economic Growth and Social Equity in Developing Countries* (Stanford: Stanford University Press, 1973).

Barnett, Tony, *Social and Economic Development: An Introduction* (New York: Guilford Press, 1989).

George, Susan, *How the Other Half Dies: The Real Reasons for World Hunger* (Montclair, N.J.: Allanheld, Osmond and Co., 1977).

Harrington, Michael, *The Vast Majority: A Journey to the World's Poor* (New York: Simon & Schuster, 1977).

Harrison, Paul, *Inside the Third World: The Anatomy of Poverty*, 2nd ed. rev. (Harmondsworth, UK: Penguin Books, 1987).

Hayter, Teresa, *The Creation of World Poverty: An Alternative View to the Brandt Report* (London: Pluto Press, 1982).

Hirschman, Albert O., *Journeys Toward Progress* (New York: Twentieth Century Fund, 1963).

Independent Commission on International Development, Willy Brandt, Chairperson, *North-South: A Program for Survival* (Cambridge: MIT Press, 1980).

Safa, H. I., ed., *Toward a Political Economy of Urbanization in Third World Countries* (New Delhi: Oxford University Press, 1982).

Thomas, A., and H. Bernstein, *The Third World and Development* (London: Open University Press, 1983).

Uphoff, N., and W. Ilchman, *The Political Economy of Development* (Berkeley: University of California Press, 1972).

Explaining Development: Models and Measurements

3 Any attempt to characterize competing models of development is handicapped by overlap and underlap and fuzziness at the margins. Most dichotomies coincide to some degree with what might be labeled First World and Third World perspectives. Such a division, however, fails to account for the fact that Third World elites, pursuing class interests, often adopt First World perspectives, and that a great many scholars and practitioners of development from the First World choose to identify with the nonelites of the Third World. Furthermore, the Second World, involved only modestly in either donor or client categories of the development game, is often overlooked entirely.

We might circumvent the fallacies of a territorial approach by speaking of concentrational versus redistributive, or elitist versus egalitarian, approaches, but such categorization would call for imputing to some players motives and values that are not acknowledged. We will begin therefore by segregating models and approaches into two very broad categories having their modern theoretical and philosophical roots in Europe in the eighteenth and nineteenth centuries. The categories had in common the assumption that progress, or development, was possible and desirable, but they differed in that one viewed the economic interests of nations and classes as being in harmony while the other viewed those interests as being in conflict. Not surprisingly, the states that promoted the view of harmonious interests have been those that were expanding their economic horizons and seeking to penetrate markets previously closed by colonial arrangements or nationalistic protectionism. Those same states, however, have not been averse to placing pragmatism over principle when their own interests called for protecting domestic markets or colonial or neocolonial relations. In fact, due to the fierce trade competition the United States has encountered since the early 1980s, particularly from Japan, the familiar call for "free" trade has recently been supplanted by a call for "fair" trade.

ASSUMING HARMONIC INTERESTS

Liberal Internationalist School

The Liberal Internationalist School attributes its paternity to Adam Smith, author of *The Wealth of Nations* (1776). Developed in reaction to mercantilism, which held that the maximization of a nation's wealth called for strict governmental control of international trade and investment and other economic activities, the new school called for the minimization of government intervention in economic transactions.

Liberalism, championed in particular by Great Britain in the nineteenth century and the United States in the twentieth, held that states had a common interest in the free flow of goods, services, and capital across national borders. Smith's laissez-faire principle was reinforced by David Ricardo's theory of comparative advantage.[1] That theory posited that states should take advantage of their raw materials, labor costs, technologies, or other strengths in order to specialize in those goods they could produce most efficiently, while trading for goods in which other states had the advantage. Consumers in all nations were expected to benefit from such specialization and from the elimination of tariffs, quotas, and other barriers to trade.

Development and Modernization Theorists

In the late 1950s and early 1960s, a group of scholars inspired by what appeared to be the virtually limitless opportunities and responsibilities of the United States in the postwar period began to build upon the principles of liberalism to explain economic growth and social change, or the lack of it, in the Third World. The approach posited that Third World states willing to eliminate trade barriers and other obstacles and to welcome investment and technological transfers from the industrialized states would be able to accelerate the development process. One of its proponents, Walt Rostow, even held that after achieving a stage he labeled "take-off," the process would be irreversible.[2]

Those approaching the issue from the discipline of economics chose to define development primarily in terms of economic growth and to measure it through aggregate data on gross national product (GNP) or per capita income, data that were blind to the skewing of income distribution. The accumulation, or concentration, of capital seen as necessary to promote growth was, at any rate, expected to be mitigated by a trickle-down effect. Other social sciences stressed the beneficial effects of the spread of Western-style education and communications and the attitudinal traits thus transmitted, such as rationalism, instrumentalism, and consumerism. The "revolution of rising expectations" was expected to accelerate social mobility, drawing more and more individuals previously steeped in tradition into the modern sector.

Political scientists weighed in with particular concerns for participation and institutionalization and their consequences with respect to stability. Samuel Huntington, for example, championed institutionalization, fearing that in its absence increasing participation would be destabilizing. Others saw structural differentiation, increasing governmental efficacy, or egalitarianism as more appropriate indicators.[3]

The scientific validation sought by scholars of the period eluded them, however, in part because their optimism, even implicit determinism, often led them to see what they wanted to see or to label whatever they saw as progress or development. Furthermore, their hesitance to acknowledge bias meant that arguments over values were generally presented as if they were over facts.

The optimism of that generation of scholars has been tempered by subsequent events: the spreading militarism of the 1970s, the economic deterioration of the 1980s, and, in general, the relative decline of U.S. influence. Nevertheless, paradigms underpinned by the assumption of harmonic interests continue to guide the major development programs of Western governments and international agencies.

Cultural Causation

One consequence of disappointment with political and economic trends in the Third World and of disillusionment with paradigms predictive of attitudinal and institutional change has been a reversion to emphasis on the explanatory power of culture as an independent variable. Samuel Huntington, noting that in their contemporary applications concepts of modernization and of Westernization are beginning to diverge, maintains that if we fail to see development and democratization taking place in the Third World, it may be because those are distinctively Western goals. He alleges that aspirations to wealth, equity, democracy, stability, and autonomy emerge from Western, particularly Nordic, experience, and that other cultures may prefer simplicity, austerity, hierarchy, authoritarianism, discipline, and militarism.[4]

Interdependence

As we shall see, much of the turf of harmonious and discordant approaches alike has been swallowed up in the 1980s by the encroachment of the new amalgamated discipline of international political economy. The concept of "interdependence," however, appears to encapsulate the tempered perspectives of the contemporary current in the harmonic interest approach. Deriving in part from attempts by Robert O. Keohane and Joseph S. Nye, among others, to deal with relations among industrialized states in the process of economic integration, the model (known in international relations theory as "transnational relations and complex interdependence") notes that many categories of actors other than nation-states—multinational corporations and transnational banks, for example—have gained importance in the international arena, and that economic issues and tools have become at least as important as national security issues and military force in molding relations among states.[5]

In analyzing relations between industrialized and developing states, theorists have noted a boomerang effect—that is, a new vulnerability on the part of the industrialized states to economic problems in the Third World. For example, although the high interest rates of the early 1980s in the First World, particularly the United States, were more devastating to the Third World than to the First, the consequent debt crisis in the Third World has threatened the solvency of U.S. banks and closed markets for U.S. manufacturers.

ASSUMING DISCORDANT INTERESTS

Marxism and Marxism-Leninism

Karl Marx was not the first philosopher to call attention to social injustice; even among scholars who consider themselves non-Marxist or anti-Marxist, however, he is given a prominent place among the founding fathers of social science, since so many of the concepts and analytical tools he introduced or elaborated have come into general usage for discussing inequitable social relations.

Marx posited that the manner in which individuals and society meet their basic material needs takes primacy over religious, philosophical, cultural, and other considerations in determining the broad outlines of social organization and ideology. Differing material interests, based on how one earns a living—e.g., whether through ownership of land or other assets or only through labor—result in differing perceptions of social reality and relegate individuals and families into social classes. Class conflict, in earlier times between feudal landlords and a rising class of industrialists and in modern times between those lords of industry and finance, the ruling "bourgeoisie," and workers, or the "proletariat," then becomes the driving force underlying political and social strife.[6]

Drawing from Hegel the principle of historical dialecticism, Marx theorized that any mode of production would have built-in contradictions or self-destructive tendencies that would undermine it until eventually it was replaced by a mode that was more efficient. The most important contradiction he saw in the capitalist system was the draining off of "surplus value"—the gap between what workers earned for their labor and what they paid for goods and services—into profits. This gap would lead to overproduction and underconsumption—thus to economic depression—as workers became less and less able to buy what they produced. Eventually a desperate working class would rise up in spontaneous revolution and destroy capitalism, replacing it with a socialist system, in which the workers themselves would collectively own the means of production. After a transitional period in which the working class would control the state, the state would wither away, unneeded in a classless "communist" society.

Vladimir I. Lenin, an impatient activist as well as an intellectual, did not anticipate a "spontaneous" uprising of the working class. Rather, he believed it was the responsibility of a "vanguard" of professional revolutionaries to educate and organize the proletariat and to lead them in the assumption of their historic role.

More important, though, to future analysts of unequal relations among states was Lenin's theory of imperialism. Building on the work of J. A. Hobson, Lenin asserted that capitalism had been able temporarily to circumvent the problem of overproduction through the conquest of foreign peoples and the establishment of overseas colonies. These colonies served as captive markets for the absorption both of surplus production and of surplus capital. According to his formulation, finance capital would become increasingly crucial to the process and would come to control manufacturing in the global economy.[7]

Dependency Theory

Whereas the Marxist-Leninist theory of imperialism seeks to explain why and how the dominant classes of the dominant capitalist powers expand their spheres of hegemony or control, dependency theory examines what this relationship of unequal bargaining and multilayered exploitation means to the dominated classes in the dominated countries. And whereas development and modernization theorists elaborated what they viewed as the *promises* of the diffusion of Western culture, technology, and money, dependency theorists (*dependentistas*) have seen such diffusion as an impediment to development, at least to development defined in terms of inclusiveness and egalitarianism.

Dependency theory, in a sense, represents the coming of age of a social science paradigm by and for the Third World. Its roots are to be found in the work of the UN Economic Commission for Latin America (ECLA) in the early 1960s, under the leadership of Argentinean economist Raúl Prebisch. He called attention to the deterioration in the terms of trade for producers of primary products and sought redress in Latin America through economic integration.

The search for means of understanding modern processes of perpetuating exploitative relations between First World and Third was carried on by other Latin Americans, notably Brazilians Fernando Henrique Cardoso and Teotonio dos Santos and Chilean Osvaldo Sunkel, along with German-American Andre Gunder Frank, who resided for many years in Chile.[8] It soon spread also to other Third World regions and to academic circles in the developed states. Whereas modernization and development theorists have been criticized for failure to concede biases and for confusing facts and values, *dependentistas* have been criticized for straightforward advocacy of radical structural change.

The assumptions that underpin dependency theory are in many ways opposites of those that underpin development and modernization theory. They include the following: First, economic interest has primacy over culture or attitudes in determining the distribution of power and status in national and international arenas. Second, the causes of underdevelopment are not to be found in national systems alone but must be sought in the pattern of economic relations between hegemonic, or dominant, powers and their client states. The perpetuation of the pattern of inequality within client states is managed by a clientele class, which might be seen as the modern functional equivalent of a formal colonial apparatus. Third, both within and among states, the unfettered forces of the marketplace tend to exacerbate rather than to mitigate existing inequalities. That is, the dominant foreign power benefits at the expense of its client states, and the clientele class benefits at the expense of other classes.

Implicit here are the convictions that development will not take place through the trickle-down of wealth or through the gradual diffusion of modern attitudes and modern technology; that the upward mobility of individuals expressed by their gradual absorption into the modern sector is no solution to the problem of the impoverishment of the masses; and that stability is no virtue in a system of pronounced inequality.

Whereas modernization and development theorists see foreign investment and foreign aid as critical to development in the Third World, dependency theorists see such investment and aid as means of extracting capital from client states. Even where such transfers from the developed states generate economic growth, *dependentistas* would expect it to be a distorted pattern of growth that exacerbates inequalities among classes as well as among regions within client states.

The Center-Periphery Model and World Systems Theory

The relationships hypothesized or described by dependency theorists have been incorporated by Norwegian scholar Johan Galtung into a model of elegant simplicity. According to the Center-Periphery Model, elites of the center, or metropolis, draw bounty from the periphery of their own state system (through taxes, for example) in order to be able to nurture and support co-opted elites of client or "peripheral" states. In turn, elites of those client states, dependent upon elites of the center for assistance in exploiting and suppressing their own peripheral populations, have no choice but to allow center elites to participate in or share in the product of the exploitation of the peripheral peoples of the peripheral states.[9]

World systems theory, pioneered by Immanuel Wallerstein, also views the world economy as segmented into core and periphery areas. Rather than focusing on interactions among governments, however, this approach calls attention to the transnational interactions of nonstate actors, particularly multinational corporations and banks. The international economy is said to be driven by economic elites, particularly of the developed capitalist states, whose governments normally do their bidding. The control centers of the world economy are then the financial rather than the political capitals. The farther one lives from such a center, the slower the trickle-down of its wealth.[10]

Wallerstein, who sees the ideas of *dependentistas* as generally falling within the world systems perspective, takes issue with more traditional Marxists and liberals alike for what he calls a rigidly developmentalist approach. That is, both schools assume that each nation-state must pass through the same set of stages, or modes of extracting surplus, in the same order. As he sees it, the nation-state system, which came into being in part as a convenience to economic elites of an earlier era, has ceased to be the institutional base of the global economy. The essential struggle, then, is not between rich and poor states, but rather between rich and poor classes in a global society.

INTERNATIONAL POLITICAL ECONOMY

The new field of international political economy (IPE) has been said to constitute a synthesis of modernization and dependency approaches.

Whether or not such a claim can be justified, IPE does embrace aspects of both approaches, particularly of their more modern Third World–focused versions; and it serves to diffuse, or perhaps confuse, what might otherwise appear a sharply polarized debate. At least in addressing Third World issues, the focus of international political economy theorists, like that of dependency theorists, tends to be on groups whose interests are defined with reference to social structure rather than on aggregate data relating to individual preferences. They seek to explain variation in class strength and behavior through comparative studies of agrarian production systems, industrial infrastructure, timing of development, and position in the world political economy. Drawing upon such class analysis, international political economy theorists generally accept the assertion of modernization theorists of a positive relationship between development and democracy. They accept also, to a point, the *dependentista* assertion that Third World countries have been disadvantaged by their participation in the global economy, but with the proviso that positive results have on occasion been achieved where Third World governments had the capacity to negotiate the conditions of their participation.

Thus the international political economy agenda recaptures the scope of nineteenth-century social concerns for the purpose of addressing contemporary policy issues. International political economy is not so much a new field as the resurrection of, or reestablishment of continuity with, an older one, one born of concerns about industrialization not only of the Third World but also of the First; one that recognizes the necessary interaction of economic and political factors. The artificial and inconvenient separation of social insights and data into disciplinary cubicles is, after all, a fairly recent expedient.

Rediscovered works in comparative historical development revealed that the sequenced stages modernization theorists expected to see transplanted from First World to Third had not even been characteristic of the First World. Gerschenkron's 1962 study of European trends, for example, noted that development took very different paths depending on the timing of industrialization.[11]

The observation that development follows no preordained sequence of stages is one that international political economy holds in common with the World Systems School. International political economy, however, faults the world system approach for underestimation of the role of the state in determining economic outcomes. Rejecting both the liberal preference for an unfettered market and the Marxist choice of state dominance of economic decision-making, International political economists contend that both state and market have important roles to play and that on occasion they are mutually reinforcing. Effective operation of the market may in fact be dependent upon the vigilance of a strong state, prepared to intervene where necessary. If, however, the state lacks autonomy from private economic elites, as Bates (1981) found to be the case in his study of African agriculture policies, its interventions are likely to subvert the market in developmentally detrimental ways.[12] Ultimately, the consequences of state intervention must depend to a considerable extent on the political character of the intervening state.

Like dependency theorists, adherents of the international political economy approach concern themselves in particular with "the contradiction between the geographic character of state power and the transnational character of economic power." Unlike most *dependentistas*, however, International Political Economy theorists argue that the penetration of foreign capital does not necessarily result in the contraction of the economic role of a Third World state. Studies by Peter Evans of petrochemical and iron industries in Brazil, by Frank Tugwell of the oil industry in Venezuela, and by Theodore Moran of the copper industry in Chile have shown that foreign-owned extractive sectors may provide sites for the expansion of state entrepreneurial activity.[13] Evans pointed out, however, that expansion of the state's role does not necessarily advance other categories of development, such as improved living standards for the majority.[14]

MEASUREMENTS AND FINDINGS

Saint Augustine, the original confused social scientist, reportedly said, "For so it is, oh Lord my God, I can measure it, but what it is that I measure I do not know." The empirical problems encountered in any attempt to move competing models and theories of development from the drawing board to a real-world testing ground are myriad.

Just as there are no universally accepted means of defining or explaining development, there are no value-neutral means of measuring it. Choices of definition and of explanatory models must determine how the process is to be promoted and how achievement will be assessed. Though the logic of such a sequence is clear enough, field operations may be guided by another logic entirely.

Aggregate Data
and the Law of the Instrument

It has been said that the way of least resistance makes men and rivers crooked; it can also make assessments of levels of development or evaluations of the results of development efforts unreliable or meaningless. At times the availability or acceptability of instruments of measurement is more readily apparent than is the guiding paradigm or the overriding goal. In such cases, the law of the instrument is likely to become the prevailing logic. Phenomena that are not measurable by the available instrument are then disregarded. In practice, what that ordinarily means is that the researcher wants something to count— items that can be aggregated.

The tendency to reliance on aggregate data calls for several precautions. In the first place, despite the seeming authoritativeness of numbers, it must be remembered that like other kinds of research and reporting, number-crunching not only is susceptible to human and machine error but is subject as well to intentional manipulation for political or bureaucratic advantage. A recent case in point involved the campaign in Great Britain to get motorists to switch to unleaded gas. An official of the Environment Ministry reported that the potential market for unleaded was 80 percent of the cars on British roads. At the same time, the minister for roads and traffic, having a different constituency and set of bureaucratic interests, put the proportion at 43 percent. What made this case particularly interesting was that the two officials were husband and wife.[15]

Furthermore, if we focus exclusively on aggregate indices or on means rather than ends, we easily lose sight of the central problem. Commenting in 1970 on Brazil's "economic miracle," President Emilio G. Medici said, "The economy is doing fine, but the people aren't."[16] This ultimate abstraction of the economy has by no means been uncommon in the literature of development, because the requirements of growth and those of redistribution are different and often contradictory. While some economists have included redistribution and generalized standards of living in their indices of development, many others—those who define development primarily as economic growth—have been content with such national aggregates as growth in GNP and per capita income. Countries engaged in a serious attempt to redistribute income and raise the standard of living of the majority generally have a poor showing in such indices. Thus international agencies have been more supportive of governments that gleefully announce their soaring GNP growth rates to the hungry masses.

For those who see development primarily in terms of egalitarianism or redistribution, aggregate data may also be an essential tool. The best known of the various indices providing summary measures of inequality, for comparison from state to state or from period to period in a single state, is the Gini Coefficient, based on the Lorenz Curve. The researcher may, however, wish to delve more deeply into the distribution of income within a particular population, in which case he might compare the income shares of groups of individuals or households with their population shares or compare the income shares of deciles of the population from the poorest to the richest. For example, at the same time U.S. economists were hailing the Brazilian miracle, Brazilian economist Celso Furtado was pointing out that the richest 900,000 Brazilians had the same total income as the poorest 45 million.[17]

In addition to measures of relative inequality, the researcher might want to examine absolute levels of deprivation and to compare them country to country or over time in a single country. Indices useful for that purpose are more varied and perhaps less reliable. They might include caloric or protein intake, the number of doctors or health practitioners serving a particular segment of the population, or the number of hours of work required to purchase some basic commodity. An index that has proved useful for that purpose—despite obvious drawbacks—is the physical quality of life index (PQLI) devised by the Overseas Development Council of Washington, D.C. It combines in a single number life expectancy, infant mortality, and literacy, each being assigned equal weight. The United Nations Development Program in 1990 released a report ranking 130 countries according to a new "human development index." Like the PQLI, the new index uses a combination of criteria to measure the quality of people's lives. It also measures inequalities within countries as well as between classes, regions, rural and urban areas, age groups, and sexes.[18]

The use of such data, however, may serve to befuddle rather than to clarify if it is incorrectly analyzed, a particular danger if researchers are dealing in data on countries or areas with which they are otherwise unfamiliar. A recent study indicating declining infant- and child-mortality rates in Chile in the 1970s, for example, might be doubly confusing. For one who had known Chile in earlier decades but knew nothing of Chile's political apocalypse of the 1970s, such findings might appear simply a continuation of earlier progress. Or the nonspecialist, unaware of the deterioration of living standards for the poorest after the coup d'état of 1973, might assume that the military dictatorship had pursued an enlightened social-welfare policy. In fact, even among the poorest in Chile there is considerable understanding of population planning. Thus the decline in mortality reflects in part a decline in the birthrate among the poor, owing to high levels of unemployment.[19]

Another problem associated with the law of the instrument has been the tendency of researchers to undertake an unwarranted leap in logic from what the instrument can reveal to what it cannot. It is far easier, for example, to establish correlation than to trace cause and effect. Thus correlations found to hold for a particular point in time have been assumed to be necessary and to suggest a causal relationship. A number of cross-national statistical studies, beginning with that of Seymour Martin Lipset in 1959, established a positive relationship between high levels of economic development and democracy, and it was assumed that that correlation reflected a functional interdependence between the two attributes.[20]

Such studies fell into disrepute in the 1960s and 1970s when the most highly developed of the Latin American states fell victim to brutal military-led counterrevolutions and when a few East Asian states achieved remarkable strides in economic development without a corresponding move toward democracy. More-recent studies have fallen back upon the more modest claim that industrial capitalism creates conditions that facilitate organization among middle and working classes, thus making it more difficult for elites to exclude them from political participation. It must be conceded, however, that elites may respond by reinforcing mechanisms of repression rather than by liberalizing. It must also be noted that class interests that coincide at one stage of development may not coincide at the next. The interests of middle and working classes, for example, tend to coincide early in the process of industrialization but to come into conflict at a later stage.

The Challenge of Intangibles

If the measurement of economic growth and of income distribution and inequality has proved challenging, measurement of nontangible attributes has been even more so. We have seen that since economic development was easier to measure than political development, some scholars have sought to impute the latter from the former. Likewise, in the 1960s, scholars hooked on number-crunching tried to measure the progress of democracy or "modernization" by attaching numerical values to attitudes or by counting whatever was available to count and drawing conclusions about attitudes from the results. Peter Ranis, for example, sought to correlate democracy and political stability with such "civilizing paraphernalia" as TV sets.[21]

Modernization. Problems encountered in assessing causes, levels, or consequences of "modernization" have arisen from the general fuzziness of the concept or at least the lack of consensus among users as to its meaning. There has also been considerable confusion as to whether the indices employed are intended to represent cause or effect or both and as to whether they are meant to represent a syndrome or alternative responses to Western influence.

Indices vary, but among those most commonly used have been (1) secularism and/or rationalism—that is, openness to the scientific and technological, accompanied by rejection of the religious and ideological;

(2) individualism and/or achievement orientation—that is, rejection of extended family or other collective interests in favor of unfettered pursuit of personal advancement; (3) consumption orientation; (4) geographic mobility and preference for urban living; (5) participation— that is, motivation and ability to organize, vote, and otherwise cooperate in active pursuit of individual and group interests; (6) egalitarianism and/or integration—that is, recognition of equal rights and provision of equal opportunity within families, among classes, and across multicultural or multiracial societies; and (7) expansion of literacy, education, and access to communications media. Political and sociological indicators have also included structural differentiation, stability, and organizational efficacy or institutionalization.

I suggest that this supposed "syndrome" exists only in the minds of wishful thinkers. To the extent that all of these attributes are characteristic of a single society at a given time, the conjuncture is surely an aberration. Many of these orientations, in fact, tend to be countervailing. A striving for personal advancement defined in consumer terms surely undermines a societal predilection toward egalitarianism and integration. Rapid urbanization places a heavy strain on national resources, and as Martin C. Needler has noted, increasing social mobilization and participation has a destabilizing effect on societies with limited resources.[22] The pooling of indices by scholars with underlying but unaddressed differences in values was bound to result in confused or contradictory findings as to relative levels of modernity and development.

Furthermore, it is questionable in the first place whether or to what extent these indices represent the so-called developed countries today, much less in the era when they were developing, and in the second place whether each of these values or attitudinal orientations is in fact contained in the package of influence diffused from West to non-West. Finally, it must be asked again whether each of these attitudes and trends is actually conducive to economic growth or redistribution or any of the other goals commonly associated with development.

Whether the rugged individualism of the pioneering spirit or the close ties to family and community and the cooperation that the frontier demanded bore more responsibility for development in the United States is an open question, but the "Protestant ethic," much touted as an engine of development, was hardly a secular code. Although a headlong pursuit of personal gain and avid consumerism may be more common in the United States today than pursuit of the common good and frugality, it is arguable that those orientations are detrimental to the continuing development process, and it is most unlikely that they constituted an unmixed blessing in earlier stages of development.

That the highly industrialized countries value science and technology is apparent enough, but that that orientation is accompanied by a rejection of religion and ideology is not equally apparent. The supposedly modern United States continues to rank very high in indices of religious belief and church attendance. Furthermore, while the anticommunist orientation that the United States has marketed so assiduously hardly qualifies in breadth or depth as a full-fledged ideology, it has certainly run against the current of social science. For its true believers, anticommunism has all the affective qualities that modernization theorists ascribe to ideology.

The diffusion of Western culture has contributed in various ways to urbanization, but there is considerable question both in the United States and in poorer countries as to the extent to which this demonstrates a preference for urban living. The exodus from rural areas, in North America and elsewhere, has come about not only and not necessarily because of the pull of job opportunities and cultural stimulation, but also because of the push of rural stagnation and the increasing control of land by agribusiness.

As for egalitarianism and integration, the United States hardly stands as a worthy model of those traits, and the attitudes on the subject that the country has marketed and displayed abroad have probably been even worse than the standards set in the domestic arena. Integration of the native population is not the major issue in the United States that it is in many other countries of the New World because the native population was almost obliterated, but the surviving North American Indians have by no means been integrated. The United States was among the last countries to give up outright slavery, and wherever it exercised police powers in the hemisphere in the early decades of the twentieth century, it introduced forms of discrimination previously unknown. There are many who argue that the lack of respect for human life demonstrated by the United States in Vietnam, or more recently in Libya and Panama, was indicative of the continuing force of racial prejudice.

Part of the problem in assessing the content of the cultural diffusion that has been labeled modernization derives from the fact that programmed and unprogrammed influences have not necessarily been in the same direction. In fact, they have sometimes been quite contradictory, and in those cases the programmed ones have usually been overriding. Consumerism in areas under Western influence has no doubt been spurred by the demonstration effect of material wealth and technological gadgetry in patron states but has also been generated as a matter of consistent policy, in order to expand markets for Western-based firms.

Social mobilization and participation are a different matter entirely. In the first place, participation in the United States, of late, has hardly been exemplary. In the second place, the programmed influence of colonial and neocolonial states has been brought to bear, on balance, on containing rather than promoting participation in the Third World. Certainly the U.S. and French constitutions and, more recently, European parliamentary systems served as models for newly independent states. Nevertheless, First World states have normally been hostile to social mobilization in the Third World and have continually thwarted attempts to expand participation and give substance to the form of democracy. When the American empire was young, that great crusader Woodrow Wilson sent in the marines to Central America and the Caribbean to impose free and fair elections, but marines writing of their experiences put "free and fair" in quotes.[23] Little wonder that official U.S. rhetoric of the 1980s had a familiar ring. Meanwhile the French, touting a strong democracy at home, resist the threat of democracy in the South Pacific. The islanders are not very happy with the French choice of their neighborhood as a site for nuclear-weapons testing.

The role of Western cultural diffusion in the expansion of literacy, education, and access to the communications media in the Third World is also a mixed bag. Direct foreign assistance for those efforts has often had more to do with attempting to influence content than with promoting learning for its own sake. The *concientização,* or consciousness-raising, approach to literacy training that was launched by Paulo Freire in Brazil in the early 1960s was denounced by U.S. officials as subversive. On the other hand, the commander of the U.S. military group in Brazil in the late 1960s praised military involvement in primary education "because people can't operate complex machines, such as computers, if they can't read the instructions."[24] Because of their overall socioeconomic orientations, the Third World governments most dedicated to the promotion of literacy and education have often been those most strongly opposed by the First World.

Formal education is not necessarily a prerequisite to other aspects of development, much less a panacea. There is considerable evidence, whether as a consequence of content or structure, that it may even serve to delay the presentation of majority demands. Formal education provides yet another channel for misinformation as well as for information. The process is not necessarily humanizing; nor does it necessarily confer self-esteem and a sense of efficacy. Rolland Paulston noted that Quechua-speaking Indian children in Peru subjected to education about alien traditions taught in Spanish by whites learned to depreciate themselves and their own culture.[25] Furthermore, advanced training for nonexistent jobs contributes to the brain drain.

Likewise, the consequences of the expansion of the communications media are largely dependent upon flow and content. Expansion of the media facilitates communication from the top down, but it need not facilitate communication from the bottom up. On the contrary, it may contribute to "massification" as an alternative to association. As the political, socioeconomic, and even cultural content of communications in many Third World countries has been censored by dictatorships supported by First World governments, the most salient role of the media has been demand creation, or the dissemination of consumerism, which, as Alejandro Portes argued, is hardly conducive to development. Defining national development as (1) sustained economic growth and generation of self-sustained industrial growth centers; (2) income redistribution on an egalitarian basis; and (3) emergence of an enhanced national self-image, Portes saw consumerism as a serious threat to development goals. He noted that the capital accumulation and investment necessary for launching the development process calls not for individual fulfillment expressed in consumption but rather for collective discipline and sacrifice.[26] Demand by the privileged few for technologically advanced gadgetry and other durable goods generally perpetuates the drain of resources from the underdeveloped to the overdeveloped world and defers any national attempt to meet the more basic needs of the larger population. Furthermore, even when "modern" industry moves to the so-called Third World, it tends to be capital-intensive (thus offering little employment) and geared to the production of durable goods that only a small sector of the population can afford.

Portes also notes that in psychosocial terms it has been not the supposed attributes of modernity but rather ideology and revival of some aspects of tradition, generally in combination, that have actually contributed to development. Ideology has served to justify the sacrifices required, and retention of tradition has contributed to legitimation of wide-ranging transformation.

Daniel Lerner asserted in 1965 that social change everywhere was a function of the number of individuals adopting the attitudes and behavior patterns associated with modernity.[27] Social change by individual co-optation would be at best a 500-year plan. But if this social change is meant to incorporate such goals as redistribution and democracy, the available evidence suggests that the change promoted by "moderns" tends to be in a different direction.

This "modern man," having adopted the tastes, material needs, and attitudes of the stereotyped West, and finding himself awash in a sea of "traditionals," becomes alienated from, and perhaps even contemptuous of, the majority of his countrymen. (Businessmen linked to multinational corporations and military establishments dependent on foreigners for training and equipment are by definition in the modern sector.) In a context of scarce resources, modern man is likely to see popular demands for a larger share of the pie as a threat to his life-style. If this modern man were really the rugged individualist he is purported to be, and if the traditional majority were as strongly oriented toward collective pursuit of interests as they are alleged to be, modernity might pose no great danger. In fact, however, if the poor were so collectively oriented, they might not be poor in the first place. And modern man, far from depending on his own devices, unites with other individuals and entities—national and foreign—whose interests are threatened and plots to protect his life-style, at whatever cost to the nation as a whole. It appears, then, that the consequences of modern-ization have more often been the opposite of those hypothesized by modernization and development theorists.

Empowerment. The concept of empowerment, which gained popu-larity in the 1980s, particularly among village-level practitioners, applies primarily to a strategy rather than to a theoretical model. For that reason and also because of the chasm generally separating theoreticians and practitioners, the concept has been less vulnerable than those associated with theoretical models to awkward attempts to operation-alize and measure it with pretense of numerical exactitude. Most efforts to identify contributing factors and to assess levels of achievement have been subjective.

Albert O. Hirschman, one of the few major theoreticians of devel-opment who has focused on process at the grass-roots level, has noted that "the whole venture of grass-roots development has arisen in good measure from a revulsion against the worship of the 'gross national product' and of the 'rate of growth' as unique arbiters of economic and human progress." He also observes that those who engage in the venture see it as intrinsically worthwhile, without regard to macroeconomic consequences.[28]

It should be possible to come up with indices of empowerment no less reliable than those that have been used in the past to measure modernization and other such abstract concepts, but that really is not saying very much. It should be possible, for example, to count, if not on a global scale, at least on a national or regional one, the number of organizations springing from or responding to nonelite communities and to track the increase or decrease in their numbers over time. Such an effort would bog down immediately, however, in disagreement, both in principle, or definition, and in fact, over which organizations were genuinely representative of grass-roots interests as opposed to representing efforts by elites to manipulate development at the grass roots.

Measuring the effectiveness of such groups on any kind of macro scale would be even more difficult. It would run the risk of slipping into some of the fallacies that crippled modernization and development approaches—for example, assuming a kind of omniscience on the part of researchers that would allow us to know what constitutes self-reliance and successful problem-solving among peoples and environments unfamiliar to us, and falling back upon economic criteria for measuring essentially psychological, sociological, and political phenomena. That is not to say that attempts to refine indices and to measure progress toward empowerment would not be worthwhile but just to point out that at best the results would be far from precise; and whatever the results, they would be unlikely to change any minds about the value of grass-roots efforts and the appropriateness of empowerment as a goal.

While noting the dubious utility of seeking to assess the "overall" impact of grass-roots development, Hirschman has made a number of observations that should be useful to those who would understand its dynamics or seek to promote it. Among them: (1) Social energy may be conserved and transformed. Invested unsuccessfully in a particular kind of collective action, social energy is likely to reappear in a different form. Hirschman's example is that of a group frustrated in a "radical" undertaking—a land takeover—remobilizing some years later to form a successful cooperative. I would add that examples of the reverse— remobilization for more "radical" undertakings—are also common. (2) Social action projects having only economic goals initially may give rise to explicitly political activism. (3) A cooperative must break even in order to survive, but economic success is not the only kind of success; any sort of collective enterprise should serve educational purposes and may well spin off other such enterprises. (4) There is no preordained sequence in development; education, for example, may precede collective action in pursuit of economic goals, but economic pursuits may also set in relief the need for literacy or other fruits of education. (5) Grass-roots development does not necessarily require the prior seizure of the central power of the state. (6) Authoritarian or elitist rule requires that subjects concern themselves exclusively with their own welfare and that of their immediate family, distrusting their neighbors. Thus empowerment, or grass-roots development, is by nature collective or communal.[29]

Many of the ideas and ideals that characterize the concept of development as empowerment have been expressed as goals of international organizations. The idea of "integrated rural development," for example, as promoted in the 1960s and 1970s by the World Bank and the United Nations, rejected conventional planning methods in favor of an approach involving local communities in every step of the process, from expression of needs and setting of priorities to implementation of projects. The approach also called for comprehensiveness, for interrelated actions on various fronts, i.e., community organization, education, curative and preventive medicine, innovation in irrigation and water purification, and enhanced agricultural productivity.

In practice, however, the required integration of efforts rarely took place. The bureaucracies involved, international or foreign and domestic alike, generally resisted pooling personnel and funds and sharing responsibilities and credit or blame. At any rate, large bureaucracies seem incapable of genuinely involving people at the community level in decision-making. The upshot was that almost any project undertaken in rural areas fell under the rubric of integrated rural development; and the label served to confer legitimacy and a progressive cover on some very conventional projects that contributed to the further concentration of wealth in rural areas and the out-migration of peasant populations.

A report prepared by the UN Research Institute for Development in 1974, pursuant to resolutions adopted by the Economic and Social Council and the General Assembly, called for a new "unified" approach emphasizing various kinds of structural and institutional change.[30] Success should be measured not in aggregate indices of growth, like GNP, but in the involvement of the entire target community in the development process; in the enhancement of social equity; in the cultivation of human potential; and in the capacitation of the community to set and meet its own goals. Such an approach, running counter to the interests of political and economic elites, was not likely to be pursued by many governments. Empowerment, however, has been the motivating vision of a great many small nongovernmental organizations based in the First World or the Third.

NOTES

1. See Adam Smith, *An Inquiry Into the Nature and Causes of the Wealth of Nations* (New York: P. F. Collier, 1901; first published 1776); and David Ricardo, *Works and Correspondence,* ed. Piero Sraffa, with the collaboration of M. H. Dobb (Cambridge, UK: University Press for the Royal Economic Society, 1951–1957).

2. Walt W. Rostow, *The Stages of Economic Growth: A Non-Communist Manifesto* (London: Cambridge University Press, 1960).

3. Gabriel Almond and G. Bingham Powell, *Comparative Politics: A Developmental Approach* (Boston: Little, Brown and Co., 1966); and Samuel Huntington, *Political Order in Changing Societies* (New Haven: Yale University Press, 1968).

4. Samuel Huntington and Myron Weiner, eds., *Understanding Political Development* (Boston: Little, Brown and Co., 1987), pp. 21–28.

5. See Robert O. Keohane and Joseph S. Nye, *Power and Interdependence: World Politics in Transition* (Boston: Little, Brown and Co., 1977).

6. Karl Marx, *Capital* [first published 1867], *The Communist Manifesto* [first published 1848], *and Other Writings,* ed. and with an introduction by Max Eastman; with an essay on Marxism by V. I. Lenin (New York: Modern Library, 1932).

7. Vladimir I. Lenin, *Imperialism: The Latest Stage in the Development of Capitalism* (first published in Petrograd 1919), trans. J. T. Kozlowski (Detroit: Marxism Educational Society, 1924); see also Lenin, *Collected Works* (Moscow: Progress Publishers, 1960–1970).

8. See, for example, Fernando Henrique Cardoso and Enzo Faletto, *Dependencia y desarrollo en América Latina* (Mexico City: Siglo XXI, 1969); Teotonio Dos Santos, *El nuevo carácter de la dependencia* (Santiago de Chile: Facultad de Ciencias Economicas y Sociales [CESO], 1968); Andre G. Frank, *Development and Underdevelopment in Latin America* (New York: Monthly Review Press, 1968); Osvaldo Sunkel, "Política nacional de desarrollo y dependencia externa," *Estudios Internacionales* 1, April 1967.

9. See, for example, Johan Galtung, *Essays in Peace Research* (Copenhagen: Eilers, 1975); *Development, Environment, and Technology: Toward a Technology for Self-Reliance* (New York: UNCTAD Secretariat, 1979); and *The True Worlds: A Transnational Perspective* (New York: Free Press, 1980).

10. Probably the best known of several books and articles in which he has elaborated his theory of development is Immanuel Wallerstein, *The Modern World-System: Capitalist Agriculture and the Origins of the European World-Economy in the Sixteenth Century* (New York: Academic Press, 1974).

11. Alexander Gerschenkron, *Economic Backwardness in Historical Perspective* (Cambridge: Harvard University Press, 1962).

12. Robert H. Bates, *Markets and States in Tropical Africa* (Berkeley: University of California Press, 1981).

13. See Franklin Tugwell, *The Politics of Oil in Venezuela* (Stanford, Calif.: Stanford University Press, 1975); Theodore H. Moran, *Multinational Corporations and the Politics of Dependence: Copper in Chile* (Princeton: Princeton University Press, 1975); and Peter Evans, *Dependent Development: The Alliance of Multinational, State and Local Capital in Brazil* (Princeton: Princeton University Press, 1979).

14. Peter Evans, "Foreign Capital and the Third World State," pp. 319–352 in Huntington and Weiner, eds., op. cit.

15. *Economist,* March 18, 1989, p. 59.

16. Cited in Dan Griffin, "The Boom in Brazil; An Awful Lot of Everything," *Washington Post,* May 27, 1973.

17. Cited in Eduardo Galeano, "The De-Nationalization of Brazilian Industry," *Monthly Review* 21, no. 7, 1969, pp. 11–30.

18. United Nations Development Program, *Human Development Report 1990* (London: Oxford University Press, 1990).

19. David E. Hojman, "Neoliberal Economic Policies and Infant and Child Mortality: Simulation Analysis of a Chilean Paradox," *World Development* 17, no. 1, January 1989, pp. 93–108.

20. Seymour Martin Lipset, *Political Man: The Social Basis of Politics* (New York: Anchor Books, 1963).

21. Peter Ranis, *Five Latin American Nations: A Comparative Political Study* (New York: Macmillan Co., 1971).

22. Martin C. Needler, *Political Development in Latin America: Instability, Violence, and Evolutionary Change* (New York: Random House, 1968), chap. 5.

23. The attitudes and methods of the U.S. "enforcers" of "democracy" in Latin America in the early twentieth century are revealed in Ronald Schaffer, "The 1940 Small Wars Manual and the 'Lessons of History,' " *Military Affairs* 36, no. 2, April 1972, pp. 46–51.

24. Major General Richard J. Seitz, commander of the U.S. Delegation to the Joint Brazil-United States Military Mission, October 1968–July 1970. Interview, Washington, D.C., June 4, 1973.

25. Rolland G. Paulston, "Estratificación social, poder y organización educational: el caso peruano," *Aportes,* no. 16, April 1970, pp. 91–111.

26. Alejandro Portes, "Modernity and Development: A Critique," *Studies in Comparative International Development* 9, no. 2, Spring 1974, pp. 247–279.

27. Daniel Lerner, *The Passing of Traditional Society: Modernizing in the Middle East* (New York: Free Press, 1965), p. 83.

28. Albert O. Hirschman, *Getting Ahead Collectively* (New York: Pergamon Press, 1984).

29. Ibid.

30. Claude Ake, *A Political Economy of Africa* (Lagos: Longman Group, Ltd., 1981), pp. 152–156.

SUGGESTED READINGS

Brown, Michael Barratt, *Models in Political Economy: A Guide to the Arguments* (Boulder: Lynne Rienner, 1985).

Cardoso, Fernando Henrique, and Enzo Faletto, *Dependency and Development in Latin America* (Berkeley: University of California Press, 1979).

Chilcote, Ronald H., *Theories of Development and Underdevelopment* (Boulder: Westview Press, 1984).

Evans, Peter B., Dietrich Rueschemeyer, and Theda Skocpol, eds., *Bringing the State Back In* (New York: Cambridge University Press, 1985).

Evans, Peter B., and John D. Stephens, "Development and the World Economy," chap. 22 in Neil F. Smelser, ed., *The Handbook of Sociology* (Newbury Park, Calif.: Sage Publications, 1988).

Frank, Andre Gunder, "The Development of Underdevelopment," in James D. Cockcroft et al., *Dependence and Underdevelopment: Latin America's Political Economy* (New York: Doubleday, 1972).

Galtung, Johan, "A Structural Theory of Imperialism," *Journal of Peace Research* 8, no. 2, 1971.

Heilbroner, Robert L., *The Worldly Philosophers: The Lives, Times, and Ideas of the Great Economic Thinkers* (New York: Time Incorporated, 1961).

Kay, Geoffrey, *Development and Underdevelopment: A Marxist Analysis* (New York: St. Martin's Press, 1975).

Lindblom, Charles, *Politics and Markets: The World's Political Economic Systems* (New York: Basic Books, 1977).

Petras, James, *Critical Perspectives on Imperialism and Social Class in the Third World* (New York: Monthly Review Press, 1978).

Prebisch, Raúl, *Change and Development: Latin America's Great Task* (Washington, D.C.: Inter-American Development Bank, 1970).

Rodney, Walter, *How Europe Underdeveloped Africa* (London: Bogle-L'Ouverture Publications, 1972).

Seligson, Mitchell A., ed., *The Gap Between Rich and Poor: Contending Perspectives on the Political Economy of Development* (Boulder: Westview Press, 1984).

So, Alvin Y., *Social Change and Development: Modernization, Dependency, and World-System Theories* (Newbury Park, Calif.: Sage Publications, Inc., 1989).

Wallerstein, Immanuel, *The Politics of the World-Economy: The States, the Movements, and the Civilizations* (Cambridge: Cambridge University Press, 1984).

Part *2*
Development in Practice:
Strategies and Issues

Donor Strategies
and Programs

4 As noted in Chapter 1, international development as such is by no means an exclusively modern or Western phenomenon. Nevertheless, the contemporary infrastructure and modus operandi, based on globally systematized divisions into donor and client states and institutions, is an expression of the severely skewed post–World War II allocation of resources and ambitions on the one hand, needs and vulnerabilities on the other. In the aftermath of that war, with Europe and much of the Orient laid waste, U.S. economic and military superiority seemed beyond challenge.

U.S. DEVELOPMENT
AND FOREIGN ASSISTANCE POLICY

The United States emerged from that war with three-fourths of the world's invested capital and two-thirds of its industrial capacity. The national neurosis resulting from recognition of such a skewed distribution was perhaps less one of guilt than one of paranoia. Diplomat George Kennan, noted as the author of the policy of containment, observed in 1948:

We have about 50% of the world's wealth but only 3.6% of the population. Our real task in the coming period is to devise a pattern of relationships which will permit us to maintain this position of disparity. . . . We need not deceive ourselves that we can afford today the luxury of altruism and world-benefaction. . . . We should cease to talk about vague and unreal objectives such as human rights, the raising of living standards, and democratization. . . . The final answer might be an unpleasant one, but . . . we should not hesitate before police repression by the local government.[1]

The extent of U.S. dominance of the international capitalist system at that time dictated that the strategies and tactics characterizing the broader development game would conform, at least initially, to U.S. business and bureaucratic interests, and that the rhetoric would reflect the fears and passions—as perceived or inflamed by policymakers—of the tuned-in U.S. public. On the client or supplicant side of the equation, Third World states, individually or collectively, have on occasion countered with development programs of their own design, but for the most part the less-developed countries (LDCs) have had little choice but to conform or react to blueprints drawn up elsewhere.

There were a couple of catches, however, to this general scheme. In the first place, the skewing of resources in this case was so severe that without remedial action the United States would be left virtually without trading partners. Thus was born the program of massive support for European reconstruction known as the Marshall Plan. The other catch, as seen by policymakers, was that the U.S. public would be insufficiently supportive of a policy premised upon the maintenance of empire for its own sake. The remedy for that problem was supplied by the dissembling and general nastiness of Joseph Stalin, the Soviet acquisition of the atomic bomb, and the success of the Chinese Communist revolution. A set of policies designed in part to maintain and expand U.S. economic supremacy could be premised upon an all-encompassing threat to U.S. survival.

For the United States, then, and by extension for donor entities in general, the idea of development as a process and a goal for the Third World toward which the First World should be of assistance grew out of the felicitous experience with the Marshall Plan in Europe and out of Cold War fears and ambitions. Within that framework, moreover, development strategies, even more than theoretical models, have been closely associated with larger economic and political trends.

Major changes in U.S. development strategy have not always coincided, however, with changes in administration. Sometimes they constitute a part of the changing climate of opinion that is a harbinger of political change to come. And owing to bureaucratic inertia or sabotage, among other things, there is often a considerable lag between the announcement of a new policy, or the rise or peaking of a policy's popularity, and the beginnings of implementation. Furthermore, whatever the intentions of a president or administration, development policy, in the course of moving through the U.S. Congress, the U.S. bureaucracy, and then client country governments and institutions, and finally interacting with supposed beneficiaries, is certain to become an amalgam of varied, and even in some cases competing, enterprises. From an empowerment perspective, that is not necessarily disadvantageous, as we shall see in Part 3.

Security and Economic Interests

Along with reviving the economies of Western Europe, the Marshall Plan, through which some $13 billion was transferred between 1948 and 1951, was seen as serving to block the spread of Soviet influence and to undergird free-market economies in the area. Thus when it began to appear that other countries and areas were slipping out from under U.S., or "Western," control and veering toward socialism, economic aid and development programs were seen as logical accompaniments to military aid and training programs.

Initially in support of the Truman Doctrine of 1947,[2] under guise of which the United States supplanted British hegemony in Greece, Turkey, and Iran, the Truman administration initiated the Point IV foreign assistance program. The authorizing legislation, called the Act for International Development, passed in 1950, created the Technical Cooperation Administration (TCA) to direct technical assistance to developing countries. Whereas capital alone sufficed to generate reconstruction and revive economies in Europe, it was assumed that the less-developed states would require training and the transfer of the latest in Western technology as well. The appropriateness of the most advanced technology was scarcely even questioned until the mid-1960s.

The Mutual Security Act of 1951 replaced both the TCA and the Economic Cooperation Administration, which had supervised the Marshall Plan, with the Mutual Security Agency (MSA). The agency's primary responsibilities were political and military, and its economic development component was intended also to serve those ends, above all to counter the spread of Communist influence in the Far East. By the time the MSA was replaced, in 1955, by the International Cooperation Administration (ICA), the focus of concern—and about half of the MSA's $600 million economic aid disbursals—had shifted to the Middle East and South Asia. Meanwhile, in 1954, Public Law 480 had created the Food for Peace program, to be administered in part by the Department of Agriculture. It was intended to ease world hunger as well as to expand overseas markets for U.S. agricultural commodities, especially grains.

The approach to development that was undertaken in the 1950s and that in most particulars survived at least through the 1960s stressed the promotion of increased production and productivity, especially through macroeconomic planning; institution-building; public investment in large-scale infrastructure projects (e.g., highways, dams); training and technical assistance, stressing First World technologies and bureaucratic procedures; and the facilitation of private trade and investment abroad.

Planning stressed attention to comparative advantage, which for most LDCs was seen to lie in the export of primary products, and to infrastructure projects that enhanced the feasibility of foreign investments. Foreign assistance was not normally tied to specific projects but was often tied to the purchase of capital goods from the United States and to the elimination of tariffs or regulations viewed as obstacles to trade and investment. Where Third World governments resisted such pressures and continued to protect nascent industries, or where cheap labor offered an obvious advantage, U.S. and other foreign investors moved from a concentration on plantations and mineral extraction to manufacturing and service industries for domestic Third World markets.

Development plans drawn up with U.S. assistance often called for new taxes. The nature of the power structure in most client states meant that taxes would be regressive and any new tax burden would be borne by the nonaffluent. Resulting new revenues were not to be spent on the nonaffluent, however; it was argued that benefits would eventually "trickle down" to low-income sectors, but that short-term requirements of capital accumulation called for the minimization of public spending on general services and social welfare.

The Promising Ambivalence of Camelot

The advent of the 1960s brought relief from the worst of 1950s Cold War paranoia—and with it a certain intoxication with power; in some quarters, it even brought a new spirit of generosity and openness to the interests of other peoples. Above all, Camelot, the abbreviated administration of John F. Kennedy, brought into public life the profound ambivalence that is so often the mark of liberals.[3] The primacy of Cold War advantage and of economic growth fueled by foreign investment remained unchallenged; but it was argued that those objectives would be best served through the promotion of social reform.

Young Americans were challenged to "ask not what your country can do for you, but what you can do for your country," and the Peace Corps was born. A new Agency for International Development (AID—now USAID), created by the Foreign Assistance Act of 1961 to supersede the ICA, was mandated to promote reform in such areas as education, health, housing, and land-tenure policy without losing sight of the requirements of U.S. business interests. At the same time, a program of aid and training for Third World police forces begun in 1954 was greatly reinforced and the U.S. military undertook new roles, including the training and equipping of Third World military establishments for "civic action" and counterinsurgency.

The cross-purposes of the reformist thrust were most clearly manifest in the Alliance for Progress, a program of aid and incentives directed toward Latin America. Military cooperation between the United States and the Latin American states had been stressed in the postwar period, but the United States had been relatively deaf to Latin American pleas for economic assistance until the triumph of the Cuban revolution. Latin American leaders did not fail to note that Kennedy's *Alianza* proposal preceded the abortive U.S.-sponsored invasion of Cuba at the Bay of Pigs by a single month.

The ambivalence of Camelot was soon to be resolved. By the early 1960s, Third World elites and their U.S. allies were finding that they could not promote technological and economic modernization—even to the extent necessary to expand markets for local and U.S. manufacturers—without at the same time promoting education, mass communication, and new forms of social organization, thus amplifying demands for broader political participation. The Kennedy administration tried to have it both ways: to promote development—even political and economic reform—but within limits, limits guaranteed by reinforced military and paramilitary forces. In insisting on the exclusion, and in some cases even active repression, of the Marxist and/or populist Left, this strategy left the relatively new centrist or moderately reformist political forces without bargaining power and dangerously exposed. In some cases the frustration of newly mobilized groups led to a collapse of the political center and polarization. In any case, the political fluidity alarmed Third World and U.S. business elites and the U.S. government. After Kennedy's assassination, the ambivalence was resolved in favor of an approach featuring fewer carrots and more sticks.

Fewer Carrots, More Sticks

By the late 1960s, most of the aspects of development policy that had reflected the idealism of the early 1960s had vanished, at least from the official utterings and undertakings of major donor institutions. Social reform as an objective ceased to enjoy even rhetorical currency. Community development, involving local participation, organization, and self-help—as undertaken, for example, by Peace Corps volunteers in Latin America and parts of Asia and by other organizations having field agents—came to be increasingly difficult, if not dangerous, and ultimately uncommon.

In Latin America, in particular, as more and more governments fell under right-wing dictatorships supported by the U.S. government, Peace

Corps volunteers working directly with the poor found themselves in something of a sandwich. The communities they worked in were likely to hold them in suspicion of serving surreptitious U.S. government purposes; and it was more likely still that the host governments that ultimately supervised them would regard them as hostile interlopers—being used, at least, by the Left. Even other agencies of the U.S. government often appeared to regard them as troublemakers or agents of insurrection. When the volunteers were finally ejected from most South American countries in the 1970s, it was as much for their successes as for their failures.[4]

In the United States, the idea of foreign assistance became less popular, even among liberals, as abuses and failures were revealed and as the country polarized on the issue of the Vietnam War. Bilateral development assistance was cut sharply, as funds were transferred to multilateral programs or shifted into military and security support categories. Program funds usable for general budgetary support took precedence over aid for specific projects, and loan funds increasingly edged out grants. Remaining funds were tied more tightly to trade and investment requirements or security interests.

The thrust of development policy for the period of the late 1960s and early 1970s is well represented by the establishment of the Overseas Private Investment Corporation (OPIC). Authorized by Congress in 1969, OPIC was given a mandate to provide public insurance for private overseas investment—a guarantee, in the event of unremunerated expropriation, of the socialization of losses.

A harbinger of change to come, however, was legislation adopted in 1969 that after a three-year period of gestation gave birth to the Inter-American Foundation. Like a number of other foreign assistance programs, the foundation is the offspring of strange bedfellows: in this case, Democrats distrustful of the existing foreign affairs apparatus under the Nixon administration and Republicans distrustful of AID as the incarnation of spendthrift Democratic do-gooding. Almost miraculously, the Inter-American Foundation survived as an island of nonpartisan professionalism after AID was taken over by the Reagan administration and increasingly made to serve conservative purposes.[5] The foundation's budget has always been modest, but, standing apart from the Department of State and relatively unencumbered by short-term foreign policy and private economic interests, it has managed to provide small loans and grants directly to organizations representing the poor. It has also, more recently, strengthened intermediary organizations in Latin American countries that nurture networks of organizations representing the poor.

"New Directions" for the 1970s

Although U.S. development assistance policy has seen as many convolutions in strategy and rhetoric as has any other aspect of foreign policy, the "New Directions" amendments of 1973 represent the only major legislative overhaul to date of the still-governing Foreign Assistance Act of 1961. The amendments, redirecting attention (if not a great deal in the way of resources) to "basic human needs," reflected a general liberalizing of the national mood resulting in part from the "greening of America"—the coming of age of the baby boom population bulge and the widespread mobilization of young people in opposition to the Vietnam War. It also reflected the incorporation of a new generation of development specialists into public and private development institutions and into academic and lobbying roles; these specialists had been exposed, through Peace Corps or other field experiences, to real people and real problems among the Third World poor.

Finally, the overhaul responded to the emergence of a new development paradigm (dependency) and an accumulation of empirical studies that challenged the trickle-down assumption of prevailing theories. The studies indicated, for example, that the fruits of previous policy successes—e.g., an average 5.5 percent annual GNP growth rate and a 3.2 percent annual per capita GNP growth rate during the 1960s for the LDCs as a group—had been stingily dispersed. The poor, in most LDCs a majority of the population, had been excluded from the benefits of growth. The poor, then, had lost ground in relative terms as the distribution gap grew, and in many countries, especially those undergoing very rapid growth, they had been disadvantaged in absolute terms as well. An International Labor Organization (ILO) study of 1960s trends also found that per capita economic growth was accompanied in many countries by rising rates of unemployment. The exceptional cases were also instructive; a few East Asian states—South Korea, Taiwan, Hong Kong, and Singapore, in particular—had been able to increase growth and decrease income disparities at the same time. This appeared to be due in part to strategies maximizing employment through labor-intensive industry and directing the benefits of agrarian reform to small-scale producers.

The New Directions amendments, therefore, were intended to channel assistance directly to the poor, particularly the rural poor. Actual capital transfers were to be modest, but technical assistance would become more readily available. This new focus was adopted simultaneously by the World Bank. Its president, Robert McNamara, told the bank's Board of Governors in 1973 that whereas less than $1 billion of some $25 billion in previous loans had been devoted to subsistence agriculture, increasing productivity in that sector would henceforth be a high-priority objective. (Even so, as late as 1977 only 23 percent of the commitments of the World Bank and its sister institution, the International Development Association, were financing projects that benefited primarily the poor.)[6]

The 1973 amendments channeled development assistance into functional budget categories, originally: Food and Nutrition; Population Planning and Health; Education and Human Resources Development; Selected Development Problems; and Selected Countries and Organizations. Subsequent reorganization incorporated an energy category. For the rural areas, simultaneous attention to these several needs was to be addressed through "integrated rural development" (IRD) programs. The IRD concept, advanced by the World Bank in the mid-1960s but coming into its own only in the 1970s, was intended, above all, to promote coordination. IRD projects often combined the efforts of more than one external donor (e.g., AID and World Bank) and an array of host country ministries and agencies. Effective coordination generally proved an elusive goal.

The new approach to technical assistance, intended to maximize employment opportunities and project sustainability, came to be known as "appropriate technology." While some LDC leaders saw in this an intent to deny them the fruits of high technology, adherents of the approach stressed that the concept was comparative and situational, that "appropriate" did not necessarily mean low, and that indeed the assessment of appropriateness should lie with the prospective users. Indeed, like the community development thrust of the early 1960s, the New Directions strategy emphasized self-help and the participation of prospective beneficiaries at every step from planning through evaluation.

The concept of institution-building was revived and given new meaning as the earmarking of funds for a plethora of individual projects gave rise to a multitude of contract agencies, both profit and nonprofit, from both First World and Third. The institutions to be built also included those of would-be beneficiaries at the village or community level. As in the heyday of community development in the 1960s, the kind of institution most often promoted was the credit, consumer, or production cooperative.

New public investment was to focus more on human resources than on material ones. Along with renewed attention to education and health care, there was a particularly strong emphasis on family planning and population control as well as on the incorporation of women (heretofore generally excluded) into sponsored development programs. The energy crisis, however, hitting hard in 1973–1974 and again in 1978–1979, turned attention once again to material resources and resulted in a new emphasis on conservation, alternate energy sourcing, and, in general, resource management.

The New Directions aid legislation preceded by several years the major swing of the U.S. political pendulum it foretold. It was not until the inauguration of the Carter administration in 1977 that some in the upper echelons of the executive branch shared the concerns for the Third World poor that had been expressed by Congress. With respect to some countries, the Carter administration also paid heed to legislation passed in the mid-1970s denying military assistance to the regimes that most systematically violated human rights. But attention both to human rights and to human needs began to fade a couple of years into the new administration.

Meanwhile mounting congressional frustration with State Department foot-dragging spilled over into legislation in 1978, creating the International Development Cooperation Administration (IDCA). The IDCA was to have jurisdiction over AID, thus taking it out from under the State Department. AID's great escape was never realized, however. The IDCA continues to exist, but inconsequentially; its offices, along with the preexisting AID ones, are housed in the State Department. Thus, while the New Directions were taken seriously by meagerly funded nongovernmental organizations, they were never more than marginal to the major donor agencies.

The limited results of the New Directions thrust need not be attributed to hypocrisy, though to be sure there were many in high places whose espousal of it was poorly grounded in commitment. There was commitment to spare among some who promoted and drafted the legislation and who pursued its implementation in the field. But catalyzing self-help is not a role that comes naturally to large bureaucracies, and a mandate for such bureaucracies to penetrate to the grass roots may well serve to undermine local initiative and spread corruption. More important, the New Directions mandate amounted to swimming upstream against a strong current of political and economic interest, both in donor states and agencies and in client states. Little wonder, then, that in many areas a modicum of success sufficed to generate a fearsome backlash.

Privatization and Militarization

The demise of New Directions had less to do with either the successes or the failures of its attendant policies, or of any other development in the Third World, than with inflation in the First World. Inflation and consequent middle-class discontent coincided in the United States with a strong reaction to the "loss" of Indochina and to what appeared to

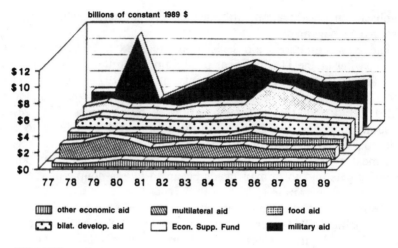

FIGURE 4.1 Program composition of U.S. aid: FY 1977–FY 1989. *Source:* U.S. House of Representatives, 101st Congress, 1st Session, Committee on Foreign Affairs, *Background Materials on Foreign Assistance,* Report of the Task Force on Foreign Assistance, February 1989 (Washington, D.C.: GPO, 1989), p. 158.

be retreat and defeat in subsequent foreign policy. Thus the coterie that came to power with Reagan in 1980 was one drawn together by frustrated chauvinism. The advent of the Reagan administration was immediately reflected in a shifting of foreign assistance funds away from development and into military and security support assistance (by then known as Economic Support Funds [ESF]), mainly in the form of grants rather than loans (Figure 4.1). There was also a sharp swing away from focus on the poor and on social infrastructure to promotion of private enterprise, domestic and foreign. The new buzz-word was *privatization.* Unlike the liberalizing trends of the 1970s, privatization was backed by far more than rhetoric. It coincided with the Third World's debt crisis and with the efforts of creditors (mainly private banks in the First World), through the IMF, to maintain a flow of interest payments that was costing many LDCs half or more of their annual export earnings. The upshot, along with foreign public assistance for private export industries in the Third World, has been a virtual fire sale by Third World governments of publicly owned assets.

The privatization thrust was multipurpose, but a companion policy, intended also to enable debt repayment, was the promotion of auster-ity—that is, primarily, the rechanneling of Third World government resources away from social programs. In dramatic contrast to Reagan

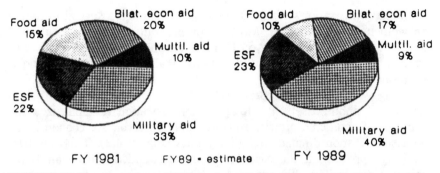

FIGURE 4.2 Program shares of U.S. foreign aid: FY 1981 and FY 1989 compared. *Source:* U.S. House of Representatives, 101st Congress, 1st Session, Committee on Foreign Affairs, *Background Materials on Foreign Assistance,* Report of the Task Force on Foreign Assistance, February 1989 (Washington, D.C.: GPO, 1989), p. 159.

administration free-market rhetoric, this called for extensive donor institution involvement, once again, in macroeconomic planning.

Likewise, while administration rhetoric condemned foreign assistance in general, and while development and humanitarian assistance as a share of all foreign aid fell from about 50 percent to less than 40 percent during Reagan's first term, the total amount of foreign aid almost doubled during that period (Figure 4.2).[7] And much of the funding that remained in the bilateral economic category, as opposed to military and ESF ones, was allocated to large-scale, private-sector initiatives administered by the new Bureau for Private Enterprise. Institutional development was once again favored, but, again, there was a change in the kind of institution to be cultivated. Now the favored institutions were to be those supporting the interests of big business, like Peru's Instituto Libertad y Democracia, to which USAID allocated some $9 million in 1989.

Since Congress (a predominantly Democratic House during Reagan's first term and a Democratic Senate as well during his second term) was never enthusiastic about the Reagan administration's basic foreign policy thrust, the New Directions amendments to the Foreign Assistance Act were never repealed; they were simply ignored. Highly publicized famine in Africa resulted in a new economic program for that continent and in funding for the new autonomous agency, the African Development Foundation, patterned after the Inter-American Development Foundation, but at congressional initiative and over executive opposition. It was established by Congress in 1980 and commenced operations in 1984. Also in the 1980s, new categories of development assistance were added for environmental concerns and for AIDS prevention and control.

The administration's 1985 aid "blueprint" retained a special initiative on women in development. Most major programs, however, continued to ignore women, and policy on family planning was turned inside out, so that U.S. funding was withdrawn from all nongovernmental organizations that promoted it.

Along with the general promotion of private enterprise and privatization of public assets, the Reagan administration reemphasized the primacy of economic growth and productivity. Even so, economic interests were subordinated to military ones (Figure 4.3). This was particularly apparent in the case of the much-heralded Caribbean Basin Initiative (CBI). The CBI, unveiled in 1981, ostensibly has as its primary mission the generation of export industry in the Caribbean. This is done by offering incentives to U.S. industry to invest or relocate in the area and by the removal of tariffs, quotas, and other obstacles to U.S. importation of their products. In fact, however, the CBI has proved to be one of many covers for channeling funds into the pursuit of a military solution to conflict in Central America.

In time, many of the Reagan administration programs and objectives were incorporated into the Foreign Assistance Act, so that AID and other agencies are authorized—in fact, instructed—to pursue the top-down strategies of the Reagan administration as well as their virtual opposite—the bottom-up strategies of the New Directions amendments. Furthermore, the legislation has been weighted over the years with the pet projects of a host of congresspersons. With such a confusing mix of projects and mandates, direct-hire aid employees have been forced to contract out most of the fieldwork and spend their time writing obfuscatory reports (Figure 4.4).

Thus, the U.S. foreign assistance program served many purposes in the 1980s—some of them mutually contradictory—but the fact that the Reagan administration found it useful was manifest in its defense of the program against sharp cuts made in the FY 1987 budget by liberals. A 1987 USAID newsletter highlighted the benefit of the program to U.S. business and industry, noting that 70 percent of the funds appropriated for bilateral assistance is spent in the United States, rather than overseas, as is half of the U.S. contribution to multilateral programs.[8]

U.S. Development Policy in Perspective

Since 1946, the U.S. Congress has appropriated the equivalent in FY 1989 dollars of $966 billion in foreign aid, including military aid, security support assistance, and food aid, as well as assistance intended for development purposes (Figure 4.5). The largest annual expenditures, both for economic and for military purposes, were those of the early

International Development and Humanitarian Assistance (Sub-Function 151)

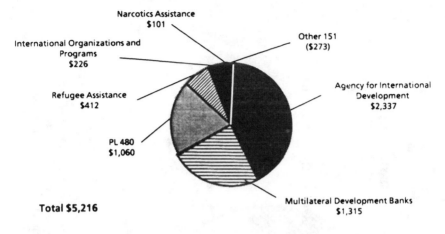

Narcotics Assistance
$101

International Organizations and
Programs
$226

Other 151
($273)

Refugee Assistance
$412

Agency for International
Development
$2,337

PL 480
$1,060

Total $5,216

Multilateral Development Banks
$1,315

International Security Assistance (Sub-Function 152)

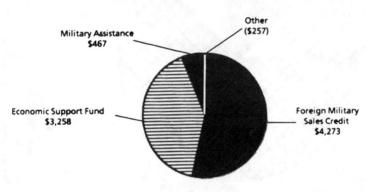

Military Assistance
$467

Other
($257)

Economic Support Fund
$3,258

Foreign Military
Sales Credit
$4,273

Total $7,741

FIGURE 4.3 Foreign aid budget: FY 1989 (millions of dollars). *Source:* U.S. House of Representatives, 101st Congress, 1st Session, Committee on Foreign Affairs, *Background Materials on Foreign Assistance,* Report of the Task Force on Foreign Assistance, February 1989 (Washington, D.C.: GPO, 1989), p. 228.

years, associated with the Marshall Plan. Since that time, the largest expenditures for development and outlays of food aid came in the early-to-mid-1960s. Overall, U.S. aid has been dropping fairly steadily, both in total outlays and as a proportion of GNP, since the late 1940s and early 1950s (Figure 4.6). During most of that period, outlays for military and security support purposes have exceeded those for development and relief purposes.

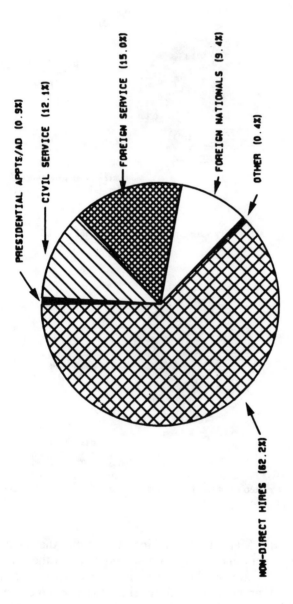

PRESIDENTIAL APPTS/AD (0.9%)

CIVIL SERVICE (12.1%)

FOREIGN SERVICE (15.0%)

FOREIGN NATIONALS (9.4%)

OTHER (0.4%)

NON-DIRECT HIRES (62.2%)

Source: Data provided by AID/PFM/PM/RP

FIGURE 4.4 A.I.D. employees by category: 1988 (including non-direct hires). *Source:* U.S. House of Representatives, 101st Congress, 1st Session, Committee on Foreign Affairs, *Background Materials on Foreign Assistance,* Report of the Task Force on Foreign Assistance, February 1989 (Washington, D.C.: GPO, 1989), p. 185.

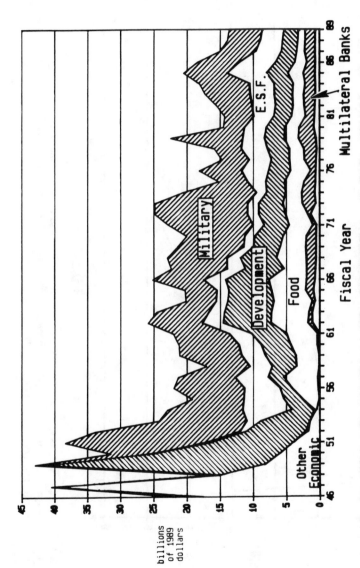

FIGURE 4.5 U.S. foreign aid, 1946–89, by major program. *Source:* U.S. House of Representatives, 101st Congress, 1st Session, Committee on Foreign Affairs, *Background Materials on Foreign Assistance*, Report of the Task Force on Foreign Assistance, February 1989 (Washington, D.C.: GPO, 1989), p. 145.

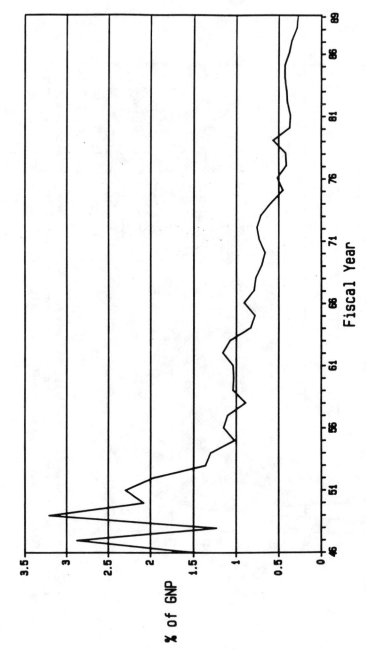

FIGURE 4.6 U.S. foreign aid, as a % of GNP, FY46–89. *Source:* U.S. House of Representatives, 101st Congress, 1st Session, Committee on Foreign Affairs, *Background Materials on Foreign Assistance*, Report of the Task Force on Foreign Assistance, February 1989 (Washington, D.C.: GPO, 1989), p. 147.

From the late 1950s to the mid-1970s, most U.S. aid was directed to Asia as a corollary of the wars in Korea and Vietnam (Figure 4.7). Since the late 1970s, most aid has been directed to the Middle East, about half of it to Israel and Egypt (Figures 4.8 and 4.9). In the late 1980s, more than 60 percent of the total U.S. foreign assistance budget of about $15 billion was allocated to military and security (ESF) categories. Bilateral economic assistance ranged between $2 and $3 billion.[9]

In time, the use of the Cold War to maintain and expand U.S. economic supremacy boomeranged, as the Machiavellians lost out to the true believers. In arming itself against all imaginable contingencies and fighting proxy wars on multiple fronts, the United States has weakened its own economy, leaving it with more sticks but fewer carrots with which to pursue its goals. Moreover, as the implementation of foreign policy devolves increasingly upon the intelligence agencies and the armed forces, so too does the making of that policy; and the economic interests that were to be pursued or protected come to be overshadowed or even undermined by the interests of the "security" bureaucracy.

In his waning years, Kennan, to his credit, declared the Cold War over and allowed that it need not have gotten so out of hand in the first place.[10] Even so, at the end of the 1980s, U.S. policy with respect to international development continued to flow largely from Cold War premises; and as Western European countries increasingly challenged U.S. guidance in development strategy and Japan surpassed the United States as a donor of economic assistance, the United States continued to expend a major portion of its shrinking aid budget in the trashing of its own neighborhood.

OTHER DONOR STATES
AND INSTITUTIONS

In the immediate postwar period, the position of the United States as a donor of official development assistance (ODA) completely dwarfed that of all other states as well as of international and nongovernmental entities. As recently as 1982, the United States continued to be the largest single contributor, accounting for 22 percent of ODA—almost double the portions of either Japan or Saudi Arabia, the two second largest contributors.

Overall disbursements of ODA have increased substantially since the 1960s; they grew from the mid-1970s to mid-1980s at the rate of about 4 percent a year, reaching some $36 billion. Counting nongovernmental and multilateral sources along with bilateral ones, there are now more

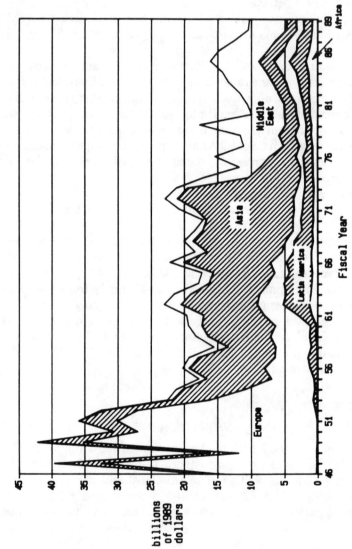

FIGURE 4.7 U.S. foreign aid, 1946–89, by region. *Source:* U.S. House of Representatives, 101st Congress, 1st Session, Committee on Foreign Affairs, *Background Materials on Foreign Assistance,* Report of the Task Force on Foreign Assistance, February 1989 (Washington, D.C.: GPO, 1989), p. 142.

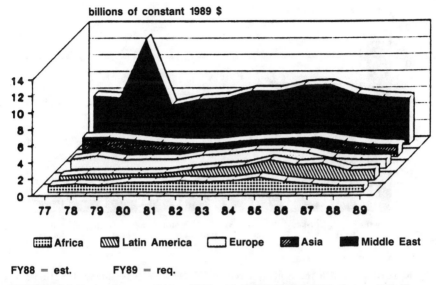

billions of constant 1989 $

Africa	Latin America	Europe	Asia	Middle East

FY88 = est.   **FY89 = req.**

FIGURE 4.8 Regional composition of U.S. aid: FY 1977–FY 1989. *Source:* U.S. House of Representatives, 101st Congress, 1st Session, Committee on Foreign Affairs, *Background Materials on Foreign Assistance,* Report of the Task Force on Foreign Assistance, February 1989 (Washington, D.C.: GPO, 1989), p. 161.

donors than there are recipient countries. As the number-one donor of nonmilitary aid, the United States was eclipsed in 1989 by Japan. And while the United States retains second place in terms of absolute amounts of funds transferred (about $8 billion in 1989), its contribution as a proportion of GNP has dropped to last place among the eighteen countries represented by the Development Advisory Committee (DAC) of the Organization for Economic Cooperation and Development[11] (Figures 4.10 and 4.11).

The Organization for Economic Cooperation and Development (OECD)

Over the past four decades, the OECD member states have contributed about one-half to two-thirds of all official development assistance. They have never approached, however, their collective goal of contributing 1 percent of GNP, or even the 0.7 percent goal set by the United Nations. Their contributions amounted to 0.35 percent of their combined GNP in 1970, rising slightly to 0.38 in 1982 and dropping back to 0.36 in 1985. Total OECD contributions rose from about $7 billion in 1970 to about $30 billion in 1985 (Figure 4.12).

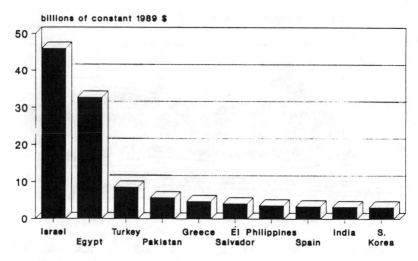

billions of constant 1989 $

| Israel | Turkey | Greece | El | Philippines | | India | S. |
| Egypt | Pakistan | | Salvador | | Spain | | Korea |

FY88 • est.   FY89 • req.

FIGURE 4.9 Major recipients of U.S. aid: FY 1977–FY 1989. *Source:* U.S. House of Representatives, 101st Congress, 1st Session, Committee on Foreign Affairs, *Background Materials on Foreign Assistance,* Report of the Task Force on Foreign Assistance, February 1989 (Washington, D.C.: GPO, 1989), p. 163.

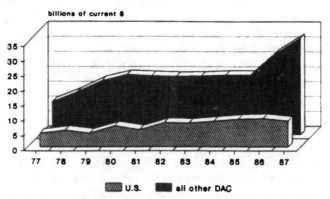

billions of current $

U.S.   all other DAC

1987 = estimates

FIGURE 4.10 Major donor economic assistance: 1977–1987. *Source:* U.S. House of Representatives, 101st Congress, 1st Session, Committee on Foreign Affairs, *Background Materials on Foreign Assistance,* Report of the Task Force on Foreign Assistance, February 1989 (Washington, D.C.: GPO, 1989), p. 164.

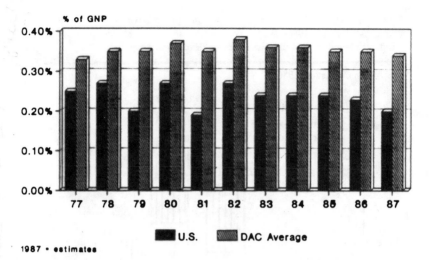

FIGURE 4.11 Major donor aid as a % of GNP: 1977–1987. *Source:* U.S. House of Representatives, 101st Congress, 1st Session, Committee on Foreign Affairs, *Background Materials on Foreign Assistance,* Report of the Task Force on Foreign Assistance, February 1989 (Washington, D.C.: GPO, 1989), p. 164.

Apart from Japan and the United States, the largest donors in the mid-1980s, contributing in the range of $1 to $4 billion each, were, in descending order: France, West Germany, Italy, the United Kingdom, Canada, and the Netherlands. For contributions as a percentage of GNP, Norway led, with the Netherlands, Sweden, and Denmark close behind. Norway's contribution amounted to 1.03 percent of GNP in 1985 and may be compared to a U.S. contribution of 0.26. Japan ranked twelfth with 0.31 percent.[12]

At the economic summit of industrialized states in Paris in July 1989, coinciding with the bicentennial of the French Revolution, Japanese Prime Minister Suzuki Onu stunned donor and LDC leaders alike by pledging a new economic aid package amounting to $43 billion to be expended by 1992. Much of Japanese aid, like that of other OECD members, has been linked to the promotion of products and investments of their nationals.

In fact, criticism of the Japanese aid program by Third World countries, other OECD members, and Japanese opposition groups sounds much like the criticism leveled earlier at the U.S. aid program. It is argued that too much of Japanese aid (some 40 percent) is in the form of loans rather than grants, that it is too tightly tied to the purchase of Japanese goods and technologies, and that too much emphasis is placed on the development of material infrastructure, such as roads,

The contraction of commercial lending and private export credits in the first half of the 1980s was largely responsible for the sharp drop in industrial-country resource transfers to developing countries.

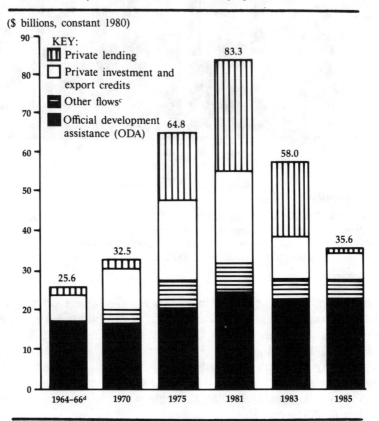

Note: Data on private voluntary grants are not available for 1964–66 average.
[a]Financial flows from DAC countries to developing countries and multilateral agencies.
[b]Deflated by the U.S. GNP deflator.
[c]Non-concessional official flows and private voluntary agency grants.
[d]Annual average.

Figure 4.12 Industrial-country net transfers to developing countries[a]: Sudden decline and change in composition ($ billions, constant 1980[b]; and percentages). Based on OECD data. *Source:* U.S. House of Representatives, 101st Congress, 1st Session, Committee on Foreign Affairs, *Background Materials on Foreign Assistance,* Report of the Task Force on Foreign Assistance, February 1989 (Washington, D.C.: GPO, 1989), p. 59.

dams, and power plants. Moreover, Japan's development professionals are quick to acknowledge that the buildup in aid projects has far outstripped their own acquisition of development expertise.

The Japanese aid program places considerably fewer staff in the field than do those of other donor states. The combined total staff of the Japan International Cooperation Agency (JICA) and Japan's Overseas Economic Cooperation Fund numbered 1,500 in 1988, compared to USAID's 5,000 employees worldwide, plus thousands of short-term contractors. JICA spokesmen boast of high performance per person but acknowledge that their personnel are seriously overloaded.

Like the United States and several other OECD countries, along with the United Nations and the Vatican, Japan also fields its own corps of volunteers. Over the past twenty-five years, approximately 10,000 Japanese, mostly young men, have served overseas under the auspices of the Japan Overseas Cooperative Volunteers (JOCV). Some 2,000 Japanese volunteers were serving in thirty-eight countries in 1989.

The general concept of foreign aid is more popular and less controversial in Japan than in the United States. Domestic critics have argued for more attention to human needs, for greater effectiveness, and for more independence. Historically, Japan has generally followed the U.S. lead in deciding where to place its aid—often giving precedence to countries where the United States claimed major strategic interests. That accommodation appears to be fading as Japan goes its own way, particularly in expanding programs in Africa. Unlike the United States, Japan rarely places strictly political conditions on the extension of aid.[13]

An OECD review of public opinion polls in member states between 1960 and 1983 indicated general public support for some forms of foreign assistance, particularly those directly addressed to the amelioration of hunger and poverty. A 1989 report of the Overseas Development Council (ODC) noted that in Canada, the Netherlands, and Sweden, in particular, and to a somewhat lesser degree in the Federal Republic of Germany (FRG), parliaments, parties, and the public are consistently supportive of foreign aid programs. This was in stark contrast to the cases of the United Kingdom (UK), where support has recently been unenthusiastic, and the United States, where the program has often been plagued by partisan and intragovernmental conflict.

According to the ODC report, the countries where foreign assistance enjoyed the greatest public support were the ones that had made the greatest commitment to public education on development issues. They were also the ones whose programs clearly stressed development objectives over political or commercial interests.[14]

The Council for Mutual
Economic Assistance (CMEA)

The overall amount of Soviet and East European economic assistance to the Third World (coordinated by the CMEA) has not been highly significant. Soviet assistance from 1954 to 1981 totaled a little more than $22 billion, while East European commitments for the period amounted to $12 billion spread among sixty countries. East Germany (GDR), with the strongest economy, was the largest contributor. Assistance from the CMEA group as a whole in 1982 represented 0.17 percent of collective GNP. It has been crucial, however, to a few countries, particularly those most in need because of credit freezes imposed by Western countries and institutions.

Such politically responsive aid has been particularly important: in the Middle East, to Egypt and Syria in the mid-1950s; in Latin America, to Cuba since the early 1960s and to Nicaragua in the 1980s; in Africa, to Angola and Mozambique in the mid-1970s and more recently to Ethiopia. Aid to India since that country's independence has had political significance but has been important commercially as well.

Like most other donor states, however, the Soviet Union and its East European allies extended credits to LDCs as a means of promoting exports, and economic assistance as a whole was increasingly neutral with respect to Cold War alignment. Technical assistance was also an important aspect of Soviet bloc programs, engaging more than 100,000 technicians in about seventy-five countries in the early 1980s. At the same time the CMEA states were hosting more than 70,000 students in their universities, half of them from Africa and half of them on scholarship in the USSR.[15]

The Organization of Petroleum
Exporting Countries (OPEC)

The OPEC donor category is a relatively new one. In 1970 total ODA from OPEC member states amounted to only $40 million. After petroleum prices rose sharply in 1973–1974, however, foreign assistance from OPEC states also rose dramatically—to $6.24 billion in 1975 and $9.59 billion in 1980. Their contribution in 1980 amounted to 16 percent of total ODA. From the early 1980s until 1990, when oil prices were dropping, however, OPEC development assistance fell by more than 40 percent. (It was not clear in late 1990 whether price hikes in reponse to Iraq's invasion of Kuwait would lead once again to higher levels of development assistance.)

Like other donor states, the OPEC countries used foreign assistance, particularly credits, as a means of promoting trade; but they also used it to strengthen political and cultural ties. Middle Eastern OPEC states, in particular, cultivated Moslem leaders and communities in Africa and Asia and sought to strengthen ties among predominantly Moslem states.

As a percentage of GNP, the contributions of OPEC states have been much greater than those of the OECD members, reaching 8.5 percent in 1975 and dropping to 2.79 percent in 1982. Saudi Arabia's contribution in 1982 amounted to 3.53 percent of GNP and that of Kuwait to 4.46 percent. Qatar's contribution for 1975 was up to 15.6 percent of GNP.[16] It should be noted, however, that not all the OPEC states benefited in the long run from the cartel's price hikes. Apart from the Gulf states, most petroleum producers saw the brief period of prosperity run up unpayable debts and uncontrollable inflation without generating additional productive capacity.

Multilateral Financial Institutions

The most important international financial institutions of the postwar era, the International Monetary Fund (IMF) and the International Bank for Reconstruction and Development (IBRD), more commonly known as the World Bank, created at the Bretton Woods Conference of 1944 by representatives of forty-four states, were designed in large measure to meet the needs of the United States. The role of the IMF was to be that of stabilizing currency exchange rates, while the World Bank's role was to facilitate foreign investment. The United States was particularly interested in eliminating colonial (especially British) and nationalistic (particularly Latin American) barriers to profitable trade and investment. To guard against the intrusion of real internationalism, it was decided that voting would be weighted in accordance with size of national contribution.

Those institutions have remained responsive to U.S. interests and, in particular, to U.S. banking interests, since it is the Department of the Treasury that represents the country in their decision-making bodies. The regional development banks, in existence since the early 1960s—Inter-American, Asian, and African—operate under similar rules, including weighted voting, with similar results. Such institutions maintain that their decisions are based entirely on economic criteria and are politically neutral. Setting aside the question, however, as to whether there can be such a thing as politically neutral economic criteria, it remains clear that U.S. political or "security" arguments, when pursued with sufficient vehemence, have almost always carried the day.

The IMF, for example, has claimed that its loan decisions were apolitical except for a general hesitancy to extend loans to unstable governments. Nevertheless, in the fall of 1980, while Jamaica's democratic socialist government, under Prime Minister Michael Manley, suffered a virtually complete banker's boycott, the IMF approved loans to the shaky juntas of El Salvador and Bolivia. The loan to Bolivia was approved despite the fact that a member of the IMF's own team was detained by the drug-dealing generals. The loan to El Salvador had to be approved without on-site inspection because the level of civil strife was such that the government could not guarantee the IMF envoy's personal safety.[17] Similarly, policymakers of the Inter-American Development Bank overrode staff recommendations on several occasions in the 1980s to deny loans to Nicaragua; and the World Bank overrode its own staff professionals to support major engineering projects in the Amazon.

Worse, perhaps, than these extreme examples of caving in to pressure is the fact that the banks systematically favor authoritarian governments over democratic ones. That is hardly surprising when one considers the kinds of options faced by leaders of debt-ridden LDCs. Since new loans, of late, are most often extended to enable the repayment of old loans, and since the funds required for debt repayment are most often squeezed out of wages and salaries and services, the leader whose tenure is not dependent on popular approval is apt to be seen as a better bet.

Liberals in the U.S. Congress, emboldened in the 1970s, attempted to deal with the problem by introducing considerations of human rights and human needs into the votes cast by U.S. representatives to the international financial institutions. They succeeded in 1980 in passing the requisite legislation, but they were never able to ensure its implementation.

In the face of the debt crisis of the 1980s, the IMF assumed the primary collection agency role on behalf of First World bankers. The World Bank, however, has greatly increased nonproject lending designed both to leverage macroeconomic policy changes and to provide governments with hard currency to pass on to their creditors.

U.S. dominance in the multilateral development banks may soon be eclipsed. Japan has become the second largest shareholder in the World Bank and the largest contributor to its cofinancing project. It has been moving up fast in the IMF as well and can be expected to challenge the U.S. position there in the 1990s.

The United Nations and Its Affiliates

Paralleling the case of the multilateral financial institutions, power relations in the United Nations in the early postwar period reflected the preeminent position of the United States on the world stage. As the process of decolonization continued, however, and as some countries ordinarily aligned with the United States began to behave more independently, the United Nations—at least its General Assembly and its specialized and affiliated agencies—came more nearly to reflect the interests of the Third World. Since the late 1960s the United Nations has increasingly been used by Third World countries as a major forum and it has taken initiatives to promote Third World development.

Among the older UN agencies and affiliates whose responsibilities include some aspect of development are the United Nations Educational, Scientific, and Cultural Organization (UNESCO); Economic and Social Council (ECOSOC); UN Children's Fund (UNICEF); Food and Agriculture Organization (FAO); World Health Organization (WHO); International Labor Organization (ILO); and, of course, the UN Development Program (UNDP). The UNDP, launched in 1965, has been accused of operating from a First World, or "modernization," paradigm, but its perspective appears to be changing. It operates a volunteer program, on the order of the Peace Corps or Papal Volunteers, with tours of duty limited to two years. The United Nations volunteers, usually better trained than their Peace Corps counterparts, work at the community level in some of the world's poorest and most strife-torn countries. The UNDP was expending over $100 million annually in the late 1980s.[18]

More recently the United Nations has spawned other programs with developmental implications, including a special development fund for women, an education and training program for southern Africa, an institute for Namibia, an environment program, a center on human settlement (HABITAT), and a center for science and technology for development.

The United Nations also created the regional economic commissions that were so influential in the early 1960s and gave shelter and legitimacy to the nonaligned movement. In the UN Conference on Trade and Development (UNCTAD), the Group of 77 (G-77) caucusing Third World countries, generally suffering from deterioration in the terms of trade for their primary products as well as from other forms of discrimination in trade, technology, and investment, found a forum for collectively airing their grievances. They have yet, however, to find the First World very responsive.

The United Nations has always had its share of critics, and its development programs have not been spared the heat. The United States has increasingly taken an adversarial stance vis-à-vis the organization. After Third World nations acquired a voting majority in the General Assembly, U.S. representatives to that body began to speak of the tyranny of the majority and of the irresponsibility of the small states. The Nixon and Reagan administrations, in fact, were vitriolic in their criticism, and the Reagan administration, in 1984, withdrew the United States from participation in (and funding for) UNESCO. The administration of George Bush, himself a former chief delegate to the United Nations, has retreated from the Reagan position, however, and in late 1989 proposed to pay the United States's full quota assessments, including the backlog of assessments withheld by the Reagan administration.

From the Left, critics have charged that UN professionals, like other international civil servants, earn too much and live too well to be able truly to empathize with the Third World's poor. Furthermore, some argue that the business of the international development establishment, including the United Nations, is merely to attend to the welfare aspects of global capital accumulation and to ensure compliance with international agreements and procedures favoring the affluent.[19]

Supporters of UN programs maintain, however, that major conferences, like those on population, women, and the environment, play an essential part in molding the consciousness of national leaders and opinion makers. They also claim that although top-down approaches to development appear to be unavoidable for large bureaucracies, UN development agencies show greater sensitivity than most to Third World needs and perspectives.

Regional organizations of general competence, such as the Organization of American States (OAS) and the Organization of African Unity (OAU), also maintain development programs. Such programs have thus far been meager, however, as the priorities of those organizations have lain elsewhere.

Nongovernmental Organizations

In contemporary development literature, the terms *nongovernmental organization* (NGO) and *private voluntary organization* (PVO) are used descriptively and interchangeably, even though in original usage their meanings were distinct and precise. The United Nations introduced "nongovernmental organization" into the literature in reference to organizations recognized as having consultative status to the UN and receiving some support from that body. The term *private voluntary organization* was reportedly coined by AID to categorize private-sector nonprofit organizations receiving AID contracts or grants.[20]

Both terms have come to be used more generally to refer to private or community-based organizations that may receive funding from governments or international organizations but are not direct appendages of them. PVO remains the more common usage, however, for U.S.-based groups, while NGO is more often used elsewhere. Thus I will use NGO as the more general term and PVO to specify U.S.-based groups. The terms may be used for organizations having purposes other than development, but we are referring here to those having development functions. Some of the literature makes a distinction as well between PVOs/NGOs as service, consultative, or intermediary funding organizations and "popular organizations," representing fund-seeking or problem-solving national or local communities. But such distinctions are not always easy; therefore, unless otherwise indicated, "popular organizations" will be subsumed in this chapter by NGOs.

There has been a remarkable proliferation of nongovernmental organizations in the past two decades. One study identified some 2,200 Northern, or First World, NGOs in 1984 expending about $4 billion in support of projects and institutions in Africa, Asia, and Latin America. This represented a threefold increase in NGO expenditures in the course of a decade. This NGO contribution to the total assistance effort was estimated to equal 10 to 20 percent of the annual budgets of bilateral and multilateral aid agencies. Meanwhile, the growth of Third World NGOs has been even more impressive; some 10,000 to 20,000 of them are now working with First World counterparts.[21] At the village or neighborhood level, very casual or partial surveys, such as those compiled by the Worldwatch Institute—reflected in Table 4.1— have identified hundreds of thousands of self-help organizations.

This proliferation has many causes—among them the growth of international exchange and area studies programs and the fact that the NGOs have offered the more adventurous, idealistic, or independent-minded a means of serving peoples without necessarily or directly serving governments. Some such organizations, in First World and Third, are composed of professionals who had served governments but were removed or chose to resign when turnovers at the top resulted in sharp changes in policy direction.

A more obvious reason for this proliferation, however, has been the recent inclination of government aid agencies to contract out their fieldwork. By 1988, 62 percent of USAID employees, for example, were nondirect hires, or contractees (compared to about 25 percent in the early 1960s). Some of those were from university faculties or from for-profit engineering or consulting firms, but a great many represented nonprofit private volunteer organizations (PVOs). USAID even contributes to a PVO-funding consortium, Private Agencies Collaborating Together (PACT).

The Canadian government and a number of European governments also contract out much of their development effort to NGOs. The Dutch government, for example, has worked through an NGO coordinating body to support the efforts of both religious and secular organizations operating overseas. The coordinating bodies serve as independent in-

TABLE 4.1   Grassroots Organizations in Selected Developing Countries, Late Eighties

Country	Description
Bangladesh	1,200 independent development organizations formed since 1971, particularly active in health and income generation with large landless population.
Brazil	Enormous growth in community action since democratization in early eighties: 100,000 Christian Base Communities with 3 million members; 1,300 neighborhood associations in São Paulo; landless peasant groups proliferating; 1,041 independent development organizations.
Burkina Faso	Naam grassroots peasant movement has 2,500 groups participating in dry-season self-help; similar movements forming in Senegal, Mauritania, Mali, Niger, and Togo.
India	Strong Gandhian self-help tradition promotes social welfare, appropriate technology, and tree planting; local groups number in at least the tens of thousands, independent development organizations estimated at 12,000.
Indonesia	600 independent development groups work in environmental protection alone; peasant irrigation groups multiplying.
Kenya	16,232 women's groups with 637,000 members registered in 1984, quadruple the 1980 number (1988 estimates range up to 25,000); many start as savings clubs.
Mexico	Massive urban grassroots movement active in squatter settlements of major cities; at least 250 independent development organizations.
Peru	Vital women's self-help movement in Lima's impoverished shantytowns, with 1,500 community kitchens; 300 independent development organizations.
Philippines	3,000–5,000 Christian Base Communities form focal points for local action.
Sri Lanka	Rapidly growing Sarvodaya Shramadana village awakening movement includes over 8,000 villages, one-third of total in country; 3 million people involved in range of efforts, particularly work parties, education, preventive health care, and cooperative crafts projects.
Zimbabwe	Small-farmer groups throughout country have estimated membership of 400,000, 80 percent women; active women's community gardens multiplying.

Source: Alan Durning, *Action at the Grassroots: Fighting Poverty and Environmental Decay,* Worldwatch Paper 88 (Washington, D.C.: Worldwatch Institute, 1989), Table 1. Reprinted by permission of Worldwatch Institute.

termediaries, funding up to 75 percent of the project costs of Dutch groups meeting established criteria, and also fund Third World NGOs directly.[22] The Canadian International Development Agency (CIDA), a governmental body, allocates $6 million (Canadian) annually (as compared to U.S. $1 million by USAID) to NGOs for use in development education.

Official support for NGO/PVO programs has come about in part because government agencies have recognized the cultural sensitivity, innovativeness, and dedication of many such groups and the advantages of decentralizing, debureaucratizing, and lowering the official profile. Contracting out also broadens the aid constituency and leaves official agencies less vulnerable to "bloated bureaucracy" epithets. For NGOs, however, and particularly for U.S. PVOs dealing with USAID, government support usually means a very considerable erosion of PVO independence; it increases dependency and regimentation and thus decreases innovation and responsiveness to beneficiary communities.

NGOs come in many categories, from those having large memberships and bureaucracies and global and comprehensive approaches to development, to those limited in size, in area addressed, and in function. Some of the major organizations with global reach, such as CARE, OXFAM, or Catholic Relief Services, were initially intended to deal with such disasters as flood and famine but have since refocused their efforts so as to concentrate on community development. Some, such as Planned Parenthood or Volunteers in Technical Assistance, limit their efforts to particular problem areas or types of assistance. Others, such as International Volunteer Service (IVS), concentrate on building local organizations and networks capable of identifying needs and addressing them. A few, like Futures for Children, make a point of eschewing government funds. Some agencies, however, that claim to accept no government funding, like World Vision (of fundamentalist religious inclination), nevertheless make a point of funding communities and projects favored also by USAID.

Religious organizations, long prominent among care givers in the Third World, have increasingly redefined their missions so as to promote income-producing activities, self-help, community organization, and other aspects of development. Liberation theology and the preference for the poor inspired by Pope John XXIII and reinforced by the Medellín Conference of 1968 have had a profound influence on the role of the Catholic church, particularly in Latin America and the Philippines, but notable in other areas as well, including the southwestern United States. In organizing *comunidades de base,* or Christian base communities, where individuals were encouraged to take collective approaches to their problems, and in supporting the organization of rural co-ops, priests and nuns based in poor communities and members of religious orders began to occupy the forefront in movements for social change— or at least to occupy a buffer zone between elite-based governments and mobilized poor communities.

The older, more established Protestant sects have followed the Roman Catholic lead in favoring the poor and challenging an order based on elite privilege. Working through the World Council of Churches, they have been particularly active in Africa. Meanwhile, newer fundamentalist sects, particularly those that mastered fund-raising through tele-vangelism, have moved in to accommodate elites feeling threatened by the new directions of the traditional religious institutions. Such sects have also competed, often with development agendas and very con-siderable resources and sometimes with local government collaboration, for the souls of poor communities. In Guatemala, for example, fun-damentalist sects had a great deal to do with the spread of Protestantism from about 5 percent of the population in 1960 to about 30 percent at the end of the 1980s.

NOTES

1. Cited in Saul Landau, *The Dangerous Doctrine: National Security and U.S. Foreign Policy* (Boulder: Westview Press, 1988), p. 33.

2. In a speech delivered to Congress in March 1947, President Harry S. Truman declared, "I believe that it must be a policy of the United States to support free peoples who are resisting attempted subjugation by armed minor-ities or by outside pressures." Cited in ibid., p. 36.

3. Professor Brady Tyson, of American University in Washington, D.C., defined a liberal as "one whose interests are not at stake."

4. The program reached its low point in the 1970s but began to rebound in the 1980s. At the beginning of the 1990s, the Peace Corps was once again in vogue, enjoying bipartisan support. In early 1990, it was functioning in seventy countries, with about 6,100 volunteers and trainees.

5. This reflected a general difference of approach of the two administrations. Nixon tended to accept the Democrat-inspired federal government as it was and work around it, while Reagan tended to bend it to his own purposes.

6. U.S. House of Representatives, 101st Congress, 1st Session, Committee on Foreign Affairs, *Background Materials on Foreign Assistance,* Report of the Task Force on Foreign Assistance, February 1989 (Washington, D.C.: GPO, 1989), p. 247; Stephen Hellinger, Douglas Hellinger, and Fred M. O'Regan, *Aid for Just Development* (Boulder: Lynne Rienner Publishers, 1988), p. 27.

7. Hellinger, Hellinger, and O'Regan, op. cit., p. 27.

8. Ibid., pp. 30–31.

9. U.S. House of Representatives, 101st Congress, 1st Session, Committee on Foreign Affairs, op. cit., pp. 152, 228.

10. No partisan of peace would want to discount Kennan's conversion; but it should be recognized that, at least since the beginning of the McCarthy era, policymakers in the United States have dared to become statesmen only after they were permanently "out of the loop," or irretrievably retired.

11. Elliott R. Morss and Victoria A. Morss, *The Future of Western Devel-opment Assistance* (Boulder: Westview Press, 1986), pp. 4–6.

12. U.S. House of Representatives, 101st Congress, 1st Session, Committee on Foreign Affairs, op. cit., p. 60.

13. Paula Hirschoff, "Yen for the World," *Worldview* (National Council of Returned Peace Corps Volunteers) 2, no. 2, Summer 1989, pp. 16–19.

14. U.S. House of Representatives, 101st Congress, 1st Session, Committee on Foreign Affairs, op. cit., p. 19.

15. U.S. Department of State, *Soviet and East European Aid to the Third World, 1981,* Department of State Publication 9345, Bureau of Intelligence and Research, February 1983.

16. Morss and Morss, op. cit., pp. 5–6, 70.

17. *Latin America Weekly Report,* October 10 and 24, 1980; *Central America Report,* November 8, 1980.

18. U.S. House of Representatives, 101st Congress, 1st Session, Committee on Foreign Affairs, op. cit., p. 180.

19. James H. Mittelman, *Out from Underdevelopment* (New York: St. Martin's Press, 1988), pp. 45–57.

20. Denise A. Wallen and Gerald R. Kinsman, "Focus on Funding: Information About U.S. Philanthropy for the Non-U.S. Grantseeker" (unpublished), December 1989.

21. Hendrick van der Heijden, "Development Impact and Effectiveness of Non-Governmental Organizations: The Record of Progress in Rural Development Co-operation," International Symposium, Royal Tropical Institute, Amsterdam, September 30–October 4, 1985, pp. 1–4.

22. Hellinger, Hellinger, and O'Regan, op. cit., p. 115.

SUGGESTED READINGS

Arnold, Stephen H., *Implementing Development Assistance: European Approaches to Basic Needs* (Boulder: Westview Press, 1982).

Arnson, Cynthia, and William Goodfellow, "OPIC: Insuring the Status Quo," *International Policy Report* 3, no. 2, September 1977.

Ayers, Robert L., *Banking on the Poor: The World Bank and Poverty* (Cambridge: MIT Press, 1983).

Chomsky, Noam, and Edward S. Herman, *The Washington Connection and Third World Fascism: The Political Economy of Human Rights,* Vol. 1 (Boston: South End Press, 1979).

Development Assistance Committee, *Twenty-five Years of Development Cooperation: A Review* (Paris: Organization for Economic Cooperation and Development, 1985).

Hayter, Teresa, *Aid as Imperialism* (Baltimore: Penguin Books, 1971).

Hayter, Teresa, and Catherine Watson, *Aid: Rhetoric and Reality* (London: Pluto Press, 1985).

Kolko, Gabriel, *Confronting the Third World: United States Foreign Policy, 1945–1980* (New York: Pantheon Books, 1988).

Lewis, John P., and Valeriana Kallab, eds., *Development Strategies Reconsidered* (Washington, D.C.: Overseas Development Council, 1986).

Massachusetts Institute of Technology, Center for International Studies, "The Objectives of United States Economic Assistance Programs," Study prepared for the Special Committee to Study the Foreign Aid Program, United States Senate, 85th Congress, 1st Session (January 1957).

Morss, Elliott R., and Victoria A. Morss, *The Future of Western Development Assistance* (Boulder: Westview Press, 1986).

Morss, Elliott R., and Victoria A. Morss, *U.S. Foreign Aid: An Assessment of New and Traditional Development Strategies* (Boulder: Westview Press, 1982).

Please, Stanley, *The Hobbled Giant: Essays on the World Bank* (Boulder: Westview Press, 1984).

Scheman, Ronald L., ed., *The Alliance for Progress: A Retrospective* (New York: Praeger, 1988).

U.S. Department of State, *Report of the Carlucci Commission on Security and Economic Assistance* (Washington, D.C.: GPO, 1985).

Third World Strategies

5 It has long been an article of faith in the West that the underdevelopment of the non-West is a consequence of its failure to become—or delay in becoming—a part of the world system. Opinion leaders of the non-West have increasingly become convinced that the opposite is the case—that their underdevelopment is a consequence of the nature of their relations with the West. Thus, while rarely lacking in advice from the First World, some Third World leaders, movements, and regional organizations have devised their own strategies for protecting their industries, expanding their markets, and even competing with First World producers. Some such strategies have been successful at times and in places. But over time First World powers have ordinarily found ways either to frustrate such strategies or to turn them to their own advantage.

IMPORT-SUBSTITUTION INDUSTRIALIZATION

The Latin American states, independent—or at least nominally so—longer than most other Third World states, got a head start in testing locally generated strategies. This was not merely by choice; it was sometimes by necessity, as in the case of import-substitution industrialization (ISI). When the devastation of World War I, followed in short order by worldwide depression, deprived those countries of the markets for their primary products and their sources of credit and manufactured goods, they had little choice but to fall back on their own devices. The strategy they adopted was one that dealt directly with the newly unmet demands, thus minimizing dislocations in the existing economic systems. That is, Latin American governments, particularly those of the more developed South American states, began to encourage domestic entrepreneurs to manufacture the products that had been imported but were now unavailable.

As elaborated later through the efforts of the UN Economic Commission for Latin America (ECLA), this strategy called for nurturing the national markets. Light industry was broadly promoted, and a few countries were able to establish heavy industries as well. Low-interest loans from government banks and financial institutions were among many fiscal incentives employed, and fledgling industries were protected by tariffs, quotas, licensing, and exchange controls. Public enterprises sprang up to support private ones, and regional development commissions sought to integrate more-backward areas into national economies.

Foreign producers, frustrated by trade barriers, began to invest directly in the manufacturing sector and produce for local markets. They were often resistant, however, to government regulation designed to promote forward and backward linkages, local reinvestment of profits, employment of nationals, protection of labor, and sharing of ownership and control with nationals. In such cases, nationalization was sometimes threatened or, more rarely, carried out.

Along with its very positive features, ISI as generally practiced in Latin America (and similar strategies undertaken subsequently in Africa and Asia, particularly in India and other states having well-developed middle classes after they gained independence) had some serious drawbacks. For one thing, such rapid industrialization called for major outlays for capital goods. In the face of chronic shortages of hard-currency reserves, this led to heavy foreign borrowing and consequent debt and inflation. For another, the technologies employed, drawn from the First World, were capital-intensive. Thus, even as the manufacturing sector grew, the proportion of the urban labor force able to find work soon began to decline. Furthermore, new industries were often unable to take advantage of economies of scale, and protective tariff barriers were conducive to inefficiency and monopoly. And given the unequal bargaining position of Third World states, the companies taking advantage of tax incentives, governmental infrastructure support, and tariff protection were all too often foreign ones anyway. Finally, production in many countries remained geared to the fortunate few—those who could afford TVs and stereo sets, washing machines and cars—while demand was growing on the part of the many for affordable shoes and building materials and bicycles—thus accelerating inflation.

One response to the mounting problems with ISI was experimentation with regional integration, as we shall explore below. The challenges of the ISI approach had never been narrowly economic, however; they were also political. And it was in the political arena that its collapse was most dramatically manifest. The real crisis of the ISI strategy was felt when it became clear that continual growth would be dependent upon expansion of the domestic market, and that such expansion implied a far-reaching redistribution of wealth and power. This recognition served to unite and mobilize elites—both domestic and foreign—who saw their interests threatened. The upshot was the suppression—in many countries through armed force—of effective demand and the adoption of a new strategy. This development will be discussed under the heading "Counterrevolutionary Strategies."

EXPORT-LED GROWTH

The Third World success stories most widely touted in the 1980s by major donor agencies and multilateral financial institutions were those of the so-called dragons, or the "gang of four": South Korea, Taiwan, Singapore, and Hong Kong. Their success and the somewhat lesser but still impressive success of Thailand and Malaysia in raising GNP per capita over the past two decades have been seen as validating the export-led growth model, especially as compared to an approach featuring import substitution.

The East Asian Gang of Four

From 1972 to 1982, the "gang of four" had experienced per capita growth rates ranging from 79 percent to 97 percent and increases in world export market shares ranging from 500 to 1,270 percent; even more remarkably, that growth had been accompanied by a diminishing gap between rich and poor. Such growth and export performance took place despite relatively modest national resource bases, but with the impetus of very considerable amounts of foreign investment and development assistance.

In promoting throughout the Third World an "adjustment" package based on export expansion, but including also monetary stabilization, trade liberalization, privatization, and deregulation, spokesmen of First World creditors (i.e., the United States, the IMF, and the World Bank) have highlighted these East Asian successes. Critics of the proposed adjustment package point out, however, that extreme stress on export promotion can lead to runaway inflation, and that Japan and Korea showed concern for bringing their postwar inflation under control before placing great stress on exports. They also became powerful exporters while resisting import liberalization and maintaining controls on foreign investment.

It was not until long after their competitive export positions were well established, critics of the creditor approach maintain, that the most successful East Asian countries turned to import liberalization, and they never accepted the now-prescribed reduction of state intervention.

Furthermore, these countries had gained policy flexibility through the prior elimination of concentrated landholdings and, in general, through concern for employment and income in both rural and urban areas.[1]

The Extraordinary Case of Taiwan

The Taiwanese case is particularly interesting in that it seems to defy all the development models. Taiwan experienced dramatic annual growth in per capita income, from about U.S. $70 at the end of World War II to about $6,000 in 1988. Meanwhile population was growing at the rate of 3.5 percent annually until the 1960s and about 2 percent thereafter. Real GNP growth averaged 9.2 percent over those years, with exports increasing from 9 percent of GNP in 1952 to 49 percent in 1980. These developments were given impetus by massive infusions of foreign investment and aid.

Surprisingly, though, this growth has been accompanied from the beginning by a trend toward reduction in income inequality. The income of the poorest 20 percent of the population rose from 3 percent of the total in 1953 to 7.7 percent in 1964, while that of the richest 5 percent dropped from 32.6 percent to 16.2 percent. Great improvement was also seen in housing, health, and education. This combination of rapid growth and diminishing inequity has been explained in large part by the land reform program undertaken between 1949 and 1953. Redistribution of the land was not in this case a revolutionary development; rather, it was a multipurpose project of a conquering new elite—the Chinese Nationalists fleeing the mainland. Thus, in redistributing the land, they not only channeled a new infusion of money into industry but also broke the power base of the native Taiwanese oligarchy. Public lands formerly held by the Japanese were also sold to farmers on reasonable terms. Along with timely attention to rural income and agricultural productivity, government policy favored technological developments that made use of abundant labor and saved land and capital.[2]

Even more surprising, however, is the fact that these economically progressive policies were undertaken by a rigidly authoritarian and socially elitist government. Through almost four decades of martial law, first under Chiang Kai-shek and later under his son Chiang Ching-Kuo, the native Taiwanese, who make up 80 percent of the population, have had precious little representation or participation in the country's political life. Nevertheless there had been a mushrooming of so-called self-help groups that were taking popular demands into the streets. There were some 1,800 street demonstrations in 1987 alone. At the end of the 1980s, Taiwan's legislative bodies were still dominated by 1949 escapees from the mainland, claiming to represent places like Szechuan and Inner Mongolia, but upon the death of Chiang Ching-Kuo, the presidency and leadership of the Kuomintang passed to a native Taiwanese; and a new opposition party, the Democratic Progressive Party, finally accorded legal recognition in 1989, was rapidly gaining in popularity.

The Drawbacks

Unlike import substitution, export promotion is not limited by the size of the domestic market, and it is less likely to protect inefficiency. Its prospects are limited, however, by external demand, a particularly vexing problem when most Third World states are pursuing the same strategy and First World countries are increasingly protecting their own markets.

In fact, at the beginning of the 1990s, most Third World countries were placing the highest priority on export promotion. It was not normally seen as a matter of choice, however; rather, it was dictated by the crushing weight of foreign debt and the obligation of maintaining debt servicing as a precondition for obtaining further credit. The strategy as promoted by creditors and the IMF differed in little more than product mix from that characteristic of an earlier period of direct colonial rule. Even where growth had been dramatic, the fruits of that growth were not normally redistributed in any form. It was the failure of that strategy to promote balanced and equitable growth in most of the Third World countries that set the East Asian experience in relief. The failures or limits of both ISI and export promotion for countries acting alone led some strategists to promote moves toward economic integration.

ECONOMIC INTEGRATION

The trend to economic integration was inspired in part by fear of saturation (at least under existing economic and political conditions) of domestic markets for industrial output. It was hoped that such integration—eliminating intraregional tariff barriers and erecting common external ones, for example—would produce economies of scale and give the ISI process a new lease on life. Like the elaborate and rationalized versions of ISI itself, the trend to economic integration, at least as it evolved in the Western Hemisphere, was largely an initiative of ECLA, under the leadership of Argentinean economist Raúl Prebisch, although it was inspired as well by the early success of the European Economic Community (EEC).

Both the Central American Common Market (CACM) and the Latin American Free Trade Association (LAFTA), linking Mexico and the South American states, were established in 1960. Both areas saw marked increases in intraregional trade. Trade among LAFTA states increased by 100 percent from 1961 to 1968. CACM results were even more impressive. Intraregional exports as a percentage of total Latin American exports rose from 6.5 percent in 1960 to 23 percent in 1970.[3] Nevertheless, serious problems plagued both organizations from the beginning. Although there were special concessions for the poorer member states, the benefits of integration accrued disproportionately to the more-developed ones. Furthermore, although the United States had resisted fiercely the trend to integration, foreign-based multinationals soon maneuvered to take advantage of the expanded markets.

The coup de grace for the CACM was the so-called Soccer War, which broke out between El Salvador and Honduras in 1969. LAFTA's disintegration, also in the late 1960s, was less dramatic, resulting primarily from the frustration of other states with the disproportionate advantages reaped by Argentina, Brazil, and Mexico. The Andean states—Bolivia, Chile, Colombia, Ecuador, and Peru, later joined by Venezuela—formed their own Andean Common Market (ANCOM). ANCOM's most interesting innovation, watched closely by other Third World states, was its approach to foreign investment. Economic plans directed foreign investors to sectors where capital was most needed. The repatriation of profits was limited. Parent companies were not allowed to restrict exports by their subsidiaries, and subsidiaries and other foreign-based enterprises were eventually (generally in fifteen years) to turn over majority control to locals. ANCOM was brought down by the early 1980s, primarily by political changes in member states, beginning with the military takeover in Chile in 1973.

LAFTA stumbled on as form without much content until it was replaced in 1980 by the even less promising Latin American Integration Association (LAIA). In the Caribbean Basin, the early measures undertaken through the Caribbean Free Trade Area (CARIFTA) proved less than impressive. The organization was superseded by the Caribbean Common Market (CARICOM), which continues to exist, though without seriously transforming trading patterns in the area.

Aspects of economic integration for other Third World regions have been proposed and discussed but have generally fallen victim to sabotage by neocolonial powers, intraregional feuds, or political and economic crises in individual states. Kwame Nkrumah's Pan-Africanist blueprint, for example, included progress in continental monetary integration as part of a larger economic and political integration process. Along with an African monetary zone, Nkrumah's plan included an

African central bank and an African payments and clearing union.[4] Nkrumah was ousted from the presidency of Ghana in 1966, but his ideas have reappeared from time to time.

In fact, several regional organizations for economic cooperation in Africa have been formed at various times, but their memberships and objectives have been limited and their successes even more so. Disparities among member states in size and levels of development have been a major obstacle to economic integration in Africa, as in Latin America. Unequal gains for Kenya, for example, to the detriment of Uganda and Tanzania, contributed to the collapse of the East African Community. Similar problems have plagued the Communauté Economique de l'Afrique de l'Ouest (CEAO), in which Ivory Coast has monopolized benefits, and the Economic Organization of West African States (ECOWAS), dominated by Nigeria. And the Customs Union of Swaziland, Botswana, Lesotho, and South Africa is an obvious case of "horse and rabbit stew" (i.e., equal parts of horse and rabbit: one horse, one rabbit).

Furthermore, export-oriented primary producers do not normally experience much demand for each other's products, and even where processed or manufactured goods are available, member states of a customs union might have to be willing to import relatively crude, inefficiently produced goods and even to give them tariff protection. Finally, the former colonial powers whose trade and aid continue to loom so large in African economies will not likely be supportive of cooperative efforts among African states unless European-based companies are the major beneficiaries. And given the political weakness and economic dependency of most African states, it does not seem likely that any regional project could long withstand concerted European opposition.

Nevertheless, the UN Economic Commission for Africa continued throughout the 1970s to promote regional economic integration as a means to collective self-reliance. The Organization of African Unity (OAU) has also lent its support to the idea. The Plan of Action drawn up at the OAU's 1980 meeting in Lagos called for the establishment of an Africa Payments Union by the end of the decade. The decade, however, has been a grim one for most of Africa, scarcely lending itself to bold regional initiatives.[5]

MULTILATERAL BARGAINING

Since the 1960s, LDCs have sought to defend their economic interests through the formation of bargaining blocs within regional and global organizations. The most important exchanges in what has become a

North-South confrontation have taken place within organs of the United Nations, particularly the General Assembly and the Economic and Social Council (ECOSOC) and in special ongoing UN conferences like the Conference on Trade and Development (UNCTAD) and the Law of the Sea Conference (UNLOS III).

Raúl Prebisch became the first executive secretary of UNCTAD, which met in 1964 in Switzerland, in 1969 in India, and in 1972 in Chile. The LDC caucus, G-77 (which actually claimed more than 120 adherents in the 1980s), found UNCTAD a receptive forum, at least in principle. The developed states accepted the G-77 proposal of granting trade concessions on a nonreciprocal basis. The concept was later incorporated into the General Agreement on Tariffs and Trade (GATT) and adopted by the EEC in the Lomé Convention of 1975.

The G-77 promotion of commodity agreements for the purpose of stabilizing primary product prices drew a mixed response. Proposals that developed states devote 1 percent of their GNP to Third World aid and that transnational corporations be subjected to a code of conduct were accepted only on a basis of voluntary compliance; thus, states and corporations with the most at stake were not likely to be accommodating.

In 1974, nevertheless, the United Nations created a commission to monitor the conduct of transnational corporations. A Mexican proposal at the 1972 UNCTAD resulted in the drafting of the UN Charter on the Economic Rights and Duties of States, which was approved by the General Assembly in 1974. Along with preferential treatment without reciprocity and stable prices for Third World exports, the charter stressed the right of expropriation of foreign assets. The charter was to be the first step toward the establishment of the New International Economic Order (NIEO). What with famine in Africa, staggering debts in Latin America, and political and ethnic strife in much of Asia, the dream of a new order appears to have receded since the 1970s, but the NIEO remains an important expression of common vision and purpose.

The Law of the Sea conferences were a response to patterns of conflict between the United States and a number of Latin American countries that claimed a 200-mile expanse of territorial waters for the purpose of regulating tuna fishing. The claim, first made by Ecuador, Peru, and Chile in the 1950s, spread through Latin America in the 1960s and from there to Africa and Asia. From the first session of UNLOS III in Venezuela in 1974 until the final one in New York in 1982, the Third World caucus presented a virtually united front. Most G-77 positions were adopted, including the 200-mile exclusive economic zone (EEZ). The United States objected vehemently, however, to the deep seabed mining provisions and voted against the convention at the United Nations in 1982. The USSR and most European states abstained.

By 1989, as a consequence of the debt crisis and the efforts of Third World countries, at the urging of First World agencies and bankers, to promote exports, many of those Third World countries had begun to participate very actively in the negotiations of the General Agreement on Tariffs and Trade (GATT). They are finding, to their dismay, that after giving in to First World pressures to open their own markets and to expand exports, the First World is now rapidly erecting barriers to keep out their products.

RESOURCE MANAGEMENT
AND COMMODITY CARTELS

The Organization of Petroleum Exporting Countries (OPEC)

For a few Third World countries—the dozen or so members of OPEC—the commodity cartel has proved a most useful strategy. The fortuitous experience of OPEC, however, is not likely to be replicated for producers of other commodities. In the first place, the petroleum cartel was not created by OPEC. The producer states had only to cut themselves into the management and the reward systems of a private cartel, the "Seven Sisters" international petroleum companies,[6] that had already proved its potential.

Before World War II, and as recently as the late 1950s, the seven international majors, controlling at least 80 percent of oil production outside of North America and the Soviet bloc, kept the industry wildly profitable through understandings on market shares and pricing policies. The minimal cost of production, especially in the Middle East, meant that despite dramatic growth in the industry in the postwar period, the companies were able to keep prices and profits high. As economic nationalism spread through the Third World, however, and host governments began to demand more in the way of royalties and regulation, the majors began to expand into new areas, playing off one country against another. Such maneuvers, plus a potential oil surplus and a reduction in prices posted by the companies for crude oil, led to the formation of OPEC in 1960.

Thus, the impetus for the creation of OPEC was the need to present a common front and enhance government bargaining power vis-à-vis producer companies. Ultimately, however, it was the commonality or symbiosis of interests between OPEC and the companies vis-à-vis oil

consumers, along with the clout major companies enjoyed with governments of consumer countries, particularly the United States, that led
to such spectacular success.

The global "energy crisis" of the 1970s was introduced abruptly with
the Arab oil embargo following the Egyptian invasion of Israel on
October 6, 1973, but the enduring effects were economic more than
political; the embargo was accompanied by an explosion in prices. The
OPEC countries had established, with the collaboration of the major
companies, a means of controlling production, and the fourfold rise in
oil prices of 1973–1974 was maintained thereafter.[7] It was not until
after the additional sharp price increases of 1979–1980 that market
forces struck back. With those increases, the producers had overreached;
conservation measures and alternate energy sourcing came into play,
but it was to a far greater extent the consequent global recession and
the debt crisis that seriously suppressed demand and weakened prices.

In the interim a number of countries, particularly Saudi Arabia and
the Emirates and other Persian Gulf ministates, had moved from client
to donor state categories. For some of the OPEC states, however, the
bust that followed the boom was worse than the preexisting poverty.
There was a tendency for higher levels of public spending to be maintained even as the boom was ending, and public borrowing was promoted by bankers frantic to unload their money. The Nigerian public
deficit, for example, rose from 1.1 percent of gross domestic product
(GDP) in 1979 to 9.17 percent in 1981, even as the country borrowed
$1 billion a year in 1979 and 1980. Nigerian imports increased from
$9.7 billion in 1977 to $19 billion in 1981, only to fall back sharply to
$4 billion by 1986, as credit dried up.[8]

Other Producer Associations

Even before the boom years of OPEC, other Third World countries
had experimented with producer associations and many more were
inspired by the fairy-tale success of some OPEC members. In the 1980s,
such associations included: African Groundnut Council, Association of
Natural Rubber Producing Countries, Asian and Pacific Coconut Com-
munity, Association of Iron Ore Exporting Countries, Intergovernmental
Council of Copper Exporting Countries, Cocoa Producers' Alliance,
Group of Latin American and Caribbean Sugar Exporting Countries,
Inter-African Coffee Organization, International Bauxite Association,
International Tea Promotion Association, Organization of Wood Pro-
ducing and Exporting African Countries, African and Malagasy Coffee
Organization, Pepper Community, and Union of Banana Exporting
Countries.

Achievements of such associations, however, have been modest and generally short-lived. Consumers willing to endure long lines at gasoline pumps and to pay outrageous prices for relief from such lines would not behave in a similar manner with respect to peanuts or bananas. Nor does the power of transnationals dealing in those commodities compare with that of the Seven Sisters.

Harnessing Energy: The Latin American Experience

The state petroleum corporation is now the rule in Latin America, being found in Mexico and nine of the countries of South America (all of Latin America, that is, except Central America and the Caribbean, Paraguay, and the Guianas). Argentina established the first state corporation, the Yacimientos Petroliferos Fiscales, or YPF, in 1922. Although Uruguay had no proven reserves, it followed suit in 1931 with the establishment of a state corporation to manage importation, refining, and distribution. Bolivia's state corporation was established in 1936, Colombia's in 1948, Chile's and Brazil's in 1950. PEMEX, the giant Mexican corporation, Petroleos Mexicanos, was established with the nationalization of foreign companies in 1938.

The nationalizations and establishment of state corporations were not simply expressions of nationalism in the abstract but took place often in response to specific instances of unacceptable behavior on the part of the foreign companies, which have long been notorious as poor corporate citizens. It is generally believed in Latin America that oil company ambitions were behind the initiation of war by Bolivia on Paraguay in 1936 and by Peru on Ecuador in 1944. The International Petroleum Company, a Standard Oil subsidiary, defied the Peruvian government's tax claims against it until its expropriation in 1968. It is even likely that rivalries between U.S. and British oil companies played a part in the Mexican Revolution. The son of the dictator Porfirio Díaz was a member of the board of directors of the major British-owned oil company in Mexico, El Aguila. The leader of the revolution against Díaz, Francisco Madero, was reputed to have been financed by Standard Oil and other U.S. companies jealous of the position of British interests, and after the revolution was successful, Madero's legal adviser went to work for a subsidiary of Standard Oil.[9]

Thus in much of Latin America foreign oil companies were not welcome. At the same time, obstacles have been placed in the way of the exploitation of oil resources by state-owned corporations. Even under Democratic administrations, the U.S. Export-Import Bank long refused, out of loyalty to free-enterprise principles, to make credit available to state corporations. Other creditors, including the World Bank, generally followed suit.

Today these circumstances have changed somewhat. The heavy role taken by the state in Latin American oil exploration and the limitations placed on foreign corporations are no longer as unusual as they once were. The increase in prices has rendered of little consequence the greater costs of production in Latin America as opposed to the Middle East. And the prospects of shortage have made it necessary to exploit resources wherever they can be found. But the increased assertiveness of governments and state oil corporations, and the expertise that government petroleum specialists have acquired, should not be taken to mean that the international companies have adjusted to a new role as benign and cooperative good citizens, despite the efforts of public relations firms to portray the companies as disinterested philanthropists.

The Latin American governments remain wary of the power of the companies and prefer to do without them if they can. The problem is that the companies can still make themselves indispensable, sometimes for innocent technical reasons, sometimes by more heavy-handed manipulation. Thus when, in 1969, President Alfredo Ovando nationalized Gulf's holdings in Bolivia, the company organized a worldwide boycott of Bolivian oil. The control of marketing networks by the international companies, at least at that time, was so effective that the Bolivians eventually had to give in and come to terms with the company (although the attempt was made to disguise the surrender by having it handled by the company's Spanish subsidiary, whose name did not reveal its connection with the parent corporation). Gulf followed similar tactics in its 1976 dispute with the government of Ecuador, suing in California courts to take possession of a shipment of oil consigned to Atlantic Richfield Company by the Ecuadorean state oil corporation. On that occasion the even-handed mediation of the U.S. ambassador, Richard Bloomfield, was successful in reaching a settlement generally acceptable to both sides.

The international companies' control over marketing networks was also responsible for their securing a very favorable financial settlement from the Venezuelan government at the time of the 1976 nationalization of the foreign companies.[10] Venezuela has subsequently been able to renegotiate the disadvantageous marketing and technical assistance agreements it was forced to accept because of its weak bargaining position at that time.

In addition to their control of marketing, what the companies have that state corporations may lack is technology and capital. Thus the technically most competent state corporation, PEMEX, which is capable of handling the technical requirements of on-shore petroleum production, has found it necessary to form joint companies with Houston-based U.S. drilling concerns in order to drill offshore in the Gulf of Mexico.

Where most of the state corporations have fallen down is in the feebleness of their exploratory drilling programs. The capital requirements of getting drilling equipment into the relatively inaccessible regions where oil is likely to be found, and the inherently risk-laden nature of oil exploration, are responsible here. Governments in Latin America are normally hard-pressed for funds to deal with even the most urgent demands being placed on them and are generally in no position to commit extremely large amounts of capital in ventures whose short-term success is not assured. Thus some specialists now believe the appropriate time to nationalize an oil industry is when the national territory is fully explored, all the risks have been taken, and production is going full blast. This was more or less the point in their national petroleum development at which the Venezuelans chose to nationalize. The Ecuadoreans, unfortunately, inspired by the Venezuelans' example, proceeded to nationalize Gulf's holdings when only a fraction of the national territory had been explored. The government oil corporation, Corporación Ecuatoriana de Petróleos (CEPE), did not itself have the capital to engage in further exploration, and other companies were discouraged from entering Ecuador by the example of what had happened to Gulf. The goose was killed before all the golden eggs had been laid. The government recognized its tactical error, and attempts have since been made to attract foreign companies.

REVOLUTIONARY STRATEGIES

There is no single revolutionary blueprint adequate or appropriate to inform the undertakings of Third World leaders generally. Each new revolution draws lessons from earlier ones but builds also on local needs and experience and on the dynamics unique to its own national revolutionary process.

Each is also a product of its own times. Just as most rebels at the turn of the nineteenth century drew upon the ideals of liberalism and the French enlightenment, most rebels since the turn of the twentieth have drawn to some extent upon the ideals and the analysis of Marx, as elaborated by Lenin. But the guidance to be drawn from Marx has been limited by his miscalculation as to the level of development at which a society is most susceptible to revolution.

Developments of the twentieth century have shown that it is not at the stage of advanced capitalism, but rather in the early stages of transition to capitalism—when subsistence farmers are being displaced and when the middle class seeks allies among the lower classes—that social upheaval may give rise to revolution. Once the middle class has acquired a certain size and status and has been co-opted by the power structure, the outcome of social upheaval is more likely to be counter-revolution. Thus, a development strategy that assumed the irrelevance of the peasantry and the hostility of the middle class would be off on the wrong track from the start.

The actual course a society in revolution pursues in its quest for development depends on at least three factors: (1) strategies consciously adopted by leaders; (2) more or less spontaneous popular initiatives; and (3) the domestic and international context, including a generally predictable but nonetheless awesome obstacle course laid down by external powers and business and banking interests. The course pursued—and it sometimes seems a zigzag one—grows out of the interplay of these factors.

The extent of redistribution, and thus the success of a revolution, depend in large part on how much wealth there is to redistribute. It also depends on maintaining the unity of the revolutionary coalition and, in general, the politicization of the population. Revolution is the ultimate bottom-up development strategy, and just as top-down strategies call for the minimization of political involvement, revolution calls for the maximization of it. There is no such thing as a technocratic approach to revolution. The only programs that stand much chance of success are those that spring from the aspirations, the imagination, and the capabilities of the common people.

While most spokesmen of Third World interests charge that those interests are continuously damaged by the more powerful forces that calibrate the workings of the international capitalist economic system, few such spokesmen—whether of revolutionary or of more conventional bent—would actually seek to withdraw their countries from participation in that system. Tendencies toward autarky are more likely to be imposed than chosen.

Even the Chinese of the People's Republic, who should have been better able than most to go it alone, opted to maintain commercial and other ties with the West. Those ties were severed early on by the United States and its allies. The Soviet Union extended technical assistance in the early years, particularly in the start-up stages of heavy industry; but after the mid-1950s, the Soviets also pulled out, leaving the Chinese without access even to spare parts and with little alternative to "self-reliance."

Soviet assistance has proved crucial and more reliable for a number of other revolutionary regimes subjected to trade and credit embargoes by the West. But such rescue operations have brought the Soviet Union few tangible rewards; and the all-out supporting role it undertook in the case of Cuba has not been and is not likely to be repeated. Meanwhile, being forced into self-reliance has had marginal benefits for some countries. Nicaraguans have rediscovered traditional remedies, for example, that are just as effective and far less costly than equivalent drugs previously imported. Such benefits, however, have generally been heavily outweighed by the economic and political costs of trade disruption.

Soviet credit and technical assistance, incidentally, has not necessarily inclined revolutionary regimes to adopt Soviet development models. Mozambique's revolutionary party, the Mozambique Liberation Front (FRELIMO), found Chinese and Yugoslav approaches more relevant to its needs, and Nicaragua's Sandinistas have drawn particularly from the experiences and institutions of Mexico.

Since Third World rebellion has generally been against colonial and neocolonial powers as well as against domestic elites, most revolutionary ideology has been infused with economic nationalism, and revolutionary strategy has included some measure of nationalization or expropriation. Initial targets have included public utilities, the communications media, banking, and extractive or plantation industries that dominated exports. The extent of socialization actually carried out, however, has often had more to do with military or political developments than with economic planning. In Mozambique, for example, about 90 percent of the Portuguese settlers had left the country within a year of independence; thus the new revolutionary government was compelled to take control of small businesses, shops, garages, and such, which it had no preparation or desire to manage. It has since invited former residents to return and invest in the private sector.[11]

Land reform has commonly been a high priority for revolutionary governments, but approaches have varied widely. In Mexico and Bolivia, the displacement of the landowning classes was not a plan of the middle-class revolutionary leadership. Rather, it was an initiative of the peasants themselves, which the national leadership had little choice but to embrace. The brutality and counterproductivity of Stalin's forced collectivization have limited the appeal of that approach for most subsequent revolutionaries. The most notable exception was Mao Zedong; he turned to forced collectivization only in the mid-1950s after concluding that a gradualist strategy for rural transformation, based primarily on cooperatives, had failed to promote equity or to generate a surplus for diversion to industry. His turn to collectivization so offended Nikita Khrushchev, who was attempting to de-Stalinize, that it became one of the several factors generating a Sino-Soviet rift.

Elsewhere direct state control of agriculture has generally been limited to plantations expropriated from foreigners, colonial powers, or, as in the case of Nicaragua, friends and relations of the deposed tyrant, and to marketing arrangements. Some measure of redistribution of land has been common, however, either to individuals or to village or tribal cooperatives or communes (e.g., communal *ejidos* in Mexico, *Ujamaa* cooperative villages in Tanzania). The extension of credit and services to new landowners has generally been programmed, but scarcity of technicians and resources has often prevented follow-up.

Having suffered from dependence on imported manufactured goods with continuously escalating prices, countries undergoing revolutions have often sought to abandon reliance on primary commodities with unreliable markets and to industrialize rapidly. That strategy has generally bogged down early on due to capital flight and shortage of hard currency for the purchase of capital goods. In the face of trade embargoes, it has proved difficult enough just to acquire the spar parts to keep existing industries operating. A common fallback strategy has been that of promoting low-tech processing or other light industry, building upon available raw materials.

Innovations in industry have often involved some approach to worker self-management. The most elaborated and successful experiment of that sort has been that of Yugoslavia, the only East European country apart from the Soviet Union and Albania to experience its own home-grown revolution. The strategy contributed for more than two decades to raising living standards and to maintaining popular participation. Over the years, however, as conflicts have arisen between the directives of central authorities and the decisions of self-managed units, they have increasingly been resolved through the circumscription of the jurisdiction of the latter.

Ironically, perhaps, the greatest successes of revolutionary governments have been in the delivery of services—services that reformist governments promise but are usually unable to deliver: health care, education, recreation, and better wages and working conditions, at least initially, for labor. This is because, while revolutionary governments are sorely lacking in material resources—they were poor to start with and are then subjected to military and economic warfare—what they have in abundance is highly mobilized and motivated citizens, committed to a common vision. Such a citizenry can do little, in the absence of material resources or external markets, about building heavy industry; but it can accomplish near miracles in the promotion of literacy or the eradication of disease. When the population ceases to be so mobilized and motivated, it is safe to say that the revolution has run its course.

Characteristics often attributed to revolution—dogmatism, centralization of decision-making, and rigid bureaucratization, for example—

are indicative either of simple tyranny masquerading as revolution or of the onset of a postrevolutionary reconcentrational phase. The essence of revolution is the presence of common purpose in the absence of centralized control. People who have so recently risked life and limb in the pursuit of personal and national dignity will not easily be shunted aside when decisions affecting their livelihoods are to be made. In fact, dealing with a mobilized population and with the usual crises of external assault and material deprivation makes pragmatism and flexibility on the part of leadership absolutely essential.

In Nicaragua in the 1980s, policymakers and managers, far from being immobilized by centralization, were still struggling to coordinate the activities of ministries each of which had undergone its own self-contained revolution. Lacking the resources to promote change in the orderly manner they might have preferred, the Sandinistas had shown the good sense to be supportive of popular initiatives that showed promise, to give way where they had to—as in holding back the tides of new squatters pouring into already overcrowded Managua—and to revise their own policies when they confronted strong popular resistance.

COUNTERREVOLUTIONARY STRATEGIES

It might well be argued that counterrevolutionary strategies are not of the Third World but of the First. Since they are played out in the Third World, however, they will be dealt with briefly here.

The basic counterrevolutionary strategy has been less often a response or reaction to a revolutionary one than to a reformist strategy featuring economic nationalism and political liberalization. That is in part because reformist regimes and policies have been more vulnerable to overthrow and reversal than revolutionary ones.

The counterrevolutionary strategy outlined here is essentially one that characterized military dictatorship in South America's Southern Cone—Argentina, Uruguay, and Chile—and Brazil between the 1960s and the 1980s. With some variations, however, the strategy has been adopted by regimes in all major Third World areas—e.g., since the 1960s, those of Sese Seko Mobutu in Zaire; Ferdinand Marcos's Martial Law in the Philippines; Suharto's "New Order" in Indonesia; the shah in Iran; and Colonel Sitiveni Rabuka in Fiji. In some of these cases, the counterrevolutionary strategy shaded into kleptocracy, or government as theft. The strategy seeks not merely to freeze socioeconomic relationships and maintain the status quo but rather to promote accumulation or reconcentration—that is, to redistribute assets and income from the bottom up. Its political component, which will not be elaborated here, calls for the forceful expulsion of lower social strata from the political arena through the dissolution of parties, unions, and other organizations representing them.

The process of reconcentration has generally begun with a dampening of inflation through cutting back effective demand. Demand is cut through the pruning of social services, particularly those involving income transfer, and through wage freezes. Frozen wages, along with other indicators that the government has brought labor under control, can be expected to inspire the confidence of investors, both domestic and foreign. Other measures, however, such as credit, tax, and tariff policies, commonly favor foreign businesses over domestic ones. Domestic enterprises are absorbed by transnational ones, and a general denationalization and oligopolization occurs. The production system stresses exports, whether of raw materials or of manufactured goods. Domestic production favors consumer durables. Based on imported technology and product lines, its target market is the upper and middle classes. In some cases fully rationalized policies of weeding out national enterprises and, generally, of deindustrialization reversed and nullified the gains of economic development programs that had been in effect over several decades. Meanwhile, progressive forms of taxation gave way to retrogressive ones, and the easing of currency convertibility and profit repatriation accelerated the flow of capital from Third World to First.

Having successfully completed the first stage of economic transformation, the regime may then turn its attention to the promotion of industrialization, rural modernization through high-technology agribusiness, and infrastructural projects such as highways, ports, and dams. Whereas the early pruning of social services may have resulted in a general contraction of the state sector, that sector soon expands once again, but in different directions, responsive to the interests of the new ruling elite (generally the military) and its constituencies. New state activities may include the establishment of parastatal enterprises, such as weapons production, that generate income and high-level positions for elements of the new elite. Although it is uncommon, such a government may begin to play an important entrepreneurial role and to impose its own guidelines on foreign investors. Brazil, for example, was able to do so and, in general, to greatly modernize its economic system while generating economic growth. At the same time, real wages dropped dramatically. Between 1960 and 1970 every decile of the population except the top one experienced a relative loss of income.[12]

Some counterrevolutionary regimes, generally favored by foreign and international financial institutions, have had considerable early success in curbing inflation and later success in attracting foreign investment, promoting economic growth, and increasing foreign exchange earnings.

In the longer run, however, the extensive foreign borrowings, the abandonment of basic food production in favor of export agriculture, and other poorly conceived policies have brought these economies into crisis, in some cases hastening military withdrawal and the return of reformist governments.

THE PLIGHT OF THE REFORMER

One of the possible approaches to development, possible particularly in times of economic crisis, is the selection or election of a reformer to the highest political office. Such a development is an indication that political power and economic power are out of kilter. In the Third World especially, it may mean that economic growth and the elaboration of economic roles have generated a middle class that is attempting to wrench from the traditional power structure its rightful place in policy-making councils. It may mean that a more-or-less democratic system has given political representation to a working class that has yet to be expressed in economic redistribution. Or it may mean that a more-or-less counterrevolutionary regime, having arisen most likely in response to an earlier bout with reformism, has run its course or has at least come to recognize the need for an institutional buffer zone between exploiter and exploited and is now willing to share its power, or at least its stage, in exchange for sharing also the blame for inequitable policies.

The essential point is that the reformers' position is based on moral force—on the evidence of popular support for his or her ideas—rather than on economic power (e.g., ownership or control of the means of production). Organization charts notwithstanding, that generally means that the reformist president or prime minister lacks the full powers normally associated with the office—most important, control over military and paramilitary forces, including the police.

There have been times and places in which reformist leaders and movements have been able to consolidate their positions and move their societies to a higher level of development. During the first two decades of the twentieth century, for example, José Batlle y Ordóñez, having drawn a generation of European immigrants into his urban-based Colorado Party, was able to turn a politically and economically backward Uruguay into a modern social-welfare state. In India, building upon the inspiration of and the massive popular mobilization carried out by Mahatma Gandhi, Jawaharlal Nehru and the Congress Party were able to achieve far-reaching reform along with national independence. Nevertheless, the very extensive and sophisticated redistributive features built into India's constitution and laws are not much in evidence in the country's shantytowns and rural villages. Bankers, landowners, and industrialists, their actual power little diminished by reformist governments and legislation, have often been able to prevent implementation of laws running contrary to their interests.

As a rule, the position of the reformer is a most precarious one. The ritual of an election should not normally be viewed as conferring power upon the popular choice. If the winner does indeed appear to be the popular choice, and one who aspires to respond to the will of the electorate, the odds are that real power is not vested in the electorate and that the reformist leader will be straitjacketed by armed forces and/or foreign powers having motives contrary to those of the electorate. An extreme case in the late 1980s was President Vinicio Cerezo of Guatemala, who often seemed a virtual prisoner in the presidential palace.[13] President Cory Aquino of the Philippines and Prime Minister Benazir Bhutto of Pakistan appeared to have rather more latitude but hardly a full range of powers.

Directly or indirectly, First World governments and major donor institutions have often promoted political and economic reform, but within limits—limits guaranteed by flows of aid and credit as well as by First World influence on Third World armed forces. The limits might be drawn, for example, at the expropriation of foreign-owned assets, the encouragement of rural labor organization, or the trimming of military budgets.

Some reformists have rejected the limits and have come to be seen, in Cold War terms, as subversives. Others have accepted the limits and have come to be seen by their own constituencies as sellouts. The sellouts have then lost their political bases to the subversives. In the case of U.S. clients in particular, since U.S. policy has been more prone to sharp reversals than the policies of other donor states, reformists have been subject to a sort of political whiplash when limits were drawn in abruptly as a new administration replaced the old. The consequent fluidity has been unnerving to domestic and foreign elites and has sometimes led to counterrevolution.

As in the case of revolutionary governments, the most important policy breakthroughs of the reformist government are generally made early on, while supporters are mobilized and optimistic and before opponents have fully marshalled their forces. Reformers generally have more slack in the leash, however, for expanding human rights and civil liberties than for rewarding their constituencies with economic gains and opportunities. To the extent that they are able to raise the purchasing power of the lower classes, they run the risk of overstimulating the economy, creating shortages for more-affluent consumers, and generating inflation. The risk is particularly great since the increase in effective demand is likely to coincide with capital flight, domestic and international credit freezes, and other expressions of elite displeasure that interfere with production. In the end, the reformist, unable to generate employment elsewhere, may feel obliged to bloat his own bureaucracy.

Even if the reformer is utterly unsuccessful in redistributing income, his intentions alone will have sufficed to mobilize opposition on the right. Meanwhile, the high expectations of his erstwhile supporters will have turned to frustration, frustration likely to be vented in ways newly legitimated by the reformer, such as strikes and street demonstrations. Sooner or later, the police, perhaps with military backing, will turn on the strikers or demonstrators with unguarded fury. The reformist leader then has to decide whether to assume responsibility for repressive measures he did not authorize or admit publicly that he is not in control of the country's security forces. He usually chooses the former.

In Latin America and other areas where military governments have withdrawn from power in the 1980s—making way, in some cases, for genuine would-be reformers—that withdrawal has been considerably less than complete. While the military remains more or less on call, the more immediate task of protecting foreign and domestic elite interests—in particular of ensuring that debt servicing is maintained without threat to the existing economic structure—has fallen to the IMF.

When foreign creditors demand sacrifice as the price of extending further loans, the rich make the usual choice about whether to accept that sacrifice, and the sacrifice is borne by those who have no choice. Civilian elites who can no longer blame the military for such grossly inequitable policies can now pass the buck to the mysterious and seemingly omnipotent IMF.

A party such as the Dominican Republic's Dominican Revolutionary Party (PRD), popular and reformist in its origins, would ordinarily be a source of anxiety for economic elites and a target for military repression—as indeed it was throughout most of its history and as recently as 1978. Because of that history, in fact, it was a much-subdued PRD that assumed the presidency in 1978. Even so, the most modest of its promised welfare advances were thwarted by the austerity measures imposed by the IMF, while the military lurked in the background. Seeing themselves under constant threat—feeling the pull of the short leash—PRD executives, Salvador Jorge Blanco in particular, made concessions to the armed forces, to creditors, and to other foreign and domestic elite interests that even notoriously conservative presidents might have resisted.[14]

Such an outcome, allowing a reformist party to take "power" only
to discredit itself, while their own reputations are protected along with
their interests, has obvious appeal for economic elites, as for hegemonic
powers. In the United States in the 1980s, a government representing
the ideological Right finally discovered what more-seasoned conservatives had long recognized, that in a client state a civilian government
that is uninterested in acting upon or unable to act upon a popular
mandate and unwilling or unable to control military and paramilitary
forces is a better hedge against social change than a repressive military
government. That learning process was expedited by a Congress that
under popular pressure to end support for human rights violations
insisted on taking a firm position on both sides of the fence; particularly
with respect to Central America, it made the maintenance of a "democratic" civilian facade a condition for the ongoing provision of military
aid.

NOTES

1. See Vittorio Corbo, Morris Goldstein, and Mohsin Khan, *Growth-Oriented Adjustment Programs* (Washington, D.C.: International Monetary Fund and World Bank, 1987).

2. Shirley W.Y. Kuo, Gustav Ranis, and John C. Fei, *The Taiwan Success Story: Rapid Growth with Improved Distribution in the Republic of China, 1952–1979* (Boulder: Westview Press, 1981).

3. William P. Glade, "Economic Aspects of Latin America," chap. 9 in Jan Knippers Black, ed., *Latin America, Its Problems and Its Promise* (Boulder: Westview Press, 1984).

4. Claude Ake, *A Political Economy of Africa* (Lagos: Longman Group, Ltd., 1981), pp. 160–172.

5. Guy Martin, "The Franc Zone, Underdevelopment and Dependency in Francophone Africa," *Third World Quarterly* 8, no. 1, January 1986, pp. 205–235.

6. Exxon, Texaco, Gulf, Standard of California, Mobil, Royal Dutch Shell, and British Petroleum.

7. See John M. Blair, *The Control of Oil* (New York: Pantheon Books, 1976), p. 293; and Peter R. Odell, *Oil and World Power*, 4th ed. (Harmondsworth, UK: Penguin Books, 1975), pp. 9–20.

8. World Bank, *World Development Report, 1988* (New York: Oxford University Press, 1988), pp. 71–74.

9. Richard B. Mancke, *Mexican Oil and Natural Gas* (New York: Praeger, 1979), p. 26.

10. Interview with Humberto Calderón Berti, then director, Venezuelan Institute of Petroleum Technology, and subsequently minister of mines and hydrocarbons, June 9, 1977, Caracas.

11. See James H. Mittelman, *Out from Underdevelopment* (New York: St. Martin's Press, 1988), pp. 129–155; and William Finnegan, "A Reporter at Large (Mozambique—Part II: The Emergency)," *New Yorker,* May 29, 1989, pp. 69–96.

12. Albert Fishlow, "Brazil's Economic Miracle," *World Today* (London) 29, November 1973, pp. 474–494.

13. Adolfo Pérez Esquivel, Argentine Nobel Peace laureate, told this author in May 1989 that, while visiting recently with Cerezo in Guatemala City, he had the impression that there were only two civilians in the presidential palace—himself and Cerezo.

14. For elaboration on the fate of the PRD, see Jan Knippers Black, *The Dominican Republic: Politics and Development in an Unsovereign State* (Boston: Allen and Unwin, 1986).

SUGGESTED READINGS

Augustine, John S., ed., *Strategies for Third World Development* (New Delhi: Sage Publications, Inc., 1989).

Byres, T., and B. Crow, with Mae Wan Ho, *The Green Revolution in India* (London: Open University Press, 1983).

Corbo, Vittorio, Anne O. Krueger, and Fernando Ossa, *Export-Oriented Development Strategies* (Boulder: Westview Press, 1986).

Fanon, Frantz, *Toward the African Revolution* (Harmondsworth, UK: Penguin Books, 1964).

Fortmann, L., *Peasants, Officials, and Participation in Rural Tanzania* (Ithaca: Cornell University Press, 1980).

Furtado, Celso, *Accumulation and Development: The Logic of Industrial Civilization,* trans. Suzette Macedo (New York: St. Martin's Press, 1983).

Heady, Ferrel, *Public Administration: A Comparative Perspective,* 2nd ed. (New York: Marcel Dekker, 1979).

Hewlett, Sylvia Ann, *The Cruel Dilemmas of Development: Twentieth Century Brazil* (New York: Basic Books, 1980).

Hyden, G., R. Jackson, and F. Okuma, *Development Experience: The Kenyan Experience* (Nairobi: Oxford University Press, 1970).

Mittelman, James H., *Out from Underdevelopment: Prospects for the Third World* (New York: St. Martin's Press, 1988).

Nyerere, Julius K., *Freedom and Development* (Dar es Salaam: Oxford University Press, 1973).

Papanek, Gustav F., *Lectures on Development Strategy, Growth, Equity, and the Political Process in Southern Asia* (Islamabad: Pakistan Institute of Development Economics, 1986).

Ranis, Gustav, "Can the East Asian Model of Development be Generalized?" *World Development* 13, no. 4, 1985, pp. 543–546; and William R. Cline, "Reply," ibid., pp. 547–548.

Serra, José, "Three Mistaken Theses Regarding the Connection Between Industrialization and Authoritarian Regimes," in David Collier, ed., *The New*

Authoritarianism in Latin America (Princeton: Princeton University Press, 1979), pp. 99–163.

Sheahan, John, *Patterns of Development in Latin America: Poverty, Repression, and Economic Strategy* (Princeton: Princeton University Press, 1987).

Walker, Thomas W., ed., *Nicaragua: The First Five Years* (New York: Praeger, 1985).

Photos

All photos were taken by the author.

In India, as in most LDCs, women start work younger, work longer hours, eat less, and have less access to health care, education, and credit than do men.

In the village of Mudichur, in the Indian state of Tamil Nadu, a clinic run by the YWCA is the only source of health care for babies. Legislation provides for comprehensive public health care, but implementation is spotty. In India, as elsewhere, health care professionals resist living in poor rural villages.

In India, dowry-abuse—harassment of a bride by the groom's family to provide more gifts from her own family—has been getting worse since the 1970s, not in spite of modernization but because of it. Such abuse is seen as deriving from the new materialism, or consumerism, of the urban middle class. In this scene women's organizations in Bangalore demonstrate at the home of a groom whose bride committed suicide.

More than 3 million Afghanis, fleeing civil strife, poured over the border into northern Pakistan during the 1980s. Shown here is a marketplace in Peshawar, Pakistan, near the border. Meeting the needs of refugees, now some 15 million worldwide, will be a major development challenge of the 1990s.

In Tunisia, entire villages concentrate on a single craft like spinning and weaving or pottery making. Tourism, the world's fastest-growing industry in the early 1990s, helps to revive or sustain traditional crafts.

Sunshine is about the only thing not in short supply in the north African Sahel region. With assistance from a Canadian NGO, this village in Burkina Faso (formerly Upper Volta) was exploring the advantages of solar-heated water and solar-powered cook stoves.

108

Survival is a constant struggle for children such as these in an Ewe village in Togo. Togo's population continues to grow at an annual rate of 3 percent, but infant mortality averages 109 per 1,000 births, and life expectancy is only 48 years. Most people are undernourished, and there is only 1 physician for each 18,000 persons.

All dressed up for the king's birthday party in Swaziland. The royal family of Swaziland has sought assistance from foreign "experts" to modernize its ministate, but all too often foreign models have proved highly inappropriate.

China—ostracized by most potential trading partners—has developed its own "appropriate" technology for modernizing agriculture and industry. The equipment shown here is in Sun Yat-sen province. But while autarchy has been forced upon some revolutionary governments, it is most rarely undertaken by choice.

Fiji is the most modernized of the South Pacific island states. It has experienced rapid economic growth but also growing inequality, ethnic and class strife, foreign intrigue, and even, in 1987, a military coup d'état.

A co-op member in the Ecuadorean Sierra. Peasants participate enthusiastically in their local cooperative, even though the approach of co-op promoters from national organizations is often paternalistic and sometimes downright condescending.

The people of Población Victoria San Miguel, one of the largest and best-organized shantytowns in Santiago, Chile, demonstrated remarkable wit, grit, and collective self-sufficiency even though subject to military repression and discrimination in employment throughout the dictatorship of General Augusto Pinochet. The social glue that sustained the community derived in large part from a network of Mothers' Centers.

Even in the more prosperous and more highly modernized cities of the Third World, such as Caracas, Venezuela, large sectors of the population are left behind.

Salvadoran peasants, resettled under the protective arm of the Catholic church, tend their fields on the slopes of the volcano Guazapa, ignoring the military's counterrevolutionary offenses. Where donor countries perceive "security" interests, developmental goals are sure to be subverted.

Shantytowns such as this one in Santiago, the Dominican Republic's second-largest city, bear witness to the rural stagnation or commercialization of agriculture on the one hand and the illusion of opportunity on the other that draw peasants to the unwelcoming cities—cities already suffering from inadequate services and chronic unemployment. In Latin America, as in much of the Third World, there are fewer available urban jobs now per job seeker than there were a half century ago.

Quechua speakers in the Ecuadorean Sierra prepare a musical program for a radio station run by the Catholic Diocese of Riobamba. The radio programs are one aspect of the efforts of Monseñor Leonidas Proaño to educate, organize, and empower the Indians of the Sierra, efforts that have been a source of alarm to the economic elite of the area.

Contemporary Issues
and Themes

Even more than most disciplines and policy areas, that of development is subject to fads. While in the United States legislation calling for targeting assistance to the poorest of the poor and paying heed to the appropriateness of technology remained on the books through the 1980s, the advent of the Reagan administration shifted the focus of consultants and bureaucrats in short order to the promotion of private enterprise. Meanwhile, however, the influence of two new categories of pressure groups, feminists and "greens," was being felt around the world and was being translated by NGOs, with backing in particular by the United Nations, into policy agenda.

Thus, beginning in the 1970s and building to a crescendo in the 1980s, the issue of the gender gap, and of the actual and potential roles of women in development, dominated conferences and symposia, research proposals and position papers, and came finally to be reflected, at least in rhetoric, in major donor foreign assistance programs. The United Nations declared a Decade for Women that closed in 1985 with an international conference in Kenya. Although interest in women has not dissipated entirely, it has been overtaken since the late 1980s by a very broadly supported focus on environmental issues. By the end of the decade, there was hardly an agency or organization having anything to do with development that did not have a division or committee dealing with the environment, and the reorientation of academics, consultants, and even politicians served to build the momentum.

Other issues that promise to have a bearing on development or a claim on development funds in the 1990s include the "informal" sector, the "War on Drugs," refugees, endangered cultures, and, of course, debt.

DEVELOPMENT AND THE GENDER GAP

When all else fails, as it so often does, women around the world somehow summon the strength to raise their children and sustain their communities. But the price is high.

Most of the world's landless farmers are women. Centuries ago in much of what is now the Third World—Africa, the South Pacific, and parts of Europe and Asia—men hunted and made war while women farmed. Hunting now is mostly for sport. There is little game left to hunt for food; and war making has become highly specialized. But women still farm. In Africa, for example, 70 percent of the food crops are raised by women. Women, however, are rarely able to obtain credit in their own names. In cases of divorce, abandonment, or death, the woman is left with no claim, as title to the land was held in her husband's name only.

Women normally work longer hours than men. The notorious "double shift" is not limited to the First World or even to the industrialized world. Women who farm or produce handicrafts or take on odd jobs in the informal sector are subject to it, too. A recent survey in Zaire indicated that men did only 30 percent of the work women did.[1] In the Philippines women were putting in sixty-one hours weekly to men's forty-one, in Uganda fifty hours compared to twenty-three. Women in North India were working two to four hours more than men each day in the tea gardens, not counting time spent on housework and child care.[2]

Women start working younger—at seven or eight years of age—in the home or in the fields. A survey in Upper Volta (now Burkina Faso) showed seven-year-old girls working more than five hours a day, compared to forty-five minutes for boys of the same age. This means, among other things, that girls receive less schooling. One-half of the women of the Third World are illiterate, compared to one-third of the men.

Women work for less. The global standard for women who earn wages or salaries has remained remarkably steady through several decades—at about 60 percent of the earnings of men. In parts of the Third World the gap is much greater. In Nairobi, Kenya, in the early 1980s, half the working women earned less than the legal minimum wage, compared to 20 percent of the men.

Women eat less. The same women who work longer hours from an earlier age and actually produce most of the food must feed the men first. Fathers and male children get priority in both quality and quantity of food. From childhood on, women are also less likely to receive medical attention. Thus in much of the Third World, the female's natural advantage in longevity does not apply. Whereas in the developed world women had an advantage of about eight years, in the Third World generally it was only two years; and in some areas—South Asia, for example—men lived longer.[3]

But is not modernization improving the situation of women? Not necessarily.

Colonial governments in some respects improved the lot of Third World women. In some places they were responsible for drawing women into formal education systems. In India, the British prohibited the practice of suttee—immolation of the bride on her husband's funeral pyre—and in parts of Africa and the Middle East, British and other colonial administrations sought to protect women from such practices as clitorectomy. On the other hand, in areas where women had decided advantages, the colonial powers brought gender relations into line with their own male-dominant model. Social structure in India's Kerala state, for example, was matriarchal and matrilocal until the British brought practices there into line with those elsewhere in the empire—supposedly for the sake of administrative "efficiency."[4]

Higher technology may exacerbate problems rather than solve them. Despite their doing more of the work (or perhaps because of it?), women have traditionally been valued less and female infanticide has been practiced widely. With the spread to the Third World of amniocentesis, the female population is also being diminished by feticide. In India the proportion of women to men is 930 per 1,000—and dropping. The devaluation of daughters this reflects is not necessarily a vestige of traditionalism, likely to be overcome in time by the spread of modernism. It is in part a product of dowry abuse, wherein the groom's family makes excessive financial demands of the bride's family. Dowry abuse itself may well be a product of modernism.

Like so much else in India, abuse of women is a long-standing tradition. The disturbing and puzzling thing about dowry abuse, however, is that it is a relatively recent phenomenon. It is most prevalent among the urban middle class, and it is spreading fast. Registered cases of dowry death, about 1,000 in 1985, were expected to exceed 2,000 in 1988, and those registered were assumed to be only a small fraction of actual cases.

The dowry system came about, in Hindu custom, because real property could not be passed to a daughter. As the daughter would be relocating to her husband's household, she could inherit only movable goods. The dowry, then, was simply the daughter's inheritance, passed to her at the time of her marriage. The interests of the in-laws were irrelevant to the transaction.

The potential for abuse was officially recognized, however, and the system was proscribed by the Dowry Prohibition Act of 1961. The act was almost universally violated; but it was not until the 1970s that accounts of brides being killed in bizarre accidents, particularly kitchen fires, became so common as to demand the attention of researchers and law-enforcement officials. The concept of "bride-burning," once a reference to the practice of suttee, has since taken on a new meaning. The real story behind the fatal kitchen fire has all too often turned out to be that of a husband or mother-in-law spilling kerosene on the bride's sari and striking a match to it. Along with such "accidents," there has also been an upsurge in suicides. A great many brides have apparently seen suicide as their only acceptable escape from the incessant pressure to drain the livelihood of their parents to satisfy the whims of their in-laws.

Sociologists and others who have studied this trend attribute it in part to the new materialism or consumerism infecting the middle class. For the bridegroom and his family, marriage may become a means of acquiring the shiny new toys—stereos, VCRs, motorcycles, even cars— that they could never afford on their own salaries. And the extortion may go on long after the wedding, as brides rarely feel that they have the option of leaving their husbands. It is socially unacceptable for a bride to return to her parents' household. Indian women are expected to marry and stay married, and apart from a few shelters established by charities or women's groups, there are virtually no alternative living arrangements. Even for female professionals who could afford to rent their own apartments, there are few landlords who would rent to single women.

Formerly prevalent only among Hindu middle-class families in the northern states, dowry demands—and dowry deaths—have spread across lines of geography, class and caste, and even religion. The practice is now common throughout the country, even in areas of Moslem or Christian settlement. In a region where women have traditionally been undervalued, at least in modern times, the steady inflation of dowry demands has led many parents to see female offspring as a distinct liability. Thus the dowry system has exacerbated the problems of female infanticide and, where amniocentesis is available, feticide. It has also contributed to the neglect and ill-treatment of female children. India is one of the few countries where women's life expectancy is markedly shorter than men's.

The only good news with respect to this grim topic is that recognition of the seriousness of the problem has served to mobilize women. Indian women are better organized now and more active politically and socially than they had been at any time since Mahatma Gandhi tapped their energies for the independence movement.[5]

Other aspects of modernization also serve to exacerbate inequality between the sexes as well as between classes. The option of cash cropping, for example, is generally available only to men. Agricultural development programs, whether of international or domestic derivation, have been grossly discriminatory. Membership in co-ops and the availability of extension services have often been restricted to men. Labor-saving devices or technologies passed on by governments or development agencies are usually passed to men, even where the labor to which they apply is women's work. Corn grinders have been made available in Kenya, but women have not been taught to operate them. Likewise oil presses in Nigeria and tortilla-making machines in Mexico became the preserve of men, who have access to cash or credit.[6] Cash crops then claim the best land, leaving only the less-fertile and less-accessible land to women for their food crops. The food crops would have fed the peasant family. The cash crop is more likely to feed the bartender's family.

We have seen that the introduction of cash cropping often leads to greater concentration of landownership and to increasing landlessness among former subsistence farmers. With shrinking plots, the men are forced to migrate—to seek work in the cities or in more prosperous areas as migratory farm laborers. Many never return. This has resulted in a rapid increase in the number of rural households headed by women. These women, as we have seen, will have even more difficulty than their husbands did in obtaining credit and technical assistance and ultimately in holding onto the tiny patches of land left to them. The spreading feminization of poverty means the juvenilization of poverty, too.

In some areas, such as East Asia, where industrial development has been largely in the direction of labor intensity and precision work, women have become very much involved in the formal workforce. In most Third World areas, however, where factory production has wiped out the market for handicrafts, the women so displaced are less likely to be hired than men; women, then, are pushed into the unregulated and notoriously low-paying informal sector.

What, then, are the implications for development specialists to be drawn from this assessment? In the first place, targeting the poorest of the poor (as has been mandated by USAID and by the World Bank, though practiced only in a token manner) generally means targeting communities in which the role of women is preeminent. It is precisely in the villages or shantytowns where conditions are most desperate that women are most likely to be the economic mainstays as well as the care givers of their families and the organizational glue of their communities. This is partly because men can, and often do, flee from their responsibilities to another place or perhaps just into a bottle. Women cannot.

In the second place, targeting women, rather than discriminating against them, benefits the whole family. A number of studies from disparate parts of the Third World have indicated that compared to men, women spend a far greater proportion of their incomes on meeting family needs rather than on personal gratification. Thus, enhancing the income of women means also raising healthier children, male and female. It is not enough, however, for women simply to earn the income if it is only to be seized by their husbands. Women must also be able to maintain control of the income they earn, and in some areas a step in that direction will call for very considerable education, consciousness-raising, and social pressure.

In the third place, it is very generally acknowledged that the population explosion is among the major sources of frustration for development strategy. General education and the issuance of contraceptive drugs and devices through family-planning clinics may be, in the absence of major social change, a very long-term process. More drastic approaches taken to date have even less to recommend them. In India, the Congress Party suffered a terrible backlash from its short-lived efforts to impose sterilization. The Chinese government has had more success in imposing its policy of limiting couples to one child but in the process has prompted a sharp rise in female infanticide. The only really effective and morally acceptable means now known of sharply limiting family size is the education and liberation, or empowerment, of women.

For women, as for other disadvantaged categories of people, there can be no gains without political struggle, but the good news is that the struggle has been joined. In countries that have undergone successful revolution, women have been prominent among the armed combatants as well as in all other roles essential to the struggle. That mobilization has subsequently been reflected in involvement in policy-making and of varying degrees of improvement in status. In the Soviet Union, women advanced quickly into the professions, becoming particularly prominent in medicine. Professional status, however, has given them no relief from the "double shift."

Revolutionary Cuba has actually tried to deal with the double shift problem. Its path-breaking Family Code, which went into effect in 1975, specifies that marriage partners are to share equally in child care and in carrying out household chores.[7] Legislation is one thing, of course, implementation another. In Nicaragua, where one-fourth to one-third of the combatants in the revolutionary struggle had been women, women's organizations have had a prominent role in the subsequent transformation of society. Just a few months after the triumph of the revolution, however, an eighteen-year-old female military officer told me, with undisguised anger, that male chauvinism had already reappeared in the Sandinista Armed Forces and the women were being pushed out.

Elsewhere the organization of women in the Third World for the advancement of their own cause as well as the causes of human rights, child welfare, and, in general, democracy and social justice has been gathering momentum at least since the 1960s. In Taiwan, for example, where economic development has greatly outpaced political development, feminist organizations have been in the forefront of the campaign for political liberalization.[8] Even in South Asia, where most women have traditionally suffered awful repression and deprivation, some of the most effective national leaders have been women, and women's organizations have been very active in grass-roots development as well as in other aspects of political life. In India, for example, the Congress Party government did not launch any new policy affecting women or family life or broad aspects of socioeconomic development without first consulting the national confederation of women's organizations.

THE FRAGILE ECOLOGY
OF MOTHER EARTH

In development studies, as in other areas of public discourse, the bandwagon of the 1990s promises to be the garbage truck. One of the many unfortunate consequences of success in the post–World War II drive for rapid industrialization and unlimited production is the generation on a massive scale of waste. Even within the United States, the issue of dumping has aroused regional antagonisms as the more-industrialized Northeast and Midwest shop around in the South and West for communities desperate enough to take in their garbage for a few dollars or a few jobs.[9] And as other local and state governments attempt to protect their constituencies, the difficulty of finding legal means of and locales for dumping makes the waste management industry particularly attractive to organized-crime syndicates.

Exporting Garbage

Nor is the scourge of waste confined to the countries where it is produced. Like other by-products of the industrial age, it slips easily over national borders, becoming a source of friction among neighboring states. U.S. businesses and municipalities, facing ever-higher disposal costs in the United States, are shipping great quantities of waste to Mexico, Central America, and the Caribbean.

The problem would be serious enough if the foul stuff in search of an eternal resting place were relatively benign household waste. Much of it, however, is hazardous industrial waste, and some—the radioactive waste of weapons and power plants, for example—is extremely lethal, posing to air, soil, and groundwater long-term threats that we have only begun to fathom. Furthermore, the more toxic the waste, the more likely that the producers will seek to dispose of it on someone else's turf and that the dangers it poses will be understated. As the private transnational organization Greenpeace has gone to great lengths to dramatize, a great deal of the world's hazardous waste is being dumped in the oceans; this serves to blunt the jurisdictional and liability disputes so often associated with disposal, but it does not prevent the generalized contamination of the world's food chain.

The by-products of industrial development that are not dumped en masse as garbage may be doing even more damage. Hazardous chemical compounds are constantly being released into the air or filtering into rivers and streams and aquifers. Particles from one such set of compounds, chlorofluorocarbons, have made their way to the protective ozone layer and eaten a hole in it, threatening higher rates of skin cancer, among other dire consequences. (This threat was viewed as serious enough to inspire a superpower treaty, signed by Bush and Gorbachev in 1989, to limit the production of chlorofluorocarbons.)

Meanwhile the cutting and burning of forests and the consumption of fossil fuels release carbon dioxide, which traps solar radiation near the earth's surface. The resulting global warming, the "greenhouse effect," could raise sea levels, inundating coastal cities and swallowing up entire islands. The Worldwatch Institute's annual *State of the World* reported in early 1989 that the five warmest years of this century had been in the 1980s. About 40 percent of this greenhouse effect is attributable to fossil fuel combustion. The United States alone contributes one-fifth of the carbon being added annually to the atmosphere, a consequence in large part of its energy-inefficient transportation system; the average car adds its own weight in carbon to the atmosphere each year.

Also contributing to the imbalance of carbon and oxygen in our atmosphere has been the rapid depletion of the planet's rain forests. Tropical ecosystems around the world are currently being destroyed at the rate of 25 million acres a year. Much has been written about the clearing of the Amazon Basin. One-fourth of Brazil's forestry reserves had been cut down by 1974. In 1988 the country lost an area of tropical rain forest larger than Switzerland. That same year, an indigenous crusader against deforestation, Francisco (Chico) Mendes, was murdered by cattle ranchers. But the problem of deforestation, with consequent topsoil erosion, upland desertification, and downstream flooding, is of global scope.

The loss of fertile soil, in turn, takes its toll on food production. For the world as a whole, per capita grain production has decreased every year since 1984, falling by 14 percent by the end of the decade.[10] Actual grain production is not a reliable guide to productive potential, in that especially in the more-developed countries production is limited in order to maintain higher prices. Nevertheless, there is no doubt that loss of productive farmland, through industrial and urban development on the one hand and erosion on the other, is one of the several factors leading so many countries to import more and more of their basic foodstuffs.

Sharing Hardships

What does all of this have to do with development? To the extent that development is measured in production and consumption without regard to ecological balance and replenishment, it has everything to do with it. Such development must be seen, along with population growth, as the engine of this ecological crisis; and the crisis offers an intimation of the limits of the process. Furthermore, wherever there are hardships to be shared, the poor get more than their share of them; and as the ecological crisis is global, its effects are felt more immediately and more sharply in the Third World.

In the first place, much of the Third World is urbanized, if not highly industrialized; it is urbanizing at a faster rate than the First World, and its municipalities are less well equipped to deal with the consequences of such concentration.

Sewerage systems, for example, are almost everywhere inadequate. In São Paulo, a modern city of some 15 million, less than half the sewage is even collected, and of that less than 5 percent is treated. In the heart of Madras or Mexico City, Santiago or Seoul, Bangkok or Jakarta, breathing is a struggle. In some cities, cement plants and petroleum-refining facilities throw off dust and sulfur. In others, mineral- and chemical-processing plants put arsenic and other toxic compounds into the air. In almost every major city, excepting a very few essentially nonmotorized ones like Beijing and Dacca, motor vehicle pollutants, especially diesel fuel, routinely cause sore eyes and throats, chronic coughing and shortness of breath, and apparently increase the incidence of lung cancer. Illnesses caused by polluted water and air must be discounted against the gains attributable to modern medicine and health-care-delivery systems.

It is estimated that 40 million tons of hazardous industrial waste are produced in Latin America each year. For better or worse, as capital circles the globe seeking cheap land and labor, the Third World is rapidly acquiring more industry, with its attendant liabilities. Whether the fault lies with weak or corrupt host governments or with greedy foreign investors, the precautions against ordinary pollution or against ecological disaster that are less than adequate in the First World are even less adequate in the Third. The kind of accident that devastated Bhopal, India, might well threaten Union Carbide's U.S. plants also; and the 1989 Exxon oil spill in Alaska's Prince William Sound exposed the weaknesses of U.S. regulatory systems; but the fact remains that preventable industrial contamination is even more common in the Third World than in the First.

If the Third World suffers more than the First from environmental degradation, it is in part because First World companies use it as a dumping ground for products they are prohibited from marketing at home. Pesticides, in increasingly common use with the spread of plantation-style export agriculture, have been among those products. They are likely to come home to roost, as residues on the fruits and vegetables shipped back to the First World. But the price to Third World field laborers, blanketed regularly in the stuff by crop dusters, is much greater; they have been suffering in ever-larger numbers from pesticide poisoning. In El Salvador, for example, during the 1970s, 1,000 to 2,000 cases of pesticide poisoning were reported annually. In 1987, 50 children died of it in a single hospital in San Salvador.[11]

The loss of vegetation and of fertile land ultimately affects us all. But as in the case of most life-and-death struggles, the affluent are not likely to be found on the front lines. The peoples most devastated are the ones who were trying to scratch out a living on land that was already marginal. The first victims of desertification are the nomads around the edges of the Sahara and Kalahari deserts. The first to suffer from erosion are the subsistence farmers on Haiti's already severely eroded hillsides.

Deforestation has disturbing implications for the planet in general. It is estimated that one-fourth of the oxygen in our atmosphere derives from the Amazonian rain forest alone. But for the poor of many Third World countries, the retreat of the trees poses more immediate hardship. The FAO estimates that 86 percent of the wood cut in the Third World is used for fuel. Wood is an inefficient fuel, but for many there is no affordable alternative. As firewood has dwindled in south and central

India, "power packs" of cow dung must be used for heating and cooking, but that leaves little to be used as fertilizer. It is estimated that more nitrogen and phosphorous from power packs goes up in smoke than the total Indian production of chemical fertilizer.

The foothills of the Himalayas, particularly in eastern Nepal and in northeast India, are being deforested at an alarming rate. For the wood gatherers, usually women, this means that the hike in search of firewood takes them farther each year from their villages. Population pressure is partly to blame, but the locals have also sometimes found themselves in competition with major lumber companies.

In one such case, in the Indian state of Uttar Pradesh, the people decided to fight back. The Chipko movement, or "tree huggers," as they came to be known, mostly women, vowed to hug the trees so that the lumber companies could not fell them without felling the villagers with them. Similar, more or less spontaneous grass-roots movements representing a coincidence of popular and environmental interests, and building upon the Gandhian tradition of nonviolent activism, sprouted elsewhere in India in the 1980s; but few have been as successful as the tree huggers, who actually forced the lumber company out of their forests.[12]

Another major threat to forest and farmland alike in the Third World has been the relentless spread of large-scale infrastructure projects. Undertaken in the name of development, sponsored by governments, underwritten by loans from the World Bank and the regional development banks, such projects have included roads, railroads, ports, power lines, and, in particular, massive dams. The clearest beneficiaries of these projects, who have mounted impressive lobbying efforts, have been First World or transnational construction companies.

The most immediate losers from these infrastructure operations have generally been indigenous peasants. Such indigenous peoples, generally occupying remote valleys or jungle clearings on the frontier of settlement, may be unintegrated into the national community and utterly lacking in political clout, but they are the vestiges of expertise in ecological balance. The resettlement promised to Mexico's Chinantec and Brazil's Kayapo Indians when plans were drawn up in the late 1980s to construct dams flooding their ancestral lands came as scant compensation. Both groups resisted and two of the Kayapo chiefs were brought to trial under Brazil's Foreign Sedition Act. Ironically, it was for urging a role for local populations in designing the policies that affect them that the Kayapo's chiefs were tried, along with a U.S. anthropologist—under a law forbidding foreign interference in Brazilian affairs.[13]

Questions of Equity and Responsibility

An environmental perspective raises fundamental ethical questions about equity and responsibility—about assessing blame and liability, about the setting of priorities, and about the merits and the urgency of competing claims on scarce resources—that are not necessarily set in relief by other perspectives.

Some of these questions pit the First World against the Third: Is it fair or reasonable for the overdeveloped nations to demand of the underdeveloped ones that they forgo certain practices, now seen as detrimental to the global environment, that were crucial to First World development? Should certain of the LDCs choose to forgo such practices, are they entitled to extra assistance to compensate for possible losses in growth or productivity? When it is clear that First World practices are responsible for environmental degradation affecting the Third World, should the responsible countries and companies be held liable in the sense of owing compensation? If environmental degradation threatens us all, do nonnationals have an inherent right to influence the practices of particular countries? If, as is argued, all life on the planet is dependent on the oxygen produced by the Amazon rain forest, should nonnationals be able to pressure the Brazilian government to drop incentives to clearance? If so, perhaps nonnuclear nations threatened by radioactive waste should have a voice in the weapons and power development policies of countries having nuclear capabilities.

As to questions of priority and urgency, many in the development community will have no trouble deciding, in principle, which has the prior claim when the interests of profit are pitted against the interest of environmental preservation. But what about the equally common circumstances that pit the interests of Mother Nature against the interests of clearly needy local populations? Where do justice and reasonableness lie when the urgent needs of large numbers of poor people run counter to those of endangered plant and animal species and, more important, to small numbers of people representing endangered cultures?

Perhaps the most important conflict of interests with respect to environmental issues, however, lies between old and young, or between generations now seeking succor from this planet and generations to which they will leave what's left of it. In this contest, future generations are at a terrible disadvantage: They have no weapons and no vote.

It would be unrealistic to imagine that the great debates about environmental issues, whether they take place at the summit or on the street corner, will have any more influence on the actual allocation or reallocation of resources than have earlier debates on technology and change, the terms of trade, the energy crisis, the income gap, and the gender gap. But we must hope that there is something to be gained through increased awareness of what is at stake.

On April 22, 1990, the twentieth anniversary of the original Earth Day was celebrated in thousands of towns and cities across the United States and around the world. Whereas the first Earth Day, brainchild of U.S. Senator Gaylord Nelson, had been in essence a counterculture event, that of 1990 was a mainstream spectacular; speakers were the biggest names in government and show business, and underwriters included the biggest transnational corporations and conglomerates, including some of the most notorious polluters. At the largest rallies, there was no need for those in attendance even to pick up their own litter; clean-up crews had been hired. For environmentalists, the mainstreaming of the issue represented a major victory of sorts; but some aging hippies were uneasy about being sidelined as spectators while the foxes ceremoniously assumed guardianship of the chicken coop.

OTHER ISSUES AND TRENDS

Trends in donor policies have always had more to do with First World politics than with Third World needs. Policies and programs serving trade and investment interests have been fairly consistent and have constantly enjoyed a high priority. Other programs, however, have been subject to the wide pendulum swings of foreign policy that reflect a major cleavage in Western, particularly U.S., society. Aspects of policy subject to the pendulum swing—from security interests, for example, to humanitarian interests—may be more nearly expressive than instrumental, designed more for their repercussions in the First World than in the Third. Intended or not, however, repercussions in the Third may be very great indeed. Major donors have generally been unreceptive to Third World solicitations and initiatives, viewing them as threatening to the established order (that is, the order favoring major donors).

Benchmark studies of Third World needs and of foreign assistance efforts and their consequences commissioned by the U.S. Congress or the executive branch over the years (i.e., the Rostow Commission study of 1957 or the Carlucci Commission report of 1983[14]) have generally served to legitimate trends already under way rather than to launch new ones. Some developments have been traceable in part, however, to nonofficial studies, and even to particular books, although such cases have usually involved long periods of gestation. The appropriate technology trend of the 1970s, which survives into the 1990s in the work of NGOs/PVOs despite diminished interest among major donors, owes much to Ernst F. Schumacher's book, *Small Is Beautiful* (1973), as the environmentalist concerns so prominent in the 1990s are traceable to Rachel Carson's *Silent Spring* (1962).[15]

At the beginning of the 1990s, First World development strategies were undergoing yet another reappraisal. Politically, the dramatic transformation of the Second World unleashed by Soviet leader Mikhail Gorbachev's campaign for disarmament, democracy, and perestroika make it exceedingly difficult to maintain a foreign assistance program premised mainly on the Cold War.

The focus on environmental degradation also has special appeal at a time when the Cold War is waning; its threat, like that of the Cold War, is eminently elastic, and the means of countering it are susceptible to "technicalyzing"—that is, the removal from public discourse to bunkers of expertise. Thus it should prove a useful rhetorical cover for the movement of large sums of money from public to private coffers with minimal oversight. Already, the amounts proposed for the cleanup of U.S. nuclear weapons facilities rival the costs of making the mess in the first place. That is not, on this author's part, to underrate the fragility of the ecology or the importance of reaching accommodation with other life forms; it is simply to offer warning as to what the major policy thrust of ecomania is likely to be.

It appeared, also, that the "War on Drugs" was being primed to take up some of the slack and serve some of the same purposes as the Cold War—e.g., as cover or justification for the monitoring and suppressing of Third World insurrection.[16] The drug war also served as a rationale for maintaining obsolete or "underutilized" military units and weapons systems and for developing new ones. In an interview reported in September 1990, General Donald J. Kutyna, commander of the North American Air Defense (NORAD), said that the drug war had sharpened skills and boosted morale among his troops. He noted that the drug war gives his men real intercept targets, making it unnecessary to contract artificial ones for practice runs. At least until the Iraqi invasion of Kuwait in August 1990, 42 percent of the Air Force's Airborne Warning and Control System (AWACS) missions were being flown in alleged pursuit of drug smugglers. Kutyna pointed out, however, that that was a costly use of AWACS and urged instead that Congress fund the new, experimental Over-the-Horizon Backscatter Radar system.[17]

Narcotraffic

In Latin America, the squeeze on imports, forcing retrenchment in industrial development, and the unreliability of prices and markets for traditional primary products, of late including even petroleum, have served to increase the importance of the area's only reliably lucrative cash crop: narcotic drugs. The introduction of new cash crops has always had a destabilizing effect on political as well as economic systems, as it has given rise to new elites having the wherewithal to challenge previously dominant classes. New cash crops also generate new struggles over land tenure and further reduce the land area allotted to food crops, leading to shortages and higher prices for staple commodities. Any promising new source of income can also be expected to complicate relations among neighboring countries and to invite intervention, as foreigners seek to cut themselves in on profits or marketing arrangements or to suppress competition.

All the usual complications and threats, however, associated with new cash crops and industries are magnified in this case because of the peculiar characteristics of the product and the illegality of the traffic. Particularly troublesome have been the steady growth in demand, especially in the United States but more recently in Latin America as well; the remarkable profitability; the high level of violence associated with the trade; the corruption of officials and institutions; the inability of governments to tax or regulate; and the invitation to intervention by the United States. The invitation to U.S. agents, and in some cases even troops, has been in some instances enthusiastic and in others grudging—more or less coerced; but in all cases it involves a certain relinquishment of sovereignty.

U.S. officials, seeing their own society as a victim of narcotraffic (rather than the engine of it), have assumed a right—even a duty—to intercept the trade at its Latin American sources, particularly in the more inaccessible reaches of the Andes and the Amazon Basin, or at pass-through points in Mexico or the Caribbean. But the Drug Enforcement Administration (DEA) regularly offers cover for the Central Intelligence Agency (CIA), and as the Kerry Subcommittee report, released in April 1989, confirms, U.S. agents have also been known to build and use the trade—not only in Latin America, but in Southeast and Southwest Asia as well—for their own official and unofficial purposes.[18] At any rate, the priorities of U.S. agents and troops stationed in Latin American countries are not likely to coincide neatly with those of host governments, much less of the powerless masses.

This focus for U.S. foreign assistance received new impetus in September 1989 when President Bush launched his own "War on Drugs." The war was to be waged with the extension of $261 million in security assistance to Colombia, Bolivia, and Peru to support antidrug efforts. U.S. Special Forces were to join DEA agents in advising the military and police establishments of these countries. If one assumes that rhetorical objectives are to be taken seriously, this war is even stupider than most. To begin with, security assistance is more likely to strengthen the *narcotrafficantes* in the long run than the weak and impoverished civilian governments that must compete with them for the loyalty of military and paramilitary forces. One of the reasons the industry has flourished in Colombia has been the very considerable protection it has received from extreme right-wing factions of the military and police.

U.S. advisers were already training local narcotic squads in Bolivia's Chapare Valley and participating in a major offensive in Peru's Upper Huallaga River Valley. Along the Upper Huallaga, "the law" is the Sendero Luminoso (Shining Path) guerrilla organization. Their enforcement techniques are harsh; but they are said to enjoy the support of tens of thousands of coca-growing peasants in the area because for a "tax" or "dues payment" of 10 percent to 15 percent of the peasant's earnings, the guerrillas represent their interests vis-à-vis the Colombian traffickers and seek to protect them against the U.S.-funded coca-eradication program. Thus, in a sense, U.S. engagement with Sendero Luminoso represented yet another instance of the use of foreign aid funds to cripple labor representation, but the business side of the equation to be strengthened in the process might well be the Colombian cartels.

Refugees and Indigenous Peoples

Other holdover or aftermath issues from the 1970s and 1980s include the plight of refugees and of indigenous peoples. Revolutionary and counterrevolutionary struggles, compounded by ecological and economic devastation, have created millions of refugees. Ambassador Jonathan Moore, U.S. coordinator for refugee affairs, reported to a congressional committee in April 1989 that there were now some 13 million refugees in the world who had fled their countries to escape conflict or persecution; and that figure probably did not take into account people such as Salvadorans and Guatemalans, whom the United States for ideological reasons fails to classify as refugees, as well as internal refugees, who have been uprooted from their homes but remain in their own countries.[19]

The U.S. Committee for Refugees, a private organization, reported that there were more than 15 million refugees worldwide in 1989, a figure not counting internally displaced refugees or the more than 700,000 East Germans who poured into West Germany at the end of the year. The 1989 figure of 15 million represented a 50 percent increase over a five-year period.[20]

Four countries alone—Israel, Afghanistan, Mozambique, and Ethiopia—had produced more than a million refugees each. There are still some 3 million Afghani refugees in Pakistan, as the *Mujaheddin* continue to assault the Soviet-backed government in Afghanistan. The deprivations of the Palestinian refugees in the occupied territories have been compounded since the late 1980s by the *intifada* (uprising) and Israeli reprisals. Meanwhile, the Iraqi invasion and occupation of Kuwait in August 1990 has generated several hundred thousand more refugees—Kuwaitis fleeing their own country as well as foreigners, particularly from the Philippines and South Asia, who had been working in Kuwait or Iraq. The first stop for most of them was Jordan, a poor country that had yet to absorb successfully earlier waves of refugees from Palestine. Some 320,000 Cambodians remain in camps across the Thai border, and given the revived ambitions of the Khmer Rouge, it is not clear whether the pullout of Vietnamese troops from Kampuchea will allow for resettlement or lead to more conflict and more refugees. Meanwhile the tide of Vietnamese asylum seekers has scarcely abated.

The brutal suppression of student-led democratic movements in Burma in 1988 and in China in 1989 has generated new refugees within and from those countries; and several years of civil strife in Sri Lanka have uprooted thousands in that tragic land that nature had dressed only for celebration. Meanwhile, Tibetans continue to stream into India's Himalayan province of Ladakh.

The refugee population in the Horn of Africa and in southern Africa increased by a million between mid-1988 and mid-1989 alone. Since the mid-1980s, more than a million Mozambicans have fled the terror of the South African–backed guerrilla organization, the Mozambique National Resistance Movement (RENAMO). Malawi, one of the world's poorest countries, shelters at least 800,000 Mozambican refugees. While domestic conflict and famine have driven more than a million Ethiopians from their homes, some 350,000 Sudanese and 400,000 Somalis have fled to Ethiopia. Meanwhile, about 2 million refugees seek shelter in the Sudan. Thousands also fled in the late 1980s from conflict in Burundi and in Namibia.[21]

Central American conflict since the late 1970s has also produced a multidirectional exodus—from El Salvador to Honduras, from Guatemala to Mexico; from Nicaragua to Honduras and Costa Rica, and from all of those countries to the United States. Estimates of the uprooted in the area range from 2 to 3 million, though not all have crossed national borders; many remain displaced and dispossessed within their own countries.

In Kampuchea, Afghanistan, Angola, and elsewhere, U.S. policies of nurturing and prolonging conflict and sabotaging settlement efforts were playing a role in generating ever-more refugees; but such policy choices were particularly ironic in the case of Central America because the final destination of the uprooted from that area is the United States.

And the longer the United States seeks by force to contain political change there, the greater will be the flood of Central Americans across U.S. borders. Such is the price of empire—a price that, among Americans, the celebrants of empire seem least willing to pay.

Meanwhile, the U.S. contribution to world emergency-relief efforts, including aid to refugees, has leveled off even as the need has grown dramatically. The U.S. portion of the budget of the International Committee of the Red Cross dropped by one-half in the past few years, while the U.S. portion of the budget of the UN High Commission for Refugees dropped from one-third to one-fifth.[22]

Indigenous peoples have suffered disproportionately from externally provoked aggression against people as well as against nature. In some cases, they have been intentionally targeted by modern-day conquistadores who coveted their land. In other cases, they have been exploited by combatants—used as cannon fodder in wars they knew little about—or simply wiped out in passing when their ancestral homes got in the way of bombs and bullets and herbicides.

Indigenous peoples have been under assault for centuries, of course, but the plight of unintegrated vestiges of so-called primitive cultures is set in relief as their numbers dwindle. The most common means of measuring development—national aggregate data—tell us nothing about the fate of such peoples. High rates of GNP or per capita growth may well represent the success of conquering peoples or cultures in obliterating indigenous ones.

The Debt Trap

Apart from ecological damage, often implying obliteration of indigenous cultures, other issues will continue to loom as overwhelming obstacles to development by any approach or definition. The debt trap, for example, has been particularly burdensome for most Latin American and African countries, but even South Pacific island ministates, only recently drawn into the global economy, have suffered severe setbacks. And countries like India and Yugoslavia that had acquired some space for genuinely national planning and economic innovation, have felt obliged, because of debt exposure, to turn to less-independent and less-egalitarian policies.

The modern version of Third World debt servitude began to take shape in the 1950s and 1960s with such industrial white elephants as steel mills. The white elephants of the 1980s—nuclear-power plants, for example—have been even hungrier and more dangerous, but other follies and calamities have weighed in as well. Corruption, capital flight, and consumption of scarce foreign reserves for luxury imports rather than for capital goods have played their part, along with military buildups, energy crises, and, above all, interest obligations.

Extraordinarily large loans were needed in the 1970s to cover the costs of energy, but bankers, awash in petrodollars, were more than anxious to extend such loans; and for the borrowers, accelerating inflation mitigated the sting of interest. In the 1980s, however, when First World inflation rates dropped, "variable" interest rates did not drop proportionately. Those rates have been kept high in part by a U.S. deficit steadily deepened by military spending.[23]

After 1982, rising debt service and the cut in lending to developing countries led to a sharp reversal of net resource transfers. Whereas between 1977 and 1982 long-term lending had contributed to positive net resource transfers amounting to $147 billion to developing countries, net transfers between 1982 and 1988 were negative, shifting $85 billion from Third World to First (see Figure 6.1). Net loss for the highly indebted middle-income countries has been even greater, standing at $93 billion, and debt service had claimed more than a third of export earnings in the 1980s.[24]

The "Informal" Sector

As modern economic sectors in the Third World have been devastated, particularly in the 1980s, by debt, inflation, loss of markets, and the like, many savvy workers disgorged onto the streets have learned how to use the unregulated markets of the streets and the illegal sweatshops of the back alleys to survive and in some cases even to prosper. Recent studies in several countries have indicated that half or more of annual GNP derives from the "informal," or unregulated, underground sectors of the economy. This discovery has led some to see the flourishing of the informal sector as a promising wave of the future.

The ingenuity and industriousness of the poor come as no surprise to development specialists who have worked directly with them; but it is hardly edifying to be reminded that people will work longer hours for less if they are desperate enough. The glorification of the informal sector strikes this author as a sort of academic jujitsu—a matter of redefining the problem itself as the solution.

"Informals," or persons who lack the means or connections to do business on the state's terms—the street-smart shoestring entrepreneurs, finding spaces for productive activity in the interstices of underdeveloped and overregulated economies—are familiar throughout the Third World and in much of the First World as well, and almost everywhere

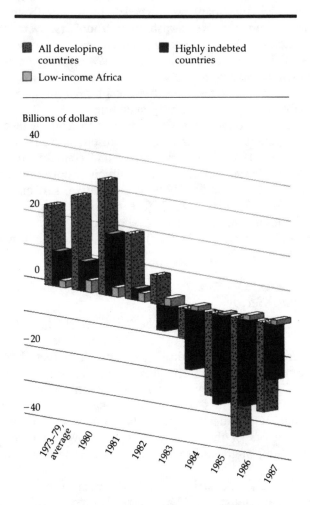

All developing
countries

Highly indebted
countries

Low-income Africa

Billions of dollars

40

20

0

−20

−40

1973–79,
average 1980 1981 1982 1983 1984 1985 1986 1987

Note: Net resource transfers are defined as disbursements of medium- and long-term external loans minus interest and amortization payments on medium- and long-term external debt.

FIGURE 6.1 Net resource transfers to developing countries, 1973 to 1987. *Source:* World Bank, *World Development Report, 1988* (New York: Oxford University Press, 1988), p. 30.

they are continually hassled and hobbled by governments responsive to the wealthier business sectors.

In Santiago, Chile, since the Pinochetazo (the military takeover of 1973), unemployment has been chronic, particularly among the one-third or more of the population who live in shantytowns. A social worker in Pudahuel, an area of spontaneous colonization and low-cost government housing, told me in the early 1980s that of the 340 families she served, only 50 individuals had jobs. Most had no recourse save the informal sector, but there they faced a merciless obstacle course.

In La Victoria, one of Santiago's oldest and largest shantytowns, a community continually persecuted because of its resistance to the dictatorship, a friend of mine tried to open a business as a seamstress in her house. She managed to scrape together the 1,500 pesos (about U.S. $30 at that time) for the license. But she had to wait six months for a visit by a municipal inspector, who told her that her premises were too primitive to qualify. She was never able to open a business, but the license fee was not returned, and she was later fined for not having filed an income tax return for her business. Her brother, a skilled carpenter, tried selling his carved wooden toys on the street; but he could not afford the license required by law of all street peddlers, so the police confiscated his wares, and he, too, was subjected to a heavy fine.

Even where governments have shown some sympathy for those in the informal sector, relief from the usual obstacle course has been hard to implement mainly because of the weakness of such governments vis-à-vis the affluent private sector. The mayor of São Paulo, for example, Luiza Erundina de Souza, elected in 1988, a Marxist representing Brazil's decade-old Workers' Party, has allowed the homeless to occupy undeveloped property, despite a daily barrage of criticism by the city's conservative newspapers. And she has allowed peddlers back onto city streets, though in response to fierce pressures from middle-class shopkeepers she has limited their numbers and the areas where they may work.

If the upshot of the current focus on the informal sector were to be fewer obstacles or more development assistance for community cooperatives or for small-scale owner-operated enterprises in slums and shantytowns, the outcome might be very positive. A considerable body of research supports the arguments that small businesses are more productive and innovative than big ones and that a multitude of locally based small businesses constitutes a sturdier base for development than a few large and potentially mobile ones. The thrust of recent studies and recommendations, however, at least those attracting major donor support, has been to reinforce pressures at the national level for pri-

vatization, relief from progressive taxation, easing of currency convert-
ability, and deregulation, including a rollback of official measures designed to protect workers or consumers. The policies proposed for
reinforcing the informal sector, for example, by Peru's Instituto de
Libertad y Democracia, which received about $9 million from USAID
in 1989, are very like those long advocated by foreign investors and
creditors and normally imposed by the IMF—policies that have contributed to such levels of unemployment and extremes of desperation
in the first place.[25]

More promising, at the end of the 1980s, was the fact that it appeared
to be dawning on First World governments and manufacturers that
countries bankrupted by debt servicing could not buy First World
products. Since Latin America had been the area hardest hit by the
debt crisis, the irony for the United States was particularly pronounced.
While the United States struggled, largely in vain, against the pressure
of Europe, Japan, and the so-called NICs on its other traditional
markets, it had virtually wiped out markets, through its staunch support
of the creditors, in the only part of the world where it had historically
had great advantage.

NOTES

1. Paul Harrison, *Inside the Third World: The Anatomy of Poverty*, 2nd ed.
(Harmondsworth, UK: Penguin Books, 1987), p. 441.

2. Tony Barnett, *Social and Economic Development: An Introduction* (New
York: Guilford Press, 1989), pp. 168–169.

3. Harrison, op. cit., pp. 444–446.

4. Discussions with Sarah Matthew, director of women's programs, Institute
for Development Education, Madras, June–July and October–November 1988.

5. While on a Fulbright-funded research program in India in 1988, this
author had occasion to meet with leaders of several women's organizations that
were dealing with the dowry-abuse problem and to become acquainted with
the family of a recent dowry-abuse victim.

6. Barnett, op. cit., pp. 157–158.

7. For more information on Cuba's family code and on the role of women
in revolutionary Cuba, see Chapter 5 in Jan Knippers Black, ed., *Area Handbook
for Cuba* (Washington, D.C.: Government Printing Office, 1976). See also several
books by Margaret Randall, including *Cuban Women Now* (Toronto: Women's
Press, 1974).

8. Feminist leaders and organizations have been in the vanguard of the
democratic movement at least since the flourishing of *Formosa* magazine in
the late 1970s. Feminist leaders, including Lu Hsui-lien and Chen Chu, were
sentenced to prison when the movement was crushed following the Kaohsiung
rally in 1979. The author was able to meet with leaders of the once-again

flourishing feminist movement in Taipei in October 1988. Lu now edits the newspaper of the new Democratic People's Party.

9. Likewise, peddling the same "economic development" incentives, private-sector prison management companies like the Nashville-based Corrections Corporation of America were approaching the same depressed and desperate communities in search of dumping sites for people. There were more than 750,000 inmates in U.S. federal and state prisons in 1990 and, like material waste management, people waste management continued to be a growth industry.

10. Worldwatch Institute, *State of the World 1989* (Washington, D.C.: Worldwatch Institute, 1989).

11. See Tom Barry, *El Salvador: A Country Profile* (Albuquerque: Resource Center, 1989).

12. Discussions with D. K. Oza, a senior officer of the Indian Administrative Service, who had done extensive studies on spontaneous grass-roots organization and the influence of Gandhi, Madras, June–July and November 1988.

13. Alexander Cockburn, "Killing Cultures," *Nation* 247, no. 13, November 7, 1988, pp. 446–447.

14. U.S. House of Representatives, 101st Congress, 1st Session, Committee on Foreign Affairs, *Background Materials on Foreign Assistance,* Report of the Task Force on Foreign Assistance, February 1989 (Washington, D.C.: GPO, 1989), pp. 257–259.

15. See Ernst Friedrich Schumacher, *Small Is Beautiful: A Study of Economics As If People Mattered* (London: Blond and Briggs, 1973); and Rachel Carson, *Silent Spring* (New York: Houghton Mifflin, 1962).

16. The priming has had its glitches. A USAID consultant told this author of an occasion in which the burning of coca fields was to be staged as a major media event; camera teams were trucked into the hinterland of Bolivia only to find that no one had brought a match.

17. Tad Bartimus, "Cold War Machine Takes on Drug Runners," *Albuquerque Journal,* September 3, 1990, pp. A1, A4.

18. U.S. Senate Committee on Foreign Relations, Subcommittee on Narcotics, Terrorism, and International Relations. Report on "Drugs, Law Enforcement, and Foreign Policy," released April 13, 1989.

19. Ambassador Jonathan Moore, U.S. Coordinator for Refugee Affairs, "Update on Immigration and Refugee Issues," Statement before the Subcommittee on Immigration, Refugees, and International Law of the House Judiciary Committee on April 6, 1989, *Department of State Bulletin* 89, no. 2148, July 1989, pp. 59–60.

20. "Refugees Top 15 Million Worldwide, Group Says," *Albuquerque Journal,* April 25, 1990, p. A7.

21. Moore, op. cit.

22. Ambassador Jonathan Moore, "Confronting Realities of Refugee Assistance," address before the Episcopal Migration Ministries Network meeting on May 26, 1989, *Department of State Bulletin* 89, no. 2149, August 1989, pp. 85–86.

23. Susan George, *A Fate Worse Than Debt: The World Financial Crisis and the Poor* (New York: Grove Press, 1988).

24. World Bank, *World Development Report, 1988* (New York: Oxford University Press, 1988), pp. 27–32.

25. Hernando de Soto, *The Other Path: The Invisible Revolution in the Third World* (New York: Harper and Row, 1988).

SUGGESTED READINGS

Boserup, E., *Woman's Role in Economic Development* (London: Allen and Unwin, 1970).

Brown, Lester R., et al., eds., *State of the World* (New York: W. W. Norton & Co., 1986).

Council on Environmental Quality, *The Global 2000 Report to the President of the United States* (New York: Pergamon Press, 1980).

Dankelman, Irene, and Joan Davidson, *Women and the Environment in the Third World: Alliance for the Future* (London: Earthscan Publications Ltd., 1988).

Deere, Carmen Diana, and Magdalena Leon, *Rural Women and State Policy: Feminist Perspectives on Latin American Agricultural Development* (Boulder: Westview Press, 1987).

Feinberg, Richard, and Ricardo French-Davis, eds., *Development and External Debt in Latin America: Basis for a New Consensus* (Notre Dame: University of Notre Dame Press, 1988).

Lappé, Frances Moore, Joseph Collins, and David Kinley, *Aid as Obstacle: Twenty Questions About our Foreign Aid and the Hungry* (San Francisco: Institute for Food and Development Policy, 1980).

Meadows, Donella H., et al., *The Limits to Growth* (Washington, D.C.: Potomac Associates, 1974).

Payer, Cheryl, *The Debt Trap: The International Monetary Fund and the Third World* (Harmondsworth, UK: Penguin Books, 1974).

Redfield, R., *The Primitive World and Its Transformations* (Ithaca: Cornell University Press, 1953).

Streeten, P., and R. Jolly, eds., *Recent Issues in Development* (Elmsford, N.Y.: Pergamon Press, 1981).

Thurow, Lester, *The Zero-Sum Society* (New York: Penguin Books, 1981).

Tinker, I., and M. Bramsen, *Women and World Development* (Washington, D.C.: Overseas Development Council, 1976).

Part 3

The Process
and the Protagonists:
Paradoxes of Development

The Process:
Games Developers Play

7 In earlier chapters we have dealt with differing perspectives on the part of theorists as to the nature and causes of underdevelopment and thus as to what should be the priorities of development programs and the approaches of development agencies. These broad discrepancies at the macro level of analysis reflect differences in values and thus in goals as between categories of donors as well as between some categories of donors and their clients. Arguments with regard to efficiency or prospects for success must ultimately deal with the question, For whom? and the answer to that one is dictated not by facts but by values.

In development, however, as in most public-policy areas, the question of values and thus of ultimate goals is not often dealt with straightforwardly. In fact, in any given program, there may be as many goals as there are institutional or even individual actors. In the case of many programs—particularly the most ambitious in terms of funding and personnel—the most crucial issues are not openly discussed at any level: not between executive and legislative branches or among supposedly cooperating agencies, not between donor and host governments, and most certainly not between donor agencies and client organizations or communities.

Thus, the ambiguities, inconsistencies, and outright but unacknowledged conflicts are pushed out of the assembly rooms and boardrooms and into the field. The goals of the game are left to be deciphered and the outcome determined by the dynamics of the process.

The unfolding of the development process, as it reflects the interplay among donor agencies and clients—often having conflicting needs and objectives—and the crossfires and minefields that field agents must negotiate, will be addressed in these chapters in a set of paradoxes. These paradoxes are drawn from the author's observations in the course of field research in a number of countries, particularly Ecuador in the early 1980s and India in the mid-to-late 1980s.[1] I believe, however, that they characterize the problems of development anywhere, including in the pockets of poverty in the United States. They are very general, impressionistic, and irreverent; they are also meant to be provocative and to serve, perhaps, as seeds of "appropriate" theory.

PARADOX NO. 1: *In public affairs, no matter how bad things appear to be, they're actually worse.* Governments and other institutions almost always try to cover up their mistakes and misdeeds and put the best face on what they have done or are doing.

Publicized rationales for policy initiatives often cover for undisclosable motives. Moreover, even when motives are relatively benign, agencies can be expected to exaggerate their successes and minimize their failures. Finally, even where publics or clients cannot avoid being less sanguine, bureaucrats tend to become convinced by their own propaganda or their own reports of successful project completion.

One need look no further than Watergate or the Iran-Contra scandal to see that beneath any government disclosure, voluntary or otherwise, lies another layer of undisclosables.[2] Nor is such mendacity confined to the U.S. government or to the superpowers. In the 1980s alone, France had its Rainbow Warrior sabotage, Great Britian its suppression of *Spycatcher* and its Falkland War cover-ups, and Japan its Recruit Company bribe scandal.

Because the concept of development is at the same time extraordinarily elastic and puffed up with positive connotations, "development" often becomes a cloak for programs with less-felicitous objectives. The British, for example, in conjunction with the World Bank, launched the Kariba hydroelectric project, which was heralded as a major contribution to the industrialization of Zambia. The Zambians were so thoroughly sold on the project that they even helped to pay for it, even though they were not to see the first payoff from their investment for thirty-five years and even though a Rhodesian company was to be appointed agent for construction.

Only later did it become clear to the Zambians that the Rhodesian company was in virtually complete control of local decision-making and that they had simply been conned. It turned out that the overriding objective of the project was to circumvent UN sanctions against the government of Ian Smith, providing huge amounts of cheap electricity to the blockaded Rhodesian regime.[3]

Misrepresentation is common also to nongovernmental institutions of First World or Third, and even relatively innocent organizational self-aggrandizement can frustrate relations among donors, field agents, and clients. When my contingent of Peace Corps volunteers arrived in Chile in 1962, our host country organization, *Techo* (Roof), which promoted community development in some of Santiago's sprawling shantytowns, briefed us on the facilities it had established and the projects we would be working with. We were told, for example, that in Población La Victoria the organization was operating nine clinics. A careful survey of the area by volunteers failed to turn up a single clinic. When we reported back to the staff that there were no *Techo* clinics in La Victoria, they responded, "Of course there are, they are right here in the files."

> PARADOX NO. 2: *Were it not for wrong reasons, there would be no right things done.* Development, even more than other political processes, makes strange bedfellows. The necessity of coalition building dictates that legislation or program planning benefiting the powerless must appeal also to some sector of the powerful.

The Food for Peace program is a case in point. Of course there were those among its proponents who were genuinely concerned about hunger in the Third World, but the program owes its existence for the most part to those whose interests are closer to home. U.S. food aid was introduced in the 1950s largely to expand markets for U.S. grain. Thus, the grain is not normally given away; it is sold to foreign governments, which in turn resell it on national markets, often at prices the poor majority cannot afford. If, on the other hand, the grain is sold cheap, it may undercut the narrow profit margins of local farmers, driving them out of business.

Moreover, food aid, like any other kind of aid, may be used for political purposes: to promote certain policies or bolster certain allies. The Ford administration, for example, used the Food for Peace program in 1974–1975 to bulwark Chile's murderous General Augusto Pinochet after Congress had cut off military assistance to his regime. Finally, such aid is under any circumstances a mixed blessing, as it diverts attention from the need for land-tenure and farm program reforms both in client countries and at home. Hunger, whether in First World or Third, does not normally reflect lack of food production or productive capacity but rather maldistribution of land, income, and opportunity.

Likewise, Ecuador's land reform of 1964 had various instigators and purposes. The reform was an outgrowth, in part, of the Kennedy administration's Alliance for Progress, which was in turn a response, in part, to the Cuban Revolution. The 1964 reform law provided that *huasipungueros,* or peons, were to receive title to the land they worked if that land was not being efficiently used or if workers were being exploited. The law was feared and staunchly opposed, of course, by some *hacendados,* or landowners. Nevertheless, it was favored—some would even say instigated—by many of the modernizing landowners who wanted to rid themselves of the medieval ties of obligation and to liquefy their assets in order to invest in industry or in construction in the cities. Some particularly well-connected landowners profited handsomely by inducing the government to pay in cash an inflated price for their land. The even more powerful barons of the northern coastal plantations also favored the 1964 agrarian reform law because it generated a larger pool of migratory wage laborers for seasonal work.

> PARADOX NO. 3: *To every solution there is a problem.* In development work, there are no happily-ever-afters. That is partly because in a nonrevolutionary situation—that is, where the material and institutional resources of most of the elite remain intact—the "haves" will soon figure out how to turn even a new law or program designed to benefit the "have-nots" to their own advantage. Reform may thus leave the have-nots having less.

In the case of land reform, peasants often exchange the problems of feudalism for the problems of capitalism. In the process of redistribution in Ecuador, the landlords, in most cases, kept the best plots—those on level land with an adequate water supply. For the majority of the former *huasipungueros,* there was no way to support a family on the tiny plots of vertical land they were left with. According to the census of 1974, half the country's landholdings were of less than 3 hectares.[4]

In the absence of a further major change in the landholding pattern, the problem of shrinkage can only get worse, as the peasant subdivides his tiny plot among his seven or eight children. Thus the cycle remains a vicious one. The peasant can't afford seed, so he is forced to hire out his labor, to migrate for several months of the year to the cities or the coastal plantations. The children left behind must help their mothers tend the crops. Unable to stay in school, they fail to acquire the skills that might enable them to earn a decent wage in the city. Marcelo

Torres, director of projects for Ecuador's Agrarian Reform Institute (IERAC), said that although the reforms of 1964 and 1973 were to have eradicated all forms of "precarious" tenure, new forms, such as sharecropping and land rental, have since appeared.

Some of the Andean peasants migrate to the cities, increasing the pressures on the limited urban market for housing and jobs. One of the motives of the Ecuadorean government in launching its land reform program was to keep the peasants on the land, reducing the pressures of urbanization and increasing production so that the peasants could feed themselves as well as the urban population. But even under the best of circumstances it would be difficult to increase production on the typical peasant's arid, eroded plot. And the "best of circumstances" do not prevail. In general, the credit—essential for any kind of improvement—that was available to the landlord is not available to the peasant. In fact, over the past decade, the importation of basic foodstuffs has been increasing sharply.

The colonization of newly opened lands in the Oriente (the Amazon Basin) and in the Santo Domingo zone, between the Sierra, or high Andes, and the coast, has eased the pressure to some extent. But the life of the pioneer in such areas has not been easy. Apart from the land itself, the government has been able to offer very little. José (Pepe) Aguilar, director of the regional office of the Ministry of Agriculture and Ranching (MAG) for the Santo Domingo zone, complained that the zone is sorely lacking in roads, potable water, electricity, basic health care, schools, technical assistance, credit—everything. Furthermore, most of the accessible land in the zone has now been claimed. Recent arrivals have to serve as wage laborers for those who are already landowners, resulting in a new social stratification. Some of the new migrants simply become squatters on land that has already been claimed, generating social tension and increasing pressures on the government.

In tandem with the proliferation of *minifundios,* or tiny plots, in the Sierra and the colonization of the jungles, there has been a reconcentration of land in the richer, more productive, area of the northern coast. Plantation owners, producing largely for export, welcomed the termination of the semifeudal *huasipungo* system, as the new tenure pattern provided them an ample supply of cheap wage labor. By the same token, however, they firmly resist any further development of the Sierra that would enable the peasants to support themselves fully on their own farms. They also, of course, resist paying the export or import taxes that would finance such development in the Sierra. As the migratory laborers begin to organize and demand higher wages, plantation owners can be expected to revise the balance between capital and labor intensity. With increasing modernization and mechanization, the danger is that in some two decades the country will have a very high proportion of workers who have neither land nor jobs.

Agrarian reform is usually presented in egalitarian terms, but even when governments mean well, development programs for the rural sector are more readily accessible to the larger landholders and often exacerbate inequality. The green revolution, regularly cited as one of the great successes of the international development agenda of the 1960s and 1970s, made available new varieties of seeds and fertilizers, new technologies and new lines of credit, but only to farmers who could afford to invest in them and who were already successful enough to be considered creditworthy. The farmers who have been able to take advantage of the program, while becoming richer, have also become more dependent.

Meanwhile, the enhanced value of land has induced the larger landowners to covet more of it, especially land held in precarious tenure arrangements, like sharecropping, by subsistence farmers. Thus, with the green revolution, India, previously subject to famine and required to import much of its food, has become self-sufficient in food production. Ironically, though, while food is more abundant, some Indians are surely eating less; the miracle of productivity has led to more concentrated landownership and increasing numbers of peasants who are landless.

On the idyllic island of Bali, the Indonesian government, in 1984, was introducing an agrarian reform program. With government encouragement and assistance to those who could afford to be innovative, cash crops, particularly vanilla and cloves, were supplanting subsistence crops, and peasants who previously worked their own land were becoming tenants or wage laborers on the land of others. Even in the South Pacific, which has suffered less in general from modernization than other Third World regions, cash cropping for export is changing patterns of life-style and of diet. Polynesians, Melanesians, and Micronesians, who used to have balanced diets of fresh fruit, root crops, and fish, are now eating canned meat and Wonder Bread and granulated sugar and are suffering from heart disease, high blood pressure, and diabetes. And Western development specialists are engaged in educating the island peoples about the virtues of their native diets.

PARADOX NO. 4: *Development programs are given impetus, not by underdevelopment, but by the fear of development that is not programmed from above.* As a rule, there is very little money for development until those who have the money and the power feel threatened—precisely by the self-activation of the poor.

All development specialists maintain that their aim is to promote self-help. It appears, however, that the primary objectives of the best financed programs are the channeling and control, if not the suppression, of the initiatives of the poor.

The big influx of development money—from AID, the World Bank, and evangelical missionaries—that came into Ecuador in the mid-1970s clearly came in response to a major mobilization of Indians in the Sierra, encouraged by the Catholic church and propelled by a belated recognition of the legal options signified by the 1964 land reform. By 1977 the peasant movement had begun to dissolve.

There are, however, many better-known examples of this paradox—like the campaign by AID in the early 1960s to suppress the Peasant Leagues of the Brazilian Northeast or, more recently, the so-called economic aid—some $700 million annually in the 1980s—directed to Central America.

Brazil's Northeast contained the country's greatest concentration of poverty generally and of rural poverty and powerlessness in particular. The area, which had 24 percent of the population but accounted for only 11 percent of the national income in 1960, remained basically feudalistic in political and socioeconomic structure and was subjected to periodic droughts that resulted in widespread starvation and emigration. The area's peasants had been untouched by the rise of populism and other developments that had expanded the urban political base and had received no benefits or protection from the extension in the 1940s of minimum-wage and union-recognition laws to the rural sector. The illiterate majority of the peasants lacked even the minimum fee for membership in the patrimonial political system—the vote.

Nevertheless, a group of tenant farmers in the state of Pernambuco had organized a mutual benefit association in the early 1950s, and when the landowner and his political allies tried to disband it in 1955, the peasants sought the support of a federal deputy named Francisco Julião. From that embryo, the movement, which came to be known as the Peasant Leagues, swelled to a following of about 100,000 at its peak in 1961. The challenge or the threat of the political awakening of the rural masses drew the attention of Brazilian nationalists as well as of the U.S. government.

Brazil's President João Goulart, along with the parties, unions, student and church groups, and other elements of the so-called leftist-nationalist movement that supported his government, responded to the challenge by joining in the fray to organize and service the peasants in hopes of drawing them into his political base. A new Rural Workers Law, promulgated in March 1963, facilitated that process. In the meantime, funding for a comprehensive approach to the problems of the area, through a new agency, had cleared the Brazilian Congress in December 1961. The Superintendency for the Development of the Northeast (SUDENE), brainchild of economist Celso Furtado, answered directly to the president and enjoyed administrative autonomy. In addition to its own responsibilities in the planning and execution of development projects, it was empowered to coordinate the delivery of both national and foreign technical assistance to the area.

U.S. administrations of liberal bent are always ambivalent, and the Kennedy administration was no exception. Thus there were those in policy-making circles who were serious about promoting redistributive reforms in Brazil and elsewhere; but the heavyweights in those circles were convinced that dealing with what they perceived as the "threat of revolt" in the most-impoverished region of Latin America's largest and most-populous state had to be the first critical test of the Alliance for Progress.

The U.S. effort there was to have two interrelated purposes. First, as part of the larger strategy to undermine the Goulart government, it aimed to assist "democratic" (pro-U.S., anti-Goulart) political leaders in defeating Leftists or other supporters of the central government.

The second purpose—undermining, containing, repressing, or destroying those organizations that gave aid and comfort to a peasant movement the United States could not control—called for manipulations at the grass-roots level. U.S. strategy on both levels spelled direct confrontation with the agency through which foreign assistance was to be channeled.

After sending a special mission to the Northeast in 1961 to draw up recommendations, the United States entered into the so-called Northeast Agreement with Brazil on April 13, 1962. The United States committed a total of $131 million, of which $760,000 was to be in dollars and the balance in local currency under PL 480 (the Food for Peace program). Thirty-three million of this amount was to be earmarked for immediate action, or "impact," projects and $98 million was reserved for long-range development projects. The Brazilian Northeast became the only subnational region in the world to merit its own AID mission.

The Northeast Agreement turned out to be, from the start, a disagreement and an utter failure in terms of both its stated and its unstated goals. U.S. attempts to co-opt political leaders and to influence the outcome of elections in the area through timely allocations of impact aid were generally unsuccessful, as were efforts to contain the peasant movement and to generate parallel organizations under covert U.S. control. Those U.S. efforts did, however, deprive SUDENE of anticipated support from the political center and drive it farther to the left. Thus the undermining of SUDENE, undertaken initially as a consequence of that agency's refusal to subordinate its own objectives to U.S. interests, had become an end in itself, and the designation of SUDENE as anti-American became a self-fulfilling prophecy.

It was only after the military coup d'état of March–April 1964, which replaced the elected civilian government with a military dictatorship, that the Peasant Leagues and other popular organizations of the Northeast were suppressed and a purged and reconstituted SUDENE adopted a policy of full cooperation with the U.S. AID mission.[5]

> PARADOX NO. 5: *Credit is extended only to those who do not need it.* The lenders' interpretation of creditworthiness generally results in discrimination against those whose holdings and ambitions are modest.

This point is obvious, but it highlights one of the gravest problems afflicting development programs in general and rural development in particular. Land reform programs are often stymied by the unavailability of credit for *minifundistas* and new settlers and thus result in a general decline in agricultural production.

The poorest peasants are often afraid even to seek loans from private banks for fear that the bank will seize their land. Such fears may be unwarranted in particular cases, but they are not irrational. Likewise, peasant communities have been hesitant to enter into contracts with government agencies; they are not confident that they understand all of the ramifications of such contracts, and they fear they might somehow be tricked.

When peasants do seek loans, they often find that banks will not honor their titles or their land-sharing or swapping arrangements among themselves. In Ecuador, peasants who want to sell land must get permission from the agrarian reform agency, IERAC. IERAC urges them to sell to owners of adjoining land or at least to others in the community, but peasants often prefer to make their own arrangements. Thus among themselves they enter into extralegal "commitments to sell." Banks, even if they were disposed to extend credit to peasants, would not recognize such extralegal arrangements. Extralegality, of course, is not their only problem.

In the Santo Domingo zone, IERAC may, under certain circumstances, sell to squatters the land they have cultivated. But the squatters cannot then get credit because banks refuse to recognize their titles. Banks also refuse to recognize collective ownership of land, even though the traditional Indian *comuna* was sanctified by law in 1937 and its provisions for participation and benefits for all community members have been strengthened by new legislation passed under the Hurtado government.

It is unfortunate but hardly surprising that private banks are rarely accessible to peasants. What is more discouraging is that even the Banco de Fomento, Ecuador's national development bank, generally refuses to make loans except to those who do not need them. Like any private bank, it is preoccupied primarily with recovering its resources, and it expects repayment in full with interest. For that reason, it was necessary to establish FODERUMA, Development Fund for the Marginal Rural Sector, as an organ of the Banco Central (Central Bank). FODERUMA does not really expect repayment, but it may direct its resources only to a very few communities; only the poorest are said to be "FODERUMAbles."

Similar problems present themselves in the establishment and the functioning of cooperatives. Almost all development agencies promote cooperatives, although most co-ops fail—at least in their function of raising incomes. In the first place, members must make investments. Therefore, those who most need help are not able to participate. For most purposes a co-op may be organized with as few as eleven members. Furthermore, cooperatives must maintain community services, draining scarce resources and making it all the more difficult for members to realize economic advantages. Investment can rarely be the solution when the problem is lack of money.

Finally, when a cooperative does succeed, it is likely to divide the community by generating new inequities. There are a few agencies, like IERAC and the literacy campaign, that at times and in places—primarily the Sierra—promote a return to traditional forms of organization, involving entire communities, rather than cooperatives. But they encounter a great deal of resistance, because the oligarchy views such *comunas* as the seeds of communism.

The unavailability of credit for those who need it most is a major problem throughout the Third World and in parts of the First World as well. Development and agriculture economists at the Universitas Udayana of Denpasar, in Indonesia, told me in 1984 that while the government provides credit for some cooperatives and resettlement projects, none is extended to the neediest, as it is assumed that they would not be able to pay it back.[6] In Indonesia, as elsewhere, co-ops usually fail. Dividends are rare, as co-op managers reinvest the meager earnings, and members, seeing no economic advantage, soon lose interest.

The poorest of the peasants, unable to obtain credit from government or from private banks, or to get ahead through membership in cooperatives, are forced to rely on traditional paternalistic—and generally exploitative—relationships. A. L. Mendiratta, serving the UN Food and Agriculture Organization in New Delhi, noted that in the 1980s rural bondage, based generally on inherited debt, was still to be found in parts of India. Such bondage had been outlawed, but peasants are poorly informed of their legal rights and poorly equipped to exercise or defend them. Defiance of landlords is risky under any circumstances, and the Indian government is unprepared to serve as an alternate patron.[7]

In Malawi, beginning in the late 1960s, the government, with a major transfusion from the World Bank's International Development Agency, undertook patronage of a set of four ambitious rural development projects. A major feature of the projects was to have been the extension of credits to peasant farmers. As it turned out, however, fewer than 5 percent of the farmers actually received any of the funds. Most of the funds were allocated to capital development and management costs, including luxurious offices and generous salaries and expense accounts for a top-heavy bureaucracy. At least one of the projects, the Lilongwe Land Development Project, received considerable praise in development-management circles, as infrastructure construction was completed roughly on schedule and productivity was increased. Participatory and distributive benefits, however, were not evident. Distribution figures for 1975 indicated that Malawi's peasantry, amounting to 95 percent of the population, received only about 11 percent of the income generated by agricultural production.[8]

PARADOX NO. 6: *Third World governments are weakened by the lack of pressures.* Pressures on such governments are fierce and incessant, but they are virtually all from one side— the side of the rich. For long-term effectiveness, development programs must build up countervailing pressures.

Victor Paz Estenssoro, perennial president of Bolivia, attributed the survival of the Bolivian revolution in its early years to the existence of the peasant militias. He told me about the visit of one such militia from a village on the altiplano to his office early in his first presidency. A spokesman for the group said the village desperately needed a telephone and a bridge to link it to the road to La Paz. Paz said, "I am very sorry, but you must understand; there are so many demands, and so few resources. There is no way I can help." The peasant leader then said, "Mr. President, do you remember how the counterrevolutionaries hanged President Villarroel from a lamppost? Well, when they come for you, you can call us on our telephone and we'll come running over our bridge and save you." Paz said they got their bridge and their telephone.[9]

In Ecuador in the early 1980s, President Osvaldo Hurtado was trying to plant the seeds of popular organizations, but it was still the *camaras*—chambers of industry and agriculture—who dominated politics. Almost all the professionals in the field of rural development in Ecuador at the time, including the militants of the government of Hurtado, acknowledged the need for another kind of agrarian reform; they conceded that even with the greatest imaginable luck and success the programs under way would not touch the structural obstacles to social change. But it would be neither fair nor realistic simply to blame the government.

With the sudden death of President Jaime Roldós in 1981, Vice President Hurtado had been propelled into the presidency before his time. He was only forty-one years old. More important, his party was relatively new and small, holding fewer than 20 percent of the seats in the single-chamber legislature, and had had little opportunity to build a popular base. Furthermore, his style—that of a soft-spoken political science professor—was puzzling to a populace accustomed to demagoguery. Finally, his administration's lack of ideological definition, though in some ways an asset, allowed critics on the left to label Hurtado a technocratic elitist, while those on the right called him a crypto-Marxist. Supporters of the government believed that it would be an accomplishment of the greatest importance if Hurtado managed to stay in power until the next scheduled elections.

Such debility was not a problem simply of that particular government, but of any Ecuadorean government, and especially of any government that proposed to incorporate the "marginalized" poor into the mainstream of national society. Rarely has a civilian government exhibited firm control of the armed forces, and no Ecuadorean government ever managed seriously to tax the oligarchy. Revenue accruing to the state from the oil boom of the 1970s had begun to provide a measure of autonomy for the government, even though 50 percent of the oil royalties were earmarked for the military. But the international petroleum glut of the early 1980s and the precipitous drop in prices left the new civilian government with heavy commitments and scant resources.

The president's administrative assistant, Ramiro Rivera, said that the country had to consider a new approach to land reform sometime in the future, perhaps in two or three decades; but the current political system simply would not permit it. The electorate in the early 1980s appeared to be abandoning traditional parties in favor of center to center-left or populistic ones. But real power does not lie with the electorate. It lies, as noted, with the chambers representing agribusiness and industry. Not only would the *camaras* react with hostility to the prospect of new structural reforms; they were still aggressively striving to roll back previous ones.

Ricardo Izurieta Mora Bowen, president of the National Federation of Chambers of Agriculture, said the *camaras* considered it their "duty" to put a stop to the policies that were ruining the economy. In addition to their objections to the Hurtado government's price controls on dairy goods and other agricultural products, their complaints focused on the agrarian reform legislation as codified in 1973. The reform of 1964 was not so bad, Izurieta said, because it removed the "irritant" of the *huasipungo* system and improved the "image" of the *hacendados*. But the codification of 1973 had left landowners insecure. Whereas under the 1964 law, land could be seized if it was unused for ten years, the modification of 1973 allowed the government to seize land that had been out of use for only two years. Izurieta conceded that the Hurtado government was not going out of its way to enforce the law, but as long as the law remained on the books the federation would see it as a threat; thus, the federation was trying to get it repealed.

Agribusiness had not failed to notice that the codification of 1973 was carried out under a military government. Izurieta said that only a minority of extremists within the *camaras* actually wanted to provoke a coup. The strategy of the majority appeared to be to keep the government intimidated by the threat of a coup without actually provoking one.

In order to deal with such extraparliamentary pressures as well as to prevail in parliament and to activate somnambulant bureaucrats—in order to address the needs of the nation as a whole—the government must be subject to counterbalancing pressure, effective pressure from the nonaffluent. No one was more conscious of that than Hurtado himself. His development programs were long-term ones, looking perhaps to the year 2000, but it appeared that all were designed to generate popular organizations that could at some point begin to serve as a balance. In the meantime, Hurtado called the military chiefs in regularly for briefings on the sad state of the economy—in hopes that they would see little promise in taking over a government that was broke.[10] He succeeded in serving out his term and turning over the office to another duly elected president; his was the first government in twenty years to do so.

PARADOX NO. 7: *The primary beneficiaries of rural development programs are the cities.* Development money settles mostly in the cities, where offices are maintained, supplies are purchased, and salaries are earned and spent.

Ouagadougou, capital of what was then Upper Volta (since renamed Burkina Faso), offered an extreme example in the late 1970s of the urban backwash of rural development. There were endless horror stories coming out of the Sahel about creeping desertification and its wake of famine and starvation; but Ouagadougou was booming. There were no tourists at all, but Ouagadougou, I was told, at that time had the highest per capita concentration of development specialists in the world. Almost any Third World capital, however, will illustrate the point.

There has been progress in Ecuador, even among the indigenous peoples in rural areas, since the beginning of banana exportation in the 1950s. Such progress has been indicated by increased consumption of commercial products and, more important, by advances in health, including a decline in infant mortality. Nevertheless, Ecuador remains a dual society, with an enormous gap in living standards between Indians and non-Indians as well as between urban and rural areas.

Ecuador's most obvious progress over the past three decades has been in social mobility—that is, the growth of the middle class. The income represented by economic growth has accrued mostly to the middle and upper classes. As banana money modernized Guayaquil, oil money has modernized Quito, and precious little of it has trickled into the countryside.

Likewise, development money, including money allocated to rural development, has been spent mostly in the city. The offices of most development agencies, including those dedicated to rural development, are located in major cities. Field agents in most rural development programs venture only infrequently and briefly into the field. Their supplies are purchased and their salaries are earned and spent, for the most part, in the cities.

Increasingly, since the International Labor Organization's Andean Mission (Misión Andina) of the 1950s, development has come to represent a major industry for Ecuador. In the late 1970s and early 1980s, the Inter-American Development Bank was investing an average of about $100 million annually in development; the World Bank $50 to $100 million; AID $15 million; the United Nations Development Program $3 million; the UN World Food Program $3 million; the Peace Corps $2.5 million; the World Health Organization $1.4 million; the UN Food and Agriculture Organization $1.4 million; the Organization of American States $1 million; and the UN Fund for Population Activity $1 million. Lesser amounts were being provided by Japan, West Germany, the United Kingdom, France, and Israel.[11]

Private development agencies also constitute a big business in Ecuador. There are at least 40 private development agencies, as such, from the United States, not to mention service, charity, and religious organizations that sponsor development programs. Don Swanson, a former Peace Corps volunteer who directs Consultants for the Development of Latin America (ASDELA), one of the major private development organizations (NGOs) in Ecuador, has identified 300 NGOs in the country without counting some 9,000 community-level "popular organizations." The nationally based Information Service for Private Organizations (SIOP), which conducted a survey of private development and welfare organizations, identified 500.

Finally, the array of development agencies of the Ecuadorean government, all known by their acronyms, constitutes a veritable alphabet soup. There are at least 60 ministries, agencies, or institutions involved in one way or another with development.

For Quito, the development boom has kept the airport busy throughout the year. It has filled office buildings, hotels, restaurants, and taxis. It has consumed tons of paper and generated a great many professional and clerical jobs. It has generated elegant proposals, plans, and evaluations. But all development programs, whether public or private, foreign or national, are top-heavy. The development boom fizzles out at the city limits.

That is not to say that there has been no development in the rural areas. But given the hundreds of millions of dollars invested and the manpower assigned to the effort, the level of development activity in the areas where it is needed most must be said to be disappointing.

NOTES

1. Much of the research reflected in Part 3 was conducted in Ecuador in June, July, and August 1982, courtesy of a Fulbright-Hays grant. It consisted primarily of interviews with about 100 development agency officials, field agents, and community leaders. For an elaboration of findings and sources, see J. K. Black, "Ten Paradoxes of Rural Development: An Ecuadorean Case Study," *Journal of Developing Areas* 19, no. 4, July 1985, pp. 527–555. A Fulbright-Hays grant also underwrote my research in India in 1988. Other research efforts represented here were funded by Mellon Foundation grants.

2. It appears now that the "arms for hostages" aspect of the Iran-Contra scandal, which the Reagan administration took such pains to deny, was itself a cover. Evidence continues to mount that while the arms shipments to Iran

were indeed related to hostages, they were not to be in exchange for the *release* of hostages held in the mid-1980s. Rather, the arms shipments appear to have been part of a deal negotiated in the fall of 1980 between the Ayatollah Khomeini's camp and Reagan's wherein Iran was to *hold* the U.S. Embassy hostages until election day, ensuring Carter's defeat. See Christopher Hitchens, "Minority Report," *Nation* 250, no. 21, May 28, 1990, p. 731.

3. David Morrell, *Indictment: Power and Politics in the Construction Industry* (London: Faber, 1987).

4. Instituto Nacional de Estadistica y Censos, *Resumen Nacional: 11 Censo Agropecuario, 1974* (Quito: Instituto Nacional de Estadistica y Censos, 1979), p. 1.

5. The best of several books dealing with the nature and consequences of U.S. foreign assistance to northeast Brazil in the early 1960s is Joseph A. Page, *The Revolution That Never Was: Northeast Brazil, 1955–1964* (New York: Grossman, 1972).

6. I. Detut Nehen and K. G. Bendesa, Facultas Ekonomi, Universitas Udayana. Personal interview, Denpasar, July 4, 1984.

7. A. L. Mendiratta, United Nations Food and Agriculture Organization. Personal interview, New Delhi, July 19, 1983.

8. Alifeyo Chilivumbo, "On Rural Development: A Note on Malawi's Programmes of Development for Exploitation," *African Development* 3, no. 2, 1978.

9. Conversations with Victor Paz Estenssoro, Albuquerque, Spring 1978.

10. Conversations with Osvaldo Hurtado, Albuquerque, April 1985.

11. U.S. Agency for International Development, Ecuador, "Briefing Book," 1981.

SUGGESTED READINGS

Bryant, Coralie, and Louise G. White, *Managing Development in the Third World* (Boulder: Westview Press, 1982).

Chambers, Robert, *Rural Development: Putting the Last First* (Harlow, UK: Longman Scientific and Technical, 1983).

Church, Frank, "Farewell to Foreign Aid: Why I Voted No," *New Republic*, November 13, 1971.

Firth, R., and B. Yamey, *Capital, Savings, and Credit in Peasant Societies* (London: Allen & Unwin, 1964).

Grindle, Merilee, *Politics and Policy Implementation in the Third World* (Princeton: Princeton University Press, 1980).

Korten, David C., and Felipe B. Alfonso, eds., *Bureaucracy and the Poor: Closing the Gap* (West Hartford, Conn.: Kumarian Press, 1981).

Korten, David C., and Rudi Klauss, *People-Centered Development: Contributions Toward Theory and Planning Frameworks* (West Hartford, Conn.: Kumarian Press, 1984).

Lipton, M., *Why the Poor Stay Poor: Urban Bias in World Development* (Cambridge: Harvard University Press, 1977).

Nef, Jorge, "Development Theory and Administration: A Fence Around an Empty Lot?" *Indian Journal of Public Administration* 27, no. 1, January to March 1981, pp. 8–22.

Schumacher, Ernst F., *Politics, Bureaucracy, and Rural Development in Senegal* (Berkeley: University of California Press, 1975).

Stout, R., *Management or Control* (Bloomington: Indiana University Press, 1980).

White, Louise G., *Creating Opportunities for Change: Approaches to Managing Development Programs* (Boulder: Lynne Rienner Publishers, 1987).

The Protagonists:
Donors, Clients,
and Field Agents

8 Development specialists are surely no less committed to their professed missions than are other categories of professionals. But along with the material and psychic rewards sometimes accrued, there are frustrations and obstacle courses that would try the patience of any saint.

An American who has spent more than twenty-five years trying to promote development in Latin America says that development work is rather like shoveling smoke. No mandates are unambiguous or irreversible; no precise boundaries can be drawn; no projects are ever concluded; no results are definitive; and no assessments are entirely reliable.

Many of the frustrations are inherent in the role of honest broker between the powerful and the powerless. In programs involving big money and big bureaucracies, the serious developmentalist, as opposed to the careerist or timeserver, will often feel like an infiltrator, able to pursue the agency's professed goals only in a surreptitious manner and forced to see his or her best efforts continuously ignored or sabotaged. Agency decision-makers, responding to the political climate that most directly affects their funding or career prospects, often override their own professional staffs and even highly paid consultants. It has not been uncommon, for example, for political appointees of the World Bank or the regional development banks to override the virtually unanimous recommendations of their professional staffs. The reverse is less common but also possible; on occasion, when the political leadership, executive or legislative, shows genuine concern for the unpowerful, it finds itself ignored or sabotaged by less-committed bureaucrats.

Even if the development specialist can count on the backing of his own agency, he must still negotiate the rapids of host country, regional, or local politics. At the local level, one can expect to encounter political reaction, loss of credibility, brain drain and budget drain, bureaucratic turf skirmishes, and overqualified, undergratified would-be field agents. And there is no guarantee that client communities will be appreciative or responsive. Still the business of development grows and attracts the best and brightest.

> PARADOX NO. 8: *The experts are always wrong.* The theories and models that guide the work of experts utilize a limited number of factors and do not allow for the unexpected. Especially when one is working in an unfamiliar setting (and experts by definition are), the unexpected always happens; in fact, if development is to be sustainable, the unexpected *must* happen.

There is a great deal of literature in circulation now on the need for culturally sensitive, ecologically sound, participatory approaches to development (empowerment being the new buzzword), and some small agencies and PVOs are demonstrably serious about it; but the big bureaucracies and high-tech or high-priced consulting agencies are not likely to be. In the first place, big bureaucracies are the creatures of political systems. They must answer first of all to the powerful, not to the powerless.

At the University of Michigan in the early 1960s, a graduate student from Venezuela, on leave from a position in his country's very reputable Ministry of Planning, explained to his fellow students how the ministry used cost-benefit analysis in making decisions on road building: "First you calculate the cost of materials, labor, purchase of right-of-way, and other expenditures, and you place that figure below the line. Then you calculate the additional income the farmers will earn through the new access to markets, multiply by the number of years the road will be serviceable, and place the product above the line. If the resulting figure is greater than 1, you build the road."

A student interjected, "But what if the figure is less than 1?"

The Venezuelan responded, "You recalculate the farmers' earnings or extend the estimated years of serviceability until the result is more than 1."

"So you always build the road?"

"Of course, we wouldn't be doing the study unless somebody important wanted the road built."[1]

The very nature of bureaucracy militates forcefully against participatory, bottom-up processes. Bureaucracies need to be able to report results—preferably quantifiable results—within a preordained and generally very limited time frame (e.g., the fiscal year). Furthermore, both concrete, or material, results and timing should be as planned or predicted. In the case of a transfer of responsibility to local counterparts or to a client organization, the process is complex and imprecise, calling for constant reappraisal, and specification of timing at the outset would probably be counterproductive.

In fact, of all the forms the termination of a program may take, a definitive intentional transfer of responsibility to community-level clients is among the rarest. Ordinarily the required reports should be of a nature that calls for further appropriations and an ongoing program. Program maintenance, the minimal objective of the institutional imperative, calls for reinforcing dependency. Likewise most consultants who claim expertise in management or technical skills are in the business of marketing those skills for money, often big money, and they are not likely to be interested in building local capacity against which they would have to compete for further contracts. Even the nonexpert, serving in a not-for-profit capacity, who has set out from the beginning to train counterparts and work himself out of a job, will often find it stressful to acknowledge that he is no longer needed and to turn his pet project over to others.

Finally, for the project manager with layers of supervisors to report to, the worst possible outcome—the development most threatening to his career—is for things to get out of control. For the client community, though, "getting out of control" is the very essence of empowerment.

The control of individual projects by bureaucrats and consultants, especially foreign ones, may result in completed projects, but it is not likely to result in the enhancement of local capacity. Nor is it likely to produce results that are well attuned to local needs. An experience of former Peace Corps volunteer Chris Searles in Swaziland in the 1970s highlights the problem. The Mbabane Urban Extension Project, to which he was assigned, involved physical and policy planning for a squatter slum with a population of about 14,000. The plans to be produced were to address land use, roads, water, sewer, and community facilities.

The expatriate-dominated project team included a U.S. architect, a South African planning firm, and a British-based multinational engineering firm. The team failed utterly to adjust plans and procedures to the local context. The master plan that was drawn up called for the strict land-use zoning common in the industrialized West, but lacking any traditional or legal basis in Swaziland, where even the concept of private property was alien. Not only did the project fail to build local capacity, but it failed even to produce a usable product. The $30,000 plan was simply discarded.

Similarly in Tunisia in 1987, in the same scorched area, on the fringes of the Sahara, where the troglodytes (cave dwellers) have for centuries found relief from the relentless heat in their naturally cooled underground dwellings, I was shown a cinder-block housing development erected in the 1970s and funded, in part, by USAID. The development simmers unoccupied in the blistering sun—an instant ruin, a monument to the arrogance of the experts who are unwilling or unable to learn from the people they would serve. Development programs that are stymied by institutional constraints, such as the need to maintain control, or by constraints of self-interest, such as hesitance to generate competing capacity or expertise, are likely also to suffer from paternalism.

PARADOX NO. 9: *Rural development is a process whereby affluent urban-dwellers teach poor peasants how to survive in the countryside without money.* All development programs and agencies are to some extent paternalistic.

The worst that might be said of a development agency is that it is paternalistic. All agencies, even religious, service, and charity groups, consider themselves of the "new wave" and say that they are not patronizing like the rest. But changing rhetoric is one thing; changing behavior patterns, particularly institutional and bureaucratic ones, is quite another.

Development specialists, for the most part, are loath to acknowledge the traces of arrogance in the operations of their own agencies but are highly sensitive to the insensitivities of other agencies. Several administrators and field agents have pointed out to me the tendency of developmentalists (in other agencies, of course) to speak to peasants in professional jargon they could not be expected to understand or to speak down to them, as if they were children. This problem was impressed on me in a personally embarrassing way in a small village in Ecuador's highland province of Chimborazo, where I appeared with the provincial director of a highly reputable development agency before a group of campesinos. He introduced me and said that "*la doctorita*" is here to find out "if you are disposed to develop yourselves or if you are apathetic and lazy like your grandparents."

Development, in theory and in practice, is a slave to fashion, and current fashion dictates the promotion of community organization and the involvement of the community in the assessment of needs and the planning of projects. All development agencies now say that this is their objective, but it appears that there are few that have put this process into practice. In Ecuador, even the Secretariat for Integrated Rural Development (SEDRI), the most stylish of them all, was having little success in this endeavor.

Distinguishing between *desarrollo* (development) and *desarrollismo* (developmentism), Monseñor Leonidas Proaño, bishop of Riobamba, said that *desarrollismo* is paternalistic. It presumes to promote change without asking the people what they need, without building on their own experience, without involving them and allowing them to take initiatives.

By way of illustration, he cited a project of the Andean Mission in a village in Chimborazo. Mission representatives arrived one day with two big healthy rams. They rounded up the villagers and asked them to bring some of their own scrawny rams for comparison. They then told the villagers that they should take the healthy rams on loan and breed them. Villagers later told the bishop that had they been consulted they would have told the mission representatives that the healthy rams would die because the area lacked water and good grazing land.

By contrast, Proaño said, *desarrollo* is above all development of the person—of his ability to think, to decide, to invest. Beneficiaries must be the subjects of their own development.

Proaño noted that traditionally the Catholic church has stressed hierarchy and ritualism. The faithful were expected simply to do as they were told. Several recent conferences, however, including those at Medellín, Colombia, in 1968, and at Puebla, Mexico, in 1979, have stressed the role of the Church as a community. When he first came to Riobamba twenty-eight years ago, Proaño said, he found the Indians—under a system of near slavery—greatly intimidated, afraid to speak to the *patrón* (landlord), to government officials, to any non-Indian, much less to a bishop. Now they are discovering that they can express themselves without fear. But true liberation from exploitation, social marginalization, and deculturation is far from being realized. Indians, he said, are still expected to go to the back of the bus.

Intimidation, of course, is the flip side of paternalism. Thus Pedro Chango, president of a Catholic student organization in Chimborazo with chapters in thirty communities, said that the primary function of his organization is consciousness-raising: instilling self-confidence and inspiring self-expression.

Among the perennial obstacles to development in the Sierra, according to Raúl do Valle, a Brazilian World Bank economist on loan to the Ecuadorean government in the early 1980s, are development agents who do not know how to relate to communities and communities that do not know how to prioritize and present demands. Raúl Gangotena, executive director of the National Pre-investment Fund (FONAPRE), conceded that integrated rural development, which was such an important theme of the Hurtado government, remained little more than a theme. Bureaucrats, he said, have generally been unwilling or unable to bridge the cultural gap, to stimulate participation, or to respond to community initiatives. As a consequence, there are no mechanisms for involving supposed beneficiaries in the planning process, or even in implementation. At the same time, the bureaucrats are unable to carry out even the simplest projects, such as the building of a school, without community participation. Thus the Indians, customarily suspicious and skeptical, for good historic reasons, see the false starts and failures of the bureaucrats as confirmation of their skepticism.

Another problem closely related to paternalism is that of ethnocentricity. Carlos Moreno, director of the Education Ministry's literacy campaign in Chimborazo, told of a UNESCO pilot project in literacy in the early 1970s that failed miserably because its imagery was utterly alien to life in the Andean highlands. The image representing the word "mama," for example, was a tall thin blond in Western dress. Pedro Bagua, an Indian leader in Chimborazo's predominantly evangelical canton of Colta, commented that along with all the programs designed to teach Indians about non-Indian culture, there should be a program to teach non-Indians—at least those involved in development—about Indian culture.

The supposedly unsophisticated may, of course, have a great deal more to teach the cosmopolitan than the mysteries of their cultures. N. Cristescu, rector of the University of Bucharest, told the author of an occasion in the late 1980s when his car developed problems as he was driving in the vicinity of the Romanian village of Bragadiru. At the village mechanic's shop where his car was being fixed, he found that ordinary car engines that ran on gasoline were being converted to use diesel fuel, which was cheaper and, in Romania, easier to filch from government supplies. Cristescu said that he mentioned the incident later to European scientists who allowed that such conversion was not possible. "Not possible," perhaps, for his scientifically trained friends, Cristescu said, but it was being done very successfully in a remote Romanian village.

In a similar vein, David Korten reported that engineers of the Philippine's National Irrigation Administration (NIA), in the Laru Project, received more advice from local farmers than they really wanted. The project proposed to strengthen the NIA's capacity to work with communally owned and operated gravity-fed irrigation systems, but project engineers were dismayed to find that local farmers objected strongly to the materials they chose for dam construction. The farmers won a Pyrrhic victory when the dam, constructed over their objections to the engineers' specifications, washed out soon after completion.[2]

> PARADOX NO. 10: *The more important an agency's mission and the more efficient its performance, the sooner it will be suppressed.* If an agency with an important mission, like land reform, has any success at all, it will generate a reaction from the privileged classes. If it has no success, it will lose credibility among its supposed beneficiaries. Worse still, it is to be expected that such agencies will generate reaction and lose credibility with beneficiaries at the same time.

As a rule, the fate of a state development agency is much like that of a reformist presidency: the longer it has been in existence, the less effective it will be. Furthermore, each new government naturally wants to leave its own mark on the bureaucracy and has little incentive to strengthen the programs of previous governments. Thus new governments and external funding sources will begin to cultivate new agencies.

But old agencies never die; they only appear to be dead. They slump into a low profile. Enough is retained in the budget for paying the salaries of bureaucrats but not enough for fulfilling their missions. Thus the professionals with the most initiative (or perhaps the most ambition) move to the new agencies or to the private sector, and the rest remain, demoralized and less productive.

In Ecuador, by the beginning of the 1980s, initiative and support had become concentrated in a few relatively new agencies, like the Secretariat for Integrated Rural Development (SEDRI), National Pre-investment Fund (FONAPRE), and the Development Fund for the Marginal Rural Sector (FODERUMA), and in the Education Ministry's literacy campaign. Agencies like the Agrarian Reform Institute (IERAC), and even the all-encompassing Ministry of Agriculture and Ranching (MAG), had become encrusted, defensive bureaucracies. For the latter agencies, budget problems were getting worse every year. When I left the office of IERAC in Santo Domingo in mid-1982, I wanted to call a taxi, but that wasn't possible; the office's telephone service had been cut for failure to pay the bill.

FONAPRE, an offspring and still technically a dependency of the National Development Council (CONADE), was created in the early 1970s through a grant from the Inter-American Development Bank (IDB). Its pivotal role is that of conducting feasibility studies for all categories of public investment, including government contracts with private firms and with foreign and international banks and agencies.

Representatives of FODERUMA, established in 1978 as the development arm of the Central Bank, sit on a permanent committee with SEDRI and MAG. Other rural development committees, involving additional agencies, are formed on a project basis. Obviously, as Políbio Córdoba, of the Central Bank, pointed out, where FODERUMA is involved, it has the last word because it controls the money. But SEDRI, established in 1980, soon came to occupy center stage. It was designed by CONADE largely as a means of circumventing the Ministry of Agriculture. Its director, Fausto Jordan, acted, for most purposes, as the Hurtado government's minister of development.

SEDRI's major functions are those of designing projects, soliciting external funding—primarily from USAID, IDB, and the World Bank—and coordinating the efforts of other agencies and ministries. Jorge Andrade, a SEDRI official in the Santo Domingo zone, noted that the various ministries are far from pleased to relinquish authority, initiative, and even budget to another bureaucratic entity.

Relations between SEDRI and IERAC have been particularly cool. A few years earlier IERAC was the agency with authority, initiative, and money, and with enthusiastic employees. By the early 1980s IERAC had lost its sense of mission; its function, Andrade said, had become technical rather than social. IERAC Project Director Marcelo Torres said IERAC had been paralyzed by lack of government support for its mission. Officials of SEDRI have chosen in general to view integrated rural development as a follow-up to the structural change of agrarian reform already carried out by IERAC. IERAC officials, however, tend to see it differently. They believe that IERAC has been intentionally weakened by successive governments in response to pressure from landowners. And they view the work of SEDRI as a nonstructural, noncontroversial alternative to agrarian reform—the way of least resistance.

IERAC officials in Chimborazo complain that they are expected to serve 100 communities with three professionals and two vehicles, and they have to beg for money for gas. Attempts to redistribute land usually get tied up in courts for several years. If they are ultimately successful, IERAC must pay the landowners in cash, whereas the peasants buy the land from IERAC over a five-to-ten-year period. Thus, a transaction on a single hacienda may absorb a large proportion of IERAC's budget—a powerful disincentive to aggressive discharge of the agency's mandate.

In the Santo Domingo zone, IERAC's task of surveying the land and issuing titles has been immensely complicated by spontaneous colonization, and IERAC has often been blamed for the ensuing chaos. Colonizers are entitled to claim only cultivated areas, and IERAC can sell to squatters if original claimants are not cultivating the land adequately. But as in the Sierra, well-connected landowners usually get their way in court. Amidst the chaos, said Estrella Velez, IERAC director for the Santo Domingo zone, IERAC has found it virtually impossible to regulate the size and shape of plots or to insist on soil conservation, reforestation, or other ecologically sound practices. Lacking the budget and personnel for follow-up technical assistance, IERAC refers peasants with newly acquired land to its stepparent, MAG; but MAG is inclined simply to refer them back to IERAC.

MAG is in a sense the pariah of the Ecuadorean bureaucracy. From intellectuals, political leaders, development professionals, peasants, even from its own personnel, it is rare to hear an appreciative word about the ministry. A former MAG official at the vice-ministerial level commented that the ministry could disappear overnight and the country would never notice—despite the fact that, in principle, MAG's authority and responsibilities are enormous. In many rural areas, at least for purposes of implementation, MAG is the government. Its role, or potential role, is eminently political. Among other things, for example, it must oversee elections for the officers of all co-ops and *comunas*.

While younger and smaller agencies may be characterized as having a sense of mission, or a sense of mission lost, MAG is too old and too big for any such characterization. Within MAG there is considerable friction and competition, most of it derived from differing regional or methodological orientations. Roque Alvarez, director of MAG's *Desarrollo Campesino* (Rural Development) program in Chimborazo observed, for example, that MAG technicians who serve the northern coast tend to defend the interests of agribusiness while those in the Sierra are more likely to be sympathetic with the peasants. For the most part, however, MAG's reputation derives from those bureaucrats who are viewed—rightly or wrongly—as serving their own interests, and in general the ministry is held in low regard by landowners and peasants alike.

MAG employees are said to treat their jobs as sinecures rather than as opportunities for service. Worse yet, in the Santo Domingo zone, accounts of corruption are rife. Pepe Aguilar, director of the MAG office for that zone, felt that the ministry's reputation is undeserved. The government's development programs, he said, are unintegrated and inadequate. Foreign and domestic development funds are now channeled into isolated projects, like those of SEDRI and FODERUMA, "*lunares en la cara de la pobreza*" (moles on the face of poverty), while MAG's provincial offices, which must deal with all the rest, are understaffed and underpaid. "We are left," he said, "with overwhelming responsibilities and no resources."

PARADOX NO. 11: *Sophistication in development processes is acquired and program continuity maintained not by donor institutions but by client organizations and individuals.* Objectives and approaches of major international agencies and of state agencies of First World and Third are adjusted in accordance with shifts in elite political climate rather than in response to experience or outcomes in client states or communities.

Since the productive life of a state development agency is very short, we see little there in the way of institutional learning. Nor is there much disposition in First World international agencies to learn from experience in the Third World; for policymakers of such agencies, it is far more important to stay attuned to policy trends in donor states. And the priorities of state agencies, in First World or Third, change somewhat with each change of administration. Nevertheless, there is continuity and there is learning.

Abrupt changes of philosophy and of objectives on the part of a foreign donor institution or of a state agency will have reverberations all the way down to community-level organizations or projects, but some threads of continuity may be retained despite the hardships and the odds. Returning to Santiago, Chile, in 1977, thirteen years after having served there as a Peace Corps volunteer, and four years after a particularly brutal military counterrevolution had destroyed most popular institutions, I found that *Techo,* one of the host-country organizations volunteers had worked with, had been "intervened"—taken over by the dictatorship to serve its own purposes.

It turned out, however, that all that had been taken over was the name, the physical assets, and perhaps the links with private and foreign funding sources. The people—shantytown dwellers who had been the institution's supposed beneficiaries and its raison d'être—were gone. *Techo*'s most important organizational component, a garment production co-op, had simply slipped out from under the institutional umbrella, changed its name, and continued its operations.

The co-op had recently fallen on hard times, though. It might have maintained itself indefinitely without subsidy or technical assistance, but the utter lack of political standing and thus of legal protection was harder to withstand. When customer firms wrote bad checks or simply refused to pay for merchandise delivered, the co-op had no recourse. "In Chile now," the manager said, "there are no courts for poor people."

Much of the continuity throughout the Third World in the planning and execution of development programs must be credited to a growing body of development professionals—dedicated and enthusiastic individuals, of the highest motivation and of great experience. These professionals—national as well as foreign—are not bureaucrats because they do not serve institutions or governments as such. They move freely between national and international organizations and between the public and private sectors. What they serve is the mystique of development, and they are the repositories of much of what has been learned about the process.

Small, private, voluntary, or nonprofit development agencies tend to be more inventive and innovative than large public ones; the former are more likely to have the flexibility to experiment with new models and approaches. The existence of such private agencies is often precarious, and there may be little direct cooperation between public and private agencies, even though private agencies seek to influence public policy and public agencies stand to profit from the experimentation of private ones.

Nevertheless, continuity is often achieved through the process of absorption—not only of projects, but more important, of people. Individuals who have cut their professional teeth in the more-competitive and innovative world of the nongovernmental agencies are a great resource to governments that aim to chart a new course. Projects initiated by foreign and international agencies may also be absorbed. USAID Director John Sanbrailo said that at least forty projects or organizations initiated by AID and its predecessor agencies had been adopted by the Ecuadorean government. A number of the Ecuadorean government's more resilient programs and dedicated development specialists were veterans of the Andean Mission, a multifaceted program launched by the International Labor Organization, with the participation of several other UN-affiliated agencies in Ecuador, Bolivia, and Peru in the mid-1950s.

Some of the more-promising government programs have grown from the seeds of volunteer efforts. The Hurtado government's literacy campaign, for example, was new to the government, but it built upon many years of experimentation and learning. The country's first literacy program was launched by the Ecuadorean journalists' union in 1944 and was carried on, without financial support, until 1960. The Ministry of Education established a Department of Adult Education in 1960, but during the 1960s and early 1970s it undertook only a few isolated, poorly conceived, and poorly funded projects.

Meanwhile in the early 1970s, a group of unemployed professionals founded a voluntary association, the Volunteer Educational Service (SEV), to promote literacy training. The group was assisted by the University of Massachusetts, under contract with AID from 1970 to

1973 to put into use the philosophy and methodology of Paulo Freire. The Inter-American Foundation became involved in 1972 and, with continuing assistance from AID, carried on the program until 1976.

Carlos Moreno, one of the founders of SEV, joined the Ministry of Education in 1976. Since 1979 the ministry has conducted a very aggressive literacy campaign. Moreno, with continuing assistance from the Inter-American Foundation, directs the very successful program in Chimborazo, a program in which content and method are determined by the campesinos themselves.

PARADOX NO. 12: *In the Third World, there is a need for technicians who are less well trained.* For the most part, those who invest their time and money in acquiring professional status do not do so in order to work in muddy shoes.

In the early 1960s, acute shortages of the well-trained were common. Juan Bosch, former president of the Dominican Republic, told this author that in 1963 he was unable to find a single Dominican electrical engineer to head up his new state electrical corporation.[3] By the 1980s, in the Dominican Republic, as in much of the Third World, training in technical and professional fields often outstripped demand and resulted in the infamous "brain drain." (An UNCTAD report estimated that as early as 1970 the value of the trained manpower resources transferred to the United States from the Third World exceeded the entire U.S. nonmilitary foreign aid budget for that year.[4]) The problem remains, however, that professionals do not normally choose to work— much less to live—in uncomfortable surroundings among slum dwellers, urban squatters, or the rural poor.

Given the medical school requirement of one year of rural service and the national glut of doctors, there is no shortage of physicians, as such, in Ecuador's rural areas. But the doctors are reputedly ill prepared and disinclined to do the kind of work that is required among the rural poor. It is widely believed that trained nurses, of whom there is an acute shortage, would do a better job.

There should also be a greater effort to train indigenous peoples in medical fields. In the province of Chimborazo, which has the nation's highest proportion of Indians, there was only one physician in 1982 who was an Indian. Even though it would be most difficult to provide adequate medical care in the Sierra without personnel who speak Quechua, Carlos Moreno, director of the education ministry's literacy campaign in Chimborazo, reported that the efforts of his ministry to teach doctors on rural service a basic medical vocabulary in Quechua had been a failure. The doctors don't learn, he said, because they are not interested.

The same problem is readily noted in other fields: One need not be an agronomist to help establish a cooperative, but one must have the patience to become acquainted with the community. Rural people customarily speak of the officials of the Ecuadorean Ministry of Agriculture as "*hombres sin piernas*" (men without legs) because, it is said, they never get out of their jeeps.

Although various foreign assistance programs still stress professional training, none of the development agents I consulted in Ecuador considered the lack of professional or technical training as such a significant problem. The problem among administrators, according to Raúl Gangotena, executive director of FONAPRE, is not so much lack of training as lack of sensitivity and motivation. As to would-be or should-be field agents, most of them simply are not. One development professional commented that MAG's agricultural extension program had always been carried out by Peace Corps volunteers. The Ecuadorean "counterparts" who should be taking over from the volunteers rarely even venture into the far-flung, sometimes nearly inaccessible, villages where the volunteers work. After twenty years of Peace Corps programs, MAG and other ministries that engage in rural development seem more dependent on the volunteers rather than less.

Many explanations have been offered for the reluctance of field agents to go to the field. Understaffing, underfunding, and bureaucratic inertia are among the most obvious. Racism and fear have also been suggested. Some agents have not bothered to conceal contempt for or exasperation with the Indians. Others have simply been fearful of venturing into Indian villages. One IERAC official commented that the highland Indians were inscrutable; they would welcome you to the village, she said, then block the road, and burn your car.

Another explanation is early burnout. A Peace Corps volunteer who said he had spent most of his time "being stood-up by MAG," observed that MAG employees who are assigned to extension work in peasant communities usually get less done and become discouraged more quickly than do those in other types of assignments. Tasks in the field are difficult to define and success is hard to measure. It is easy to understand how even those who begin their work with great enthusiasm might conclude after a few years that, as a MAG soil engineer told me, "the campesinos are not interested in development; they don't want to learn." It seems likely, however, that when bureaucrats see such apathy they are gazing at a mirror image.

In the final analysis, the career and life-style ambitions of Ecuadorean professionals are no different from those of professionals elsewhere. For the university trained, working in muddy shoes simply does not represent the pinnacle of a career, nor does it appear to be the fast track to the pinnacle. The well-trained are hardly to be blamed for wanting to live well. But surely there are those who would find a lesser degree of training, a less-than-professional salary, and the opportunity to serve, a privilege. In this, the literacy campaign may have blazed a trail. It has had outstanding success in training indigenous peoples to work in their own communities.

Technical training has become a major component of most rural development programs worldwide. Bill Douglas, a former Peace Corps volunteer in Nepal and in the 1980s a USAID officer in Kathmandu, maintained, however, that such training has created almost as many problems in Nepal as it has solved. The most highly trained are reluctant to work in the countryside, while middle-level training of villagers tends to raise their ambitions and cause them to leave their own villages. Furthermore, Douglas said, when Nepalese receive their development training outside the country or from foreigners, they learn the concepts and the jargon of development professionals, and their own local perspectives are lost or suppressed; they even find it difficult to communicate with their own people.[5]

> PARADOX NO. 13: *Distance unites.* Exploitation and racial and class discrimination may well be built into national and international systems, but the expression of these evils with which the poor must live on a daily basis is local. Thus, a requirement for changing traditional relationships may be the intervention of agents who are not local.

It is no accident that those development agents who have the will to live among the rural poor and who, for the most part, are accepted by them are so often young foreigners. Foreigners, and particularly young ones, are able to cross the lines of class in a manner that would be far more difficult for nationals (or for the same young foreigners in their own countries). In this sense distance unites. By the same token, it is easier for Indians of the Sierra, for example, to deal with national officials in Quito than with local or cantonal officials.

Furthermore, there needs to be a bridge between campesinos and development agencies that have the resources but neither the contacts with nor the confidence of the people. For now, these foreign volunteers living in rural villages are practically the only agents who have the ability and the will to serve as such a bridge.

The arguments against using foreigners, particularly from the United States, in national development programs in the Third World are many and often sound. But the most obvious and most common argument—that Peace Corps volunteers are, after all, agents of a neocolonial power and of the particular administration that happens to be in office—probably is not sound, except in the most narrow sense.

While some U.S. administrations, particularly that of Richard Nixon, have attempted to suppress the Peace Corps or to change drastically its functions, the Peace Corps as a whole appears to have changed little in approach and objectives since its course was first charted by Sargent Shriver. That is probably due in no small measure to the large proportion of midlevel contemporary Peace Corps officials who were among the founding generation of volunteers. Thus the programs of the Peace Corps in many countries even in the 1980s were more nearly reflective of a Kennedy administration than of a Reagan one.

Beyond that, however, it is arguable that Peace Corps volunteers are not, in practice, agents of anyone other than themselves. Like other kinds of "field agents," they tend to become "free agents"; that is, their performance in the field is determined in greater measure by their own imaginations and value systems and by their own personal interpretations of what their roles should be than by the objectives of funding or supervisory agencies.

A common complaint by Peace Corps and host country supervisors about the volunteers is that they tend to "do their own thing." Volunteers freely admit that is the case, and in general, "their own thing" has meant doing more rather than less—abandoning agencies that served middle-class interests to work with the poorest of the poor, shunning routine bureaucratic roles for mobilizational ones, organizing and enabling communities to bring pressure to bear on foot-dragging bureaucracies or elected officials, and denouncing corruption.

Most of the several dozen volunteers who participated, through interviews or questionnaires, in a survey this author conducted in Ecuador in 1982 said or implied that when they perceived differences between the objectives, wishes, or demands upon them of Peace Corps supervisors, host agency supervisors, and residents of their communities, they would be most likely to respond to their communities.[6] Further observations have convinced me that the more complex the superstructure of supervisory agencies, the more leverage is available to the field agent. The more leverage available to the field agent and the more intense and prolonged the contact between agent and beneficiary community, the more closely the project will respond to the aspirations of that community rather than to the objectives of the sponsoring bureaucracies.

PARADOX NO. 14: *In the land of the blind, the one-eyed man is a subversive.* Knowing too much or caring too much in modern and traditional societies alike is apt to make one an "enemy of the people."

Killing the messenger is an old and honored tradition. At the very least, the telling of unpopular truths may make one a social pariah; and in the development business, the agent who insists on allowing the real world to encroach on a program designed to meet the needs of the official world may soon find himself unemployed. In development work, however, the paradox takes on additional meanings.

Simply informing underprivileged populations of their rights and urging them to seek redress are likely to subject them to new dangers. In fact, if a solution that seems obvious to the development agent is not being tried, it may well be because locals are aware of dangers to which the nonlocal agent is oblivious. After all, to elites whose insecurity is exaggerated by the enormity of what they have to lose (e.g., El Salvador's "fourteen families"), it matters little whether those who seek to enhance the bargaining position of the poor are motivated by goals that might be designated developmental rather than revolutionary.

A redistribution of goods or benefits on any basis other than charity (that is, on any basis that challenges rather than reinforces preexisting power relationships) will be threatening to elites. Dom Helder Camara, archbishop of Olinda and Recife and spiritual leader in the 1960s of the opposition to Brazil's military dictatorship, said of his country's ruling elite, "When I feed the hungry, they call me a saint. When I ask why they are hungry, they call me a Communist."

One of the advantages of involving nonlocals in the development process is that whether such agents represent foreign governments, international organizations, or national institutions, such as the Church or the national university, they will probably be less vulnerable than members of a local underclass to reprisal by landlords or other local elites. Their links to nonlocal institutions would normally offer them at least a modicum of security. Furthermore, even if they remain very vulnerable indeed, the odds are that they will be relatively oblivious to such risk. In this sense, then, ignorance may really be bliss.

In India's rural areas, minimum-wage laws are rarely enforced. Peasants do not have the time, information, or resources to take landlords to court. Nor is the government prepared to take on the new roles that would be necessary if the legislation were to be made effective. In general, the issue is joined only when outsiders, most often university students, assist in educating and organizing the peasants. Even then, success is by no means ensured, and the price of failure may be high. Landowner reprisal against reform mongering has often been swift and brutal.

When nonlocal agents, however, become aware of risks—e.g., after underclass mobilization has generated fear and anger among elites—they may pull out, leaving locals even more exposed and vulnerable. In many areas that have seen strife, locals are keenly aware of this potential sequence of events and thus less than receptive to the message of the well-meaning but naïve or uninformed development agent. Nevertheless, the seasoned development agent has a responsibility to take such vulnerabilities into account, to discuss them fully and straightforwardly with client communities, and to subject clients to no more risk than the agent and his nonlocal colleagues are prepared to take.

There is a final possibility that should be mentioned. Given the fact that the motives of external donors and/or of host governments may be less than forthrightly stated, the field agent who takes seriously the publicly stated goals of a development project (i.e., community organization for self-help) may on occasion find himself isolated. If the field agent pursues a strategy of empowerment when the donor's purpose was actually pacification or control, the agent may find his project being sabotaged by his own supervisors or by other agencies of his own government or the host country government from which he had expected support.

Moreover, the development specialist, or field agent, may find that the information or skills he is expected to pass on to host country authorities or counterparts are likely to be used in a manner utterly at odds with his own objectives or the stated purposes of the program. In such a case, he may find it necessary to redefine his own role or to sabotage his own project.

A Peace Corps volunteer working in the public administration program in Monrovia, capital of the West African state of Liberia, in the late 1960s said: "Look, the fellow I'm working for is a crook; that's all there is to it. Here I am teaching him modern methods of administration and accounting. What do you do when you make that kind of person more efficient? You teach him how to steal more money, that's what."[7]

NOTES

1. This exchange took place in the classroom of Political Science Professor Martin C. Needler at the University of Michigan in 1963.

2. David C. Korten, "Rural Development Programming: The Learning Process Approach," chap. 18 in David C. Korten and Rudi Klauss, eds., *People-Centered Development* (West Hartford, Conn.: Kumarian Press, 1984).

3. Former President Juan Bosch, personal interview, Santo Domingo, January 12, 1988.

4. Tony Barnett, *Social and Economic Development* (New York: Guilford Press, 1989), p. 214.

5. William Douglas, USAID, Nepal, personal interview, Kathmandu, July 8, 1983.

6. Of the seventeen volunteers who sent me completed questionnaires, eight said they would respond first to their Ecuadorean communities; two to their own judgment or conscience; three to Peace Corps supervisors; two to host agency supervisors; and two did not know to whom they would respond.

7. Efrem J. Sigel, "The Peace Corps As a Development Service," *International Development Review* 10, no. 1 (10th Anniversary Issue), March 1968, pp. 34–38.

SUGGESTED READINGS

Bates, R., "People in Villages: Micro-Level Studies in Political Economy," *World Politics* 31, 1978, pp. 129–149.

Bryant, Coralie, and Louise G. White, *Managing Rural Development: Peasant Participation in Rural Development* (West Hartford, Conn.: Kumarian Press, 1980).

Chambers, Robert, *Managing Rural Development* (New York: Holmes and Meier, 1974).

Gorman, Robert F., ed., *Private Voluntary Organizations as Agents of Development* (Boulder: Westview Press, 1984).

Hancock, Graham, *Lords of Poverty: The Free-Wheeling Lifestyles, Power, Prestige, and Corruption of the Multi-Billion Dollar Aid Business* (London: Macmillan Press, Ltd., 1989).

Heginbotham, Stanley, *Cultures in Conflict* (New York: Columbia University Press, 1975).

Hirschman, Albert O., *Development Projects Observed* (Washington, D.C.: Brookings Institution, 1967).

Jedlicka, A., *Organization for Rural Development: Risk-Taking and Appropriate Technology* (New York: Praeger, 1977).

Korten, David, "Community Organization and Rural Development: A Learning Process Approach," *Public Administration Review* 40, September-October 1980, pp. 480–512.

Nelson, J., *Access to Power: Politics and the Urban Poor in Developing Nations* (Princeton: Princeton University Press, 1979).

Reeves, T. Zane, *The Politics of the Peace Corps and Vista* (Tuscaloosa: University of Alabama Press, 1988).

Tendler, Judith, *Turning Private Voluntary Organizations into Development Agencies: Questions for Evaluation* (Washington, D.C.: Agency for International Development, April 1982).

Wynia, Gary, *Politics and Planners: Economic Policy in Central America* (Madison: University of Wisconsin Press, 1972).

On Motives
and Consequences

9 We have seen that development professionals and field agents are sometimes overcome by a feeling of helplessness. They may find that the priorities of their supervisors deviate greatly from the professed mission of the agency, or that their own projects appear to be veering off in a direction that was never anticipated. In fact, the process of development, involving a complex interplay of interests and motives and impersonal forces, has many authors and many points of departure.

Outcomes reflect far more than any particular identifiable set of motives. For development professionals, as for community leaders, such complexity is sure to mean frequent bouts with disappointment and failure. But it also means opportunity; and what looks at one point like failure may be merely a pause, or a new staging area for a better calculated assault against the barricades.

PARADOX NO. 15: *The more important the decision, the fewer and less well informed will be those involved in making it.* Decisions viewed as most crucial to the system (e.g., war and peace)—or as most crucial to the fortunes of its leaders—will be made by those having general responsibility rather than by those having expertise on the issue.

Among the costliest decisions ever made have been those that have given shape to the modern mosaic of nation-states. Most such decisions have been made at the highest levels—by conquistadores and kings, by alien colonizers most likely unaware and most certainly unconcerned that in drawing frontiers they were cutting across tribal homelands and ancient kingdoms and giving rise to endless conflicts. Spanish and Portuguese rulers divided Latin America between them along an imaginary line drawn by a pope who had never set foot in the New World. The carving up of Asia and Africa by northern European empire builders was equally arbitrary, resulting in the erosion of preexisting political community and the fabrication of externally oriented economies. It remains difficult to travel from one national capital to another in Africa without going by way of London or Paris.

One would like to believe that such high-handed decisions, having dire consequences for so many, must be a thing of the past. Certainly the revolutionary technological advancements in transportation and communications, information gathering and processing, and the proliferation of agencies and institutions of education, research, and "intelligence," should make ignorance on the part of decision-makers less readily excusable. Furthermore, decision-making in most modern governments is formally structured so as to ensure power sharing and accountability. But the availability of good information and the mandating of socially accountable decision-making procedures by no means assures that they will be used. In fact, it is precisely when they are most needed—when the stakes are highest—that they are least likely to be used.

In the United States at the beginning of the 1980s, an administration determined for ideological and partisan reasons to seek military solutions to political and economic crises in Central America not only studiously avoided the counsel of nongovernmental specialists in the area but made a point of purging or reassigning State Department and other governmental area-specialists and replacing them with specialists in counterinsurgency and guerrilla warfare. Before the end of the decade, it had been revealed that Reagan's coterie, in pursuing the Iran-Contra affair, had defied and deceived the Congress as well. The effort so conceived and implemented involved the expenditure of billions of dollars, much of it supposedly economic aid extended in the name of development; the upshot for the Central American states, however, was economic devastation rather than development and the loss of more than 150,000 lives.

As indicated by the case of the U.S. role in Central America in the 1980s, one of the reasons why the most ambitious development programs—as measured by the money and manpower invested—fail so dramatically is that "development" may be only a cover for the pursuit of crasser interests. But even where decision-makers have the general welfare in mind, the attachment of the highest priority to a program or project and/or the allocation to it of extraordinary sums generally means that it will be tightly controlled from the top. Even where counsel is sought from beyond the constricted circle of policymakers— on highly technical matters, for example—those consulted will sense a need to tailor their reports to what they presume superiors want to hear.

Egypt's Aswan High Dam, planned with Western funding in the 1950s and completed with Soviet funds and technical assistance in the 1960s, was such a project. The effort to control an entire river basin system was also to serve as a reaffirmation of Egyptian nationalism, as a means to regional hegemony, and as a pyramid of sorts, guaranteeing immortality to its sponsor, Gamal Abd al-Nasser. The need to control flooding, to generate power for industry, to secure year-round navigation, and to regulate water supplies so as to increase food production and fish catch had long been recognized. But the urgency attached to the high dam project, due in large part to national and international political considerations, ensured that preexisting studies and alternative plans for the development of the Nile Basin would be ignored and drawbacks of the new project would be underestimated. Nasser sought through the project to strengthen his socialist movement by breaking the monopoly of the traditional Nile River fishing oligarchy, to extend his influence over the Sudan, and ultimately to underscore Egypt's economic and political independence from the West.

There were, to be sure, some very positive outcomes of the dam project, especially in the short term. Periodic flooding was overcome; water stored in the reservoir could be released as needed; river transportation became more dependable; and the fish catch from the reservoir was impressive. But many of the expected benefits were not realized, and there were innumerable unanticipated negative consequences.

Drainage problems on cultivated land were intensified, for example; salinity and the incidence of schistosomiasis in newly irrigated areas were greatly increased. As silt previously deposited in the delta was captured instead by the reservoir, downstream soils were impoverished. Furthermore, the reduced amounts of fresh water and silt reaching coastal areas decimated the sardine industry. Finally, more than 100,000 Nubian villagers had to be relocated owing to construction and flooding of the reservoir. The housing and agricultural lands provided to them failed to meet minimum needs and expectations, and this formerly self-sufficient people was rendered dependent on Egyptian government and foreign assistance.[1]

To be sure, miscalculation is common even in less-ambitious schemes, and outcomes rarely coincide with intentions, but one of the saddest things about this case is that so many of the unanticipated costs and adverse effects might have been avoided if the best scientific and technical assessments had been systematically sought, uninhibitedly offered, and faithfully heeded. In fact, the politicization of the project was such that across a broad range of issues and objectives, essential elements and possible pitfalls were overlooked, costs were consistently underestimated, and benefits were exaggerated.

Such narrowly shared and seemingly ignorant decision-making sometimes reflects simple corruption. An irrigation minister in the Indian state of Bihar in the 1970s, charged with controlling floods along the tributaries of the Ganges and improving irrigation, appointed unqualified henchmen to the highest administrative and engineering posts. Through them he milked the system, manipulating tender requirements, for example, to favor contractors offering kickbacks. Levels of competence were disregarded and construction standards were not enforced. Consequently, the barriers protecting the river valleys collapsed under flooding, ruining crops and leaving millions homeless.[2]

Idiosyncratic and uninformed decision-making, however, need not imply corruption or the intrusion of "high politics." Unfortunately, top-down approaches are the rule rather than the exception for large national and international bureaucracies. The World Bank, in the mid-1970s, emerged from a housing project in Manila with egg on its face, as worldwide attention was drawn to the mobilization of community groups opposed to the project. The bank had helped to create a National Housing Authority, which then undertook an urban upgrading effort in the large Tondo slum area. The 4,500 squatter families that were to be relocated, making room for port facilities for foreign firms, and the remaining residents who were to pay higher rents were not even informed in advance of the plans being made, much less consulted about them.[3] One of the reasons why the bank favors such large, authoritarian-oriented institutions as implementers is that project officers are pressured to commit large sums over a brief period.

PARADOX NO. 16: *Before a people can determine its own future, it must take back its past;* that is, it must reinterpret a history constructed by its oppressors.

Brazilian educator Paulo Freire has observed that the oppressed internalize their oppressors' opinion of them and ultimately become convinced of their own unfitness. Thus liberation must begin with a realization of self-worth.[4] Most systems of pronounced inequality, especially those in which inequality is compounded and reinforced by racial or ethnic difference, are traceable to armed conquest. Previously self-governing and self-sufficient tribes or nations may have been subjugated and transformed into slaves or serfs on what was once their own land. Or they may have been pushed off the land and left with little recourse but to compete for menial work at meager pay.

Over time the violent roots of such exploitative systems are progressively obscured from subsequent generations of the conquered. The systems acquire a measure of legitimacy through the implantation of the myth that differential reward and punishment and limitations of access to wealth and power rest somehow on divine will or on merit. Challengers of the myth are seen as troublemakers or even "subversives." Thus any movement that embraces empowerment as means or end must begin by discrediting the prevailing myth and replacing it with one—which may or may not be based in historical fact—that serves to enhance individual and collective self-esteem.

Such myths or, in highly elaborated form, ideologies often incorporate imported parts—the ideals of liberalism, for example, or the explanatory power of Marxism—but for the cultivation of a broad base it appears essential that the raw materials be homegrown; that is, the empowering myth must be also a popular history that draws upon elements of religion or culture distinguishing the underclass from its oppressors and that revives popular heroes or incidents of courageous confrontation or successful counterattack against the conquerors or their progeny.

Indigenismo, or nativism, in Mexico and the Andean highlands, Black Power in the Caribbean, and Negritude in Sub-Saharan Africa have offered psychological sustenance to oppressed underclasses. They have also, on occasion, provided momentum and a sense of direction to otherwise sporadic or unfocused expressions of social unrest. Popularly based independence movements in Africa and Asia sought to underpin their new nations with the symbolism of precolonial civilizations. Ghana and Zimbabwe, for example, took their names from ancient African empires.

Mahatma Gandhi, in mobilizing the peoples of the South Asian subcontinent to throw off British rule, employing a relentless campaign of nonviolent civil disobedience, drew upon the works of Tolstoy and Thoreau, upon elements of Western liberal and socialist thought, and upon Christianity. But the integrating principles of his philosophy, particularly the centrality of truth seeking and the conviction that moral ends could be achieved only through equally moral means, he drew from Hinduism; and his concept of a democratic society was that of decentralized village self-rule through the ancient *panchayati* system—ideally a system drawing upon the participation of all members of the community. To him, national liberation meant the uplifting of all the people—women as well as men, and the untouchables, whom he redesignated "harijans," or children of God. It also meant the investment of new pride in indigenous cultures. The grounding of his campaign in indigenous values, customs, and symbols turned the Congress Party into a broadly based movement. The spinning wheel, in particular, at which

Gandhi himself worked regularly, came to symbolize the cottage industry that had been highly developed in precolonial times. Such industry
had been systematically suppressed by the British, and Gandhi taught
that it had to be revived to break the colonial chains of dependency.[5]

Popular history or revindicating myths may be at the service of
rogues, of course, as well as of statesmen. Until about thirty-five years
ago, the peoples of highland Papua New Guinea thought they were the
only people in the world. The first airplane that arrived, bearing
Australian explorers, was seen as a great silver bird bringing back the
blanched ghosts of their ancestors. The technologically advanced gadgetry they bore could not have been fabricated by mortals, so it was
believed to represent the magic of the spirit world. The appearance
there and elsewhere to previously isolated populations in the South
Pacific of these miraculous artifacts gave rise to the so-called cargo
cult, which assumed that the great silver birds bearing gifts from
ancestors could alight only on specially prepared landing strips.

As highlanders and other poor country people of Papua New Guinea
flocked to the capital city, Port Moresby, in search of work, they found
jobs scarce and the miraculous artifacts generally unobtainable by legal
means. Thus illegal means—robberies, accompanied by rape, beatings,
and other behaviors characteristic of intertribal revenge warfare—have
become all too common. Some of the cleverest leaders of outlaw gangs
have devised a means—a kind of stone-age Marxism—for justifying
their actions. Their argument is that the dramatic disparity in wealth
between themselves and the white foreigners comes about because the
gifts sent by their ancestors are being hijacked and monopolized by the
foreigners. In burglarizing, therefore, they are only taking back what
was rightfully theirs.[6]

> PARADOX NO. 17: *Maintaining stability at the apex of a
> sharply graduated social pyramid requires perpetuating in-
> stability at the base.* To maintain their position, those at the
> top must keep those at the bottom fighting among themselves.
> Structural change therefore requires an unaccustomed unity
> among the underclasses and deepening cleavages among elites.[7]

In political discourse, "stability" may have any one of three meanings.
It may mean (1) the routinization of political and social change in the
absence of conflict; (2) the absence of conflict and the absence of change;
or (3) the absence of structural change, even if such change must be
staved off through conflict. When *stability* is used as a term of art—
that is, for political or diplomatic effect—the implication is generally

that it is intended to mean the absence of conflict. In fact, however, national elites and/or colonial or hegemonic powers often fall back upon the old principle of divide and rule; that is, they generate conflict or the threat of it in order to establish or maintain dominance.

Tribal and ethnic animosities were not invented by colonial and neocolonial powers; but those powers have often played upon them and exacerbated them to their own considerable advantage. In fact, where social stratification or political centralization did not in itself provide a Herodian class, or co-optable elite, colonial or neocolonial powers often found it necessary to rule through a racial or ethnic minority. Such minorities are more readily manipulable, as they may be able to maintain a privileged position in their own societies only through external support.

In Haiti, the first modern state born of a slave revolt, U.S. forces occupying the country from 1915 to 1934 suppressed Black leadership and ruled through a facade leadership of the French-oriented mulatto minority. In the heart of Africa, in the territory that was to become the states of Burundi and Rwanda, European rule—first German, then Belgian—reinforced the dominance of the minority Tutsi over the Hutu majority. A revolution in Rwanda at the beginning of the 1960s toppled the Tutsi, but in Burundi the Tutsi elite continues to benefit from foreign aid and to rule through intimidation. Periodic massacres have resulted in several hundred thousand deaths, mostly of Hutus, since independence in 1962.

The migration of labor, voluntarily or otherwise, has always given rise to intra-working-class hostilities that elites could play upon as a distraction from equity, or class, issues. The transplantation of labor for plantation economies, particularly slaves from Black Africa and South Asian laborers distributed around the territories of the British Empire, has left deep ethnic divisions that seem to invite manipulation by domestic elites and foreign powers. In Fiji, for example, the British and, since independence in 1970, other aid donors have sought to reinforce the dominance of the indigenous chiefly oligarchy, even as the population of South Asian origin was overtaking the islanders numerically. When a coalition headed by South Asians and having a nationalist, prolabor, and antinuclear orientation won national elections in 1987, the United States—edging out Great Britain in its hegemonic role—apparently encouraged military officers responsive to the chiefly oligarchy to stage a coup in order to reassert ethnic Fijian preeminence.[8]

In South Africa, it is no accident that the ruling Afrikaners have referred to Blacks as "plurals" and have gone out of their way to "accommodate" separate tribal identities. Many of the policies designed to separate Whites, Asians, and Coloreds from Blacks have also aimed to segregate Blacks from Blacks. Designated leaders of Black homelands, for example, acquire a vested interest in the system and might be expected to feel threatened by Black unity leading to a unified state.

In courting Mangosuthu Gatsha Buthelezi, chief minister of KwaZulu, the Zulu homeland, the Nationalist Party succeeded to some extent in deepening divisions within the numerically dominant Zulus and between the Zulus and less numerous Black tribes even as the African National Congress (ANC) and other groups sought to unite Black South Africans in active opposition to the White minority's power monopoly. ANC leader Nelson Mandela charged that it was government policy to keep members of Buthelezi's political organization, Inkatha, fighting ANC supporters in Natal province, where more than 5,000 people died during the last half of the 1980s. Such conflict appeared in the townships around Johannesburg in August 1990 and in little more than a month had claimed 800 lives. The ruling party also sought through such tactics to convey to Western trading partners the impression that the social conflict that plagued their society was not a consequence of apartheid but rather of traditional intertribal hostility.

The unity of the White population, however, has always been tenuous at best, and the Afrikaner leaders fell into the trap that has so often destabilized minority rule—that of violent overreaction to relatively nonviolent opposition. Such overreaction alienates passive or tentative allies who enjoy the perquisites of minority rule but prefer not to be associated with its brutal underpinnings.

For some decades, the English-speaking press has been a source of persistent, hard-hitting criticism of the Nationalist government. In general, members of South Africa's English-speaking minority have been quick to dissociate themselves from the crude racism of the more numerous Afrikaners, descendants of Dutch and French Huguenot settlers, who maintain their own distinctive language. But one need not doubt the selfless courage of some and the sincerity of many to note that, until recently at least, English-speaking liberals were the most comfortable group in the country. Enjoying the comforts and privileges of being White, they also had the luxury of clear consciences; they could protest their liberalism and blame the brutalities of the system on the Afrikaners.

The intensified strife of the 1980s, however—overwhelmingly, government violence against unarmed protesters, often children—left no viable space for passive scorn. While official violence served to unite and mobilize Blacks, it served to detach definitively from the Nationalist Party camp many of its tentative, uncomfortable allies. Along with the English speakers, there has been increasing alienation among Afrikaners themselves, especially those of the generation now coming of age. And finally, the gratuitous violence has made it more difficult for Western allies to continue to do business as usual. Trade embargoes and disinvestment finally began seriously to threaten major business interests.

Such tidal changes in public opinion and political alignment led the government in early 1990 to release Mandela, the country's most-revered political prisoner, and to begin formal talks with the African National Congress. The battle for an end to apartheid remains far from won, and even if the most blatant manifestations of racial prejudice are delegitimated, it remains to be seen whether far-reaching structural change will follow. With respect to egalitarianism, the standards set by "the West," and even by Black-ruled Africa, are not so very high. Nevertheless, for the first time in almost half a century, momentum is clearly on the side of empowerment for South Africa's Black minority.

> PARADOX NO. 18: *Treating the symptoms may prolong the disorder.* Even with the best of intentions, a development program that simply meets immediate needs rather than enabling communities to organize sustainable means of meeting their own needs is likely to kill local initiative and build dependency. Sometimes, of course, pacification (rather than empowerment) appears to be precisely what was intended.

Monseñor Leonidas Proaño, Ecuador's bishop of Riobamba, said that an important difference between *desarrollo* (development) and *desarrollismo* (developmentism) is that *desarrollismo* treats the symptoms of poverty without dealing with its structural roots. Proaño, spiritual leader of the Catholics of Chimborazo and a "liberation theologist" of international reputation, said that most development agencies, like most political parties, are in the business of co-opting indigenous leaders and dividing, rather than uniting, communities.

Monseñor Proaño has been, for more than a decade, one of Ecuador's most controversial figures. He is considered a radical, he said, because he speaks of social justice. One high-ranking official of the U.S. Embassy told me in no uncertain terms that Proaño was a Communist. Another asked, with lowered voice, if he was "his own man." Proaño would answer that he is not his own man, but rather a servant of Christ. He noted that Christ showed a preference for working with the poor, that he surrounded himself with the poor and chose his disciples from among them. "We try to live that teaching here," he said.

Proaño holds office hours every weekday afternoon, and the humble premises of his bishopric in Riobamba are indeed filled every afternoon with the poor seeking guidance in dealing with their everyday problems.

The bishopric promotes the organization of *comunidades de base,* grass-roots Christian communities in which the peasants discuss their problems and propose means of dealing with them. The bishopric also sponsors various organizations and educational programs and a radio station that transmits in Quechua. Proaño's preference for ministering to the poor has gained him the enmity of local landowners as well as of governments, domestic and foreign. He and his followers are widely accredited or blamed for the peasant mobilization that was under way in the mid-1970s.

In fact, that mobilization was catalyzed indirectly by the 1964 agrarian reform law. The law was enforced only sporadically, and IERAC, the agency charged with its enforcement, was meagerly funded and kept on a short leash. IERAC was not authorized to institute expropriation proceedings until the *huasipungueros,* on their own, "denounced" their *patrones,* or landlords. Any employee of IERAC who tried to inform peasants of their rights or encouraged them to denounce their landlords was subject to disciplinary action. Nevertheless, word of the legal option spread among the peasants and by the early 1970s, according to Antonio Jurado and Armanda Philco of IERAC's Chimborazo office, IERAC offices in the Sierra were swamped with denunciations.

Meanwhile, after the bishops' conference in Medellín in 1968, the Catholic church decided to divide its own lands among the peasants who worked them. The redistribution program was to be carried out through the efforts of the Campesinos' Labor Federation (CEDOC), organized by a very conservative faction of the Church. The work was later carried on by the Ecuadorean Institute of Development Studies (INEDES), which grew out of CEDOC, and, in turn, by the Ecuadorean Agricultural Service Center (CESA), which grew out of INEDES.

In terms of methods and objectives, both CEDOC and its offspring organizations were moving across the political spectrum toward the left and identifying more and more with the Indians rather than with the founders of the original CEDOC or with the Church. Nevertheless, the peasants working with CESA began to organize on their own and ultimately took over control of the movement. Ramón Espinel, who worked with CESA in the early-to-mid-1970s, said that the non-Indians who had launched the movement, not knowing how to respond to this usurpation of their role, became demoralized and divided, and many resigned.

The quixotic president of Ecuador, José María Velasco Ibarra, under assault from both the Right and the Left, decided to court the peasants and, in 1969, began more serious enforcement of the agrarian reform law, especially in the rice-producing coastal areas. The military conspirators who prematurely terminated Velasco Ibarra's fifth term, in

February 1972, were ideologically inconsistent, but following up on his revolutionary rhetoric, the new president, General Guillermo Rodríguez Lara, in 1973 codified the agrarian reform laws and, in the process, strengthened them. Moreover, the government, temporarily solvent as a consequence of the new oil-exportation bonanza, greatly increased the budget and authority of IERAC.

Rodríguez Lara soon backed away from the promotion of reform, and the junta that replaced him in 1975 proved very conservative. Nevertheless, the peasant mobilization begun in the late 1960s continued to build until it reached a peak of militance, particularly in Chimborazo, in 1975 and 1976. In response to this mobilization, the World Bank, building on a project already started by AID, underwrote a major program of integrated rural development, which has since been absorbed by SEDRI. Meanwhile, there was an enormous influx into Chimborazo province of Evangelical missionaries, who invested large sums in their own unintegrated development efforts.

Evangelical missionaries had begun to establish a base in Chimborazo, in the canton of Colta, in the 1940s. Their operations grew in the 1960s, but it was in the 1970s, particularly the mid-1970s, that missionaries arrived in large numbers with large sums of money to distribute. For communities that were prepared to convert, the missionaries and their technicians built potable water systems, community centers, schools, and clinics. An Ecuadorean development specialist in the Sierra noted that the missionaries took over the management of infrastructure projects that were already under way, wilting campesino initiative and dissolving campesino organizations. The Evangelicals' Indian converts also adopted a different frame of mind; they became passive, willing to wait for handouts that, in fact, were coming, but only to Evangelical communities. A Peace Corps volunteer working in Colta observed that the Evangelicals were highly materialistic and paranoid about "communism."

The upshot of this influx of missionaries was the demobilization of the peasant movement. Many Ecuadoreans suspect that was hardly coincidental. They note that most AID funds and other foreign assistance programs also favor the Evangelical communities. The Ecuadorean Institute of Cooperativism (ICE), funded predominantly by the German Konrad Adenauer Foundation, is one of many agencies that tends to favor Evangelical communities. Its provincial director, Vicente Cardoso, who had worked for many years with AID, told me that "with co-ops, people get what they need and are satisfied—not rebellious or revolutionary."

Among the Evangelicals working in Chimborazo are fourteen sects, united for practical purposes in the Gospel Missionary Union. One of the sects operating in Colta, known as *Hoy Cristo Jesus Bendice (HCJB)*, transmits radio programs in Quechua from the village of Majipamba.

It also has a transmitter in Quito that is among the strongest in the world, exceeding even the power of the Voice of America. Radio operations in Majipamba have been turned over to indigenous Evangelicals, but the contract stipulates that the parent organization may take it back if locals stray from the gospel according to *HCJB*.

The bête noir of Catholics and nationalists throughout Ecuador until it was expelled from the country in 1981 was the missionary organization known as the Summer Institute of Linguistics (SIL). Suspicions of covert operations masquerading as evangelism or development have since focused on an organization called World Vision. Whereas SIL was based in the Oriente, World Vision works mainly in the Sierra.

Frank Boshold, director of the World Vision program in Ecuador in the early 1980s, said that World Vision had come to Ecuador in 1978 and had been growing each year since. Its local budget for 1982 was $1.5 million and Boshold expected it to continue to grow. In Chimborazo, World Vision had five "development" promoters on salary overseeing more than thirty projects. Each project was also monitored by community leaders who received token payment.

Boshold conceded that World Vision is often accused of being a CIA front. He maintained that the organization receives no government money, although USAID and other funding agencies may contribute to the same projects or the same communities.[9]

The people of Chimborazo were still rigidly divided into Catholic and Evangelical camps in the early 1980s. The Catholics maintained that the Evangelicals were apathetic and the Evangelicals said the same of the Catholics. It seemed, though, that there was a great deal of mobilization and consciousness-raising taking place in both communities. The events of the 1970s suggest that, in the short run, efforts to divide and pacify may be effective; the long run, however, is another matter.

> PARADOX NO. 19: *He who pays the piper does not necessarily call the tune.* At any rate, development is a complicated process, deriving from many different sources and motives— an art rather than a science and a creature of fortune as much as of planning. No one, not even those who pay the bill, can control it.

Of course there are mixed motives among those who support development programs. It would be most naïve to suppose, for example, that those who underwrite the foreign policy of the United States are greatly concerned about the welfare of Ecuadorean campesinos.

There is always a danger for would-be change agents, as for supposed beneficiaries of development programs, of being co-opted and manipulated. But for people of goodwill to withdraw from the development process or deny themselves the use of development resources is hardly a solution. Those whose motives are covert, or at least less than forthrightly stated, will continue their work under any circumstances. And there is also the possibility that in the development game the agents and agencies of occult motives are deceiving themselves—that projects that are begun for the purpose of pacification, for example, may result ultimately in further mobilization instead.

It is quite common for agents in the field, or even agency directors, to have motives very different from those of the governments they are presumed to represent. Even USAID, which has been drawn into U.S. efforts in several countries to destabilize democratic governments, is a multifaceted agency with as many motives as it has officers, field agents, and contractees. Along with projects undoubtedly designed to propagandize, divide, or pacify, it also funds many projects having the potential of promoting *desarrollo* as opposed to *desarrollismo*. And even those that are launched as *desarrollismo* may eventually be turned inside out by their intended beneficiaries. Paul Fritz, deputy director of AID-Ecuador in 1982, said that the agency's most effective programs happen by serendipity—through informal contacts and response to "targets of opportunity," which have nothing to do with whatever Washington happens to be pushing.

Furthermore, funding agencies, for better or worse—most development specialists would say for the better—do not necessarily monitor what their contract organizations are doing. The International Volunteer Service (IVS), for example, a small development agency that recruits worldwide for trained technicians to work at the village level in developing countries, is funded in part by USAID, but IVS's contractual accountability consists only of one annual global report. USAID country officers have a veto over taking IVS volunteers, but they have nothing to say about the in-country program. Hank Beder, IVS country director in Ecuador in the early 1980s, supervising about six volunteers, said that AID had initially requested quarterly reports, but that, in fact, he had only spoken with AID officials three times in four years and that at times AID seemed to lose track of the fact that there was an IVS program in Ecuador.

Another agency that has been colonized by professionals dedicated to the mystique of development is the Inter-American Foundation. Despite the zigs and zags of U.S. policy from one administration to another and despite the long-term thrust of U.S. policy toward Latin

America, the Inter-American Foundation has consistently pursued a course that might be called liberational, or empowering.

Both the Inter-American Foundation and AID, as previously noted, underwrote a literacy program in Ecuador based on the philosophy and methodology of Paulo Freire—and they did so during the administration of Richard Nixon! Carlos Moreno, who directed the program, had easy responses for its critics. When the Left charged that he and his colleagues were promoting imperialism, he asked, "By spreading revolutionary ideas among the peasants?" When the Right charged that they were fomenting revolution, he challenged, "With AID funds?"

The Inter-American Foundation was still contributing to the literacy campaign in Chimborazo in 1982 through a program known as *Pan para la Educación* (Bread for Education). Bakeries were established and operated collectively by and for individual *comunas*. Earnings were used for maintenance of the bakery, for the purchase of books, paper, and other educational tools, and for other community projects. The literacy program itself held that there are three kinds of illiterates: (1) those who cannot read and write; (2) those who can read and write, but don't understand their own reality; and (3) those who see reality but don't do anything about it.

Programs of *desarrollismo* posing as *desarrollo* may indeed divide and pacify in the short term, but any program that involves collective action is hostage to many wills and subject to abrupt change of direction. Thus CEDOC, organized by conservatives for the purpose of controlling the campesinos, had come under the control of campesinos and had become split between the Catholic Left and the Marxist Left. U.S. Embassy officials admitted through gritted teeth in 1982 that an Ecuadorean labor union organized by the American Institute for Free Labor Development (AIFLD)—a strange bedfellow creation of the AFL-CIO, AID, and the CIA—had slipped under the umbrella of the country's major Marxist federation.

Even the supposedly pacified Evangelicals of Chimborazo do not seem so passive anymore. Moreno said that whereas a few years earlier the Evangelicals scorned all secular music, in the early 1980s some *conjuntos* (ensembles) of young musicians began to compose their own songs of social protest. Under a contract with *HCJB*, the Ministry of Education uses its powerful transmitter in the literacy campaign; it has also hired five Evangelicals from Majipamba to design radio programs. An Education Ministry official recently complained to Moreno that their radio programs were becoming overly critical of the government; one of the offensive scripts had said that the government was obligated to respond to the needs of the campesinos, and that if it failed to do so the campesinos should take matters into their own hands.

Moreno said that the Evangelicals had become better organized than the Catholics, and that some of the U.S. missionaries had left due to pressure from indigenous Evangelicals. The indigenous community of Chimborazo remained divided, but some leaders both of Catholic and Evangelical communities were attempting to bridge the gap and to reach out to poor mestizos as well.

The demonstration effect of seemingly modest development projects is often very strong. Once a few schools have been built or a few co-ops organized, once a potential source of assistance has been identified, the energy that propels the process generally comes from the peasants themselves. The Sierra Indians I encountered in no way fit the stereo-type of sullenness, shyness, or lethargy. After I had explained, in one small village, that my mission was only of research, one of the villagers approached me and asked, "Are you sure you can't do anything for us?" I replied regretfully that I could not. Nodding toward the Peace Corps volunteer who had accompanied me, the villager asked, "Then what can he do for us?"

Furthermore, development programs often reinforce each other and acquire political significance through unforeseen multiplier effects. Ecuador's literacy campaign has been given impetus by agrarian reform. Since the agrarian reforms of 1964 and 1973 have taken effect, peasants often find themselves involved in legal transactions; they want to be able to read in order to make sure that they are not being cheated. Now that they are learning to read and now that they have the vote (they say that the exclusion of illiterates from the franchise until 1979 had nothing to do with literacy; it was simply a cover for excluding Indians), they are getting together to study and discuss the platforms of the various parties.

The relatively new Party of the Democratic Left (Izquierda Demo-crática—ID), was already the strongest party in Chimborazo in 1982 and was competing fiercely with Popular Democracy (Democrácia Pop-ular—DP), the Christian Democratic heir of the rural following of the near-defunct Conservative Party—in other rural areas, as well. At-tempting to compete with the governing DP, ID in 1981 and 1982 launched a number of rural development projects of its own. For efforts in political instruction to have credibility, party leaders had found it necessary to offer the peasants something they needed.

Rodrigo Borja, national ID party leader, and Arnaldo Merino, federal deputy and leader of ID in Chimborazo province, expressed the belief that all development efforts are worthwhile among a people who need so much and that all contribute in one way or another to the general process of mobilization. They also believed, incidentally, that peasant mobilization would, in the long run, favor their party. In fact, it appears that it did; Borja was elected president of Ecuador in 1988 with particularly strong support in the Sierra.

Pedro Bagua, a leader of the indigenous Evangelicals of Colta province, said that after much study and discussion, his people decided that ID was the right party for them. He saw the party's goal, and his own goal for his people, as socialism, and he believed the party was the best vehicle for development, because through it his people could go directly to the parliament with their demands. Bagua developed his various skills—in language, medical arts, teaching, and leadership—through association with the Summer Institute of Linguistics and with the Evangelical mission in Colta. He said that the sources of assistance and the motives of benefactors are unimportant. "The campesinos," he said, "know how to take advantage without being co-opted."

NOTES

1. John P. Metzelaar, "The Itaipu and Aswan High Dams: Two Generations of Dams Compared" (unpublished), November 1989.

2. Paul Harrison, *Inside the Third World: The Anatomy of Poverty,* 2nd ed. (Harmondsworth, UK: Penguin Books, 1987), pp. 372–373.

3. Stephen Hellinger, Douglas Hellinger, and Fred M. O'Regan, *Aid for Just Development* (Boulder: Lynne Rienner Publishers, 1988), pp. 131–134.

4. Paulo Freire, *Pedagogy of the Oppressed* (New York: Seabury Press, 1970).

5. K. Seshadri, *Indian Politics: Then and Now* (Delhi: Pragatee Prakashan, 1976), pp. 57–66.

6. As explained to the author by political scientist Yaw Saffu, of the University of Papua New Guinea, Port Moresby, July 1985.

7. Plato, in the eighth book of the Republic, made the latter point. "You cannot make a successful revolution," he said, "if the ruling class is not weakened by internal dissension or defeat in war." Cited in Karl R. Popper, *The Poverty of Historicism* (Boston: Beacon Press, 1957), p. 62.

8. Michael Howard, "Strategic Interests and Foreign Aid in Fiji," chap. 8 in Jan K. Black, ed., *Development on a Human Scale* (Boulder: Westview Press, forthcoming).

9. World Vision has come under suspicion in other areas as well, such as Fiji—where its operations, like those of U.S. aid programs, were highly supportive of political factions that staged a coup d'état in 1987—and Central America. The organization withdrew from the administration of a camp for Salvadoran refugees in Honduras after being accused of turning two refugees over to the Salvadoran government.

SUGGESTED READINGS

Andrain, Charles F., *Political Change in the Third World* (Boston: Unwin Hyman, 1988).

Breslin, Patrick, *Development and Dignity: Grassroots Development and the Inter-American Foundation* (Rosslyn, Va.: Inter-American Foundation, 1987).

Brockett, Charles D., *Land, Power, and Poverty: Agrarian Transformation and Political Conflict in Central America* (Boston: Unwin Hyman, 1988).

Brundtland, Gro Harlem, Chairperson, World Commission on Environment and Development, *Our Common Future* (New York: Oxford University Press, 1987).

Foster, G., *Traditional Cultures and the Impact of Technological Change* (New York: Harper and Row, 1962).

Goulet, Denis, *The Cruel Choice: A New Concept in the Theory of Development* (New York: Atheneum, 1977).

Gran, Guy, *Development by People: Citizen Construction of a Just World* (New York: Praeger, 1983).

Hirschman, Albert O., *Getting Ahead Collectively* (Elmsford, N.Y.: Pergamon Press, 1984).

Lernoux, Penny, *Cry of the People* (Harmondsworth, UK: Penguin Books, 1982).

Salmen, Lawrence F., *Listen to the People: Participant-Observer Evaluation of Development Projects* (New York: Oxford University Press, published for the World Bank, 1989).

Uphoff, Norman, *Local Institutional Development: An Analytic Sourcebook with Cases* (West Hartford, Conn.: Kumarian Press, 1986).

Conclusion:
Leaning on the Limits

10 Some years ago Representative Dante Fascell, chairman of the U.S. House Foreign Affairs Committee, quipped that foreign assistance is a means whereby the poor of the rich countries contribute to the rich of the poor countries. It is also, of course, yet another means whereby the poor of the rich countries further enrich their own pampered elites.

Few of our readers will be surprised to find that there is a dark underside to the aid game, as played by the overdeveloped states and the multilateral financial institutions they control. But is that all there is? With respect to big-money, high-visibility, major-donor programs, optimists will find little encouragement in these pages.

The Central American quagmire of the late twentieth century makes it abundantly clear that collective self-help, or empowerment, remains the provocation rather that the objective of most major U.S. programs, including economic assistance programs. As demonstrated repeatedly in other times and places, the big money for development purposes kicks in only when the wealthy and powerful come to feel that the organization, or mobilization, of the poor and oppressed threaten their interests.

Perhaps we should find some satisfaction, therefore, in the fact that so much of the money appropriated for development is simply stolen. In the final analysis, if economic development is to mean more than occasional spurts of economic growth, if it is to mean a higher standard of living and a greater measure of self-reliance for the majority, it will not be accomplished by placing the military might of the world's greatest power at the service of those who have perpetually blocked just such development. It should be apparent at any rate that where "security" interests are engaged, economic aid is directed toward pacification, not pump priming, much less empowerment.

Central America, of course, is an exception. Or is it? In 1986 one-quarter of all U.S. aid, about $4.9 billion, was in the category of Economic Support Funds (ESF). Funds in this category grew by 84 percent in real terms between 1981 and 1986, and the number of countries receiving such aid doubled. As explained by the State Department, ESF moneys "provide the resources needed to stem the spread of economic and political disruption and to help allies in dealing with threats to their security and independence"[1]—allies at that time like Marcos in the Philippines, and Pakistan's General Zia, and Liberia's Sergeant Samuel Doe, and Zaire's multimillionaire Mobutu.

By the end of the decade, the Cold War, which had provided the rationale for economic aid as pacification on behalf of tyrants, was on the wane, mainly because the Soviet Union, under Gorbachev's leadership, had opted out of it. Many of the same functions, however, such as the strengthening of Third World military and paramilitary organizations and surveillance and suppression of peasant rebellion, would be carried out through the escalating "War on Drugs." That, too, was to be characterized as foreign aid. Moreover, even where major donor foreign economic assistance is not providing support or cover for political or military undertakings, its objectives are likely to be set with a view toward the debt exposure of commercial banks, the infrastructure needs of private investors, the institutional imperatives of donor agencies, or the interests of other economic or bureaucratic elites.

But what about food aid? Surely it is genuinely meant to address the problem of Third World hunger. Not so, say the Food First folks.[2] Food aid is above all aid from the U.S. taxpayer to the U.S. grain farmer. Moreover, like any other kind of aid, it may be used for political purposes: to promote certain policies or to bolster allies. Finally, it may distort domestic and international markets and divert attention from the need for land-tenure and farm program reforms both in "beneficiary" countries and at home. Hunger, whether in First World or Third, does not normally reflect lack of food production or productive capacity but rather maldistribution of land, income, and opportunity.

Then what about agrarian reform? Indeed the green revolution has been a great success—to the extent that productivity was its goal. If the goal, however, was redistribution of the land and the strengthening of the position of poor peasants, the outcome has been very much the reverse. For the most part, new products, technologies, and credits have been available or usable only for the already-affluent landowner, and enhanced land values have intensified struggles that peasants were sure to lose. Nor are its gains likely to be sustainable, since the approach has featured importation of seeds, fertilizers, pesticides, and modern farm machinery.

The miracle seeds, genetically engineered, cannot be used for future crops; so the farmer remains dependent upon the company supplying the seeds—for most farmers a foreign company. According to John Kinney, whose Talavaya Center, a nonprofit conservancy and seed bank in Espanola, New Mexico, won the 1985 UN environmental program award, 70 percent of the world's open-pollinated (as opposed to genetically engineered) crops have become extinct in the last fifty years because of the spread of the hybrids. And if the hybrid plants are stronger, so are the bugs; many have become immune to commonly used pesticides.

Perhaps what is needed, then, is a simple transfer of money, in huge amounts, from the First World to the Third. That has, in fact, taken place, at least on paper, and the upshot is the international debt crisis— for the Third World, a combined foreign debt at the end of the 1980s of more than a trillion dollars.

The fact that the U.S. debt now dwarfs the debts of the Third World is scant comfort to those countries spending half or more of their annual foreign exchange earnings and virtually all of their new borrowings just to cover interest on earlier loans. According to the United Nations' 1989 *World Economic Survey,* there was again in 1988, for the sixth consecutive year, a net transfer of financial resources from poor countries to rich ones. In 1988, the transfer set a new record, $33 billion.

In this drama, there is plenty of blame to spread around—to public and private sector elites of First World and Third. The people who can claim *no* share of the blame are the same ones who claimed no share of the benefits. They are also the ones who will bear the cost. As the rich make the usual choice as to whether or not to accept sacrifice, the unavoidable sacrifice is borne by those who have no choice.

For much of South America, the debt and the "austerity" regimen (i.e., higher prices and interest rates, lower wages and longer working hours, fewer subsidies and fewer services, and a fire sale of government assets) imposed by the creditors' enforcer, the International Monetary Fund, have accomplished in the 1980s what seemed in the 1970s to require military rule: the freezing of socioeconomic and political relationships, or even a rollback of previous political and economic gains by the working or would-be-working classes. Mexico's experience was similar. The number of government-owned enterprises had dropped during the 1980s from more than 1,100 to fewer than 200, while real wages had been cut in half.[3] Ruling elites in the Third World are placed in the enviable position of being able to claim that they would like to adopt more equitable policies but are prevented from doing so by the IMF.

The flotsam of modernization that threatens to bury all hope of development in Latin America floats even more incongruously over Africa. In Kinshasa, sleek modern skyscrapers, monuments to Mobutu's creditworthiness, hover mockingly over a society in near-total disintegration. When I visited a few years ago, I was warned not to venture out onto the city streets. If I failed to have my pockets picked by hungry civilians, I was told, I would surely be mugged by marauding soldiers, whose pay was then several weeks in arrears. Even Second World countries, just beginning to disassemble their own faulty development models, have already become entangled in the First World's debt trap.

Is there a way out? There might be if First World policymakers and officers of the multilateral financial institutions could be held to their protestations about commitment to democracy. There might be incorporated into international law a ruling to the effect that a people cannot be held liable for debts incurred by a government not of their choosing. There might be general accord on a strategy, like that attempted in vulnerable isolation by Peru's President Alan García, to limit debt servicing to a modest percentage of annual foreign exchange earnings. In fact, were reason or fairness to prevail, there might be many plausible exits. But the Age of Aquarius missed its cue.

None of our theoretical models offers a creditable vision as to how current trends and relationships, so often inimical to the interests of people and other living things, are to be transformed. So long as national borders pose no obstacle to the movement of capital and autarky remains virtually universally unfeasible or unappealing, it is hard to see how nationalistic and/or egalitarian policies could fail to provoke severe punishment.

I find some hope, however, in the boomerang effect—that is, in the belated recognition on the part of First World leaders that their policies are self-defeating. Even the largely co-opted leadership of the AFL-CIO finally noticed that the U.S. policy of keeping labor in client states weak and disorganized (and thus cheap) was depriving U.S. workers of their jobs. It cannot forever escape the attention of First World farmers and industrialists that the bankrupting of the Third World by Western financial institutions is depriving them of customers.

Furthermore, the ultimate limits to a pattern of development characterized by unfettered growth are posed by a fragile and already dangerously contaminated environment. It remains to be seen whether the global community will take the steps necessary to decelerate the destruction; but the issue at least has been joined.

What then might be said for the prospects for a bottom-up, "empowerment" approach to development? Does a deck so heavily stacked leave any space at all for maneuver by those who hold no aces? There are those who would say that nonrevolutionary development programs— that is, programs designed to induce changes gradually, from the bottom up, to improve the standard of living and the problem-solving capacity of the poorest without immediately and obviously threatening the per- quisites of the affluent—are at best foredoomed to failure, at worst sheer hypocrisy, intended to fail. On my more pessimistic days I am one of them. Nevertheless, it must be recognized that most revolutionary movements also fail and that, whether they succeed or fail, they are almost certain to be very costly in lives and in human suffering. Furthermore, no social arrangements are permanent, not even the redistributive benefits of successful revolution. Thus, for those of us who, for reasons of realism, pacifism, or cowardice, are not likely to engage in direct instigation of revolution, there must be some alternative to acceptance of a shamefully inequitable status quo.

In fact, it might be argued that the very grimness of prospects for meaningful political and economic change at the state level at the beginning of the 1990s makes grass-roots development efforts all the more essential and perhaps even inevitable. It has been said that necessity is the mother of invention. Crisis often gives rise to creativity and to mobilization for the common good.

Even in the United States, as the federal government, in the 1980s, shed responsibility for assistance to economically depressed areas and sectors, communities were reaching inward and rediscovering the strength to be found in common purpose and collective action. In north-central Maine, several rural communities lacking a physician pooled their money to send one of their own to medical school. Eugene, Oregon, reeling from the collapse of the timber industry, has turned to a strategy most recently tried and abandoned in the Third World: import substi- tution. A similar and similarly successful program, starting with the matching of local buyers and sellers, has been undertaken in Duluth, Minnesota. This revival of localism has infected even the New South, where leaders have finally despaired of competing not only with each other but also with the Third World in cutting taxes and labor costs to lure industry. In September 1989, the Southern Governors' Associ- ation unveiled its new strategy of "growth from within." Along with assistance to local businesses, the governors will stress the enhancement of infrastructure and of education and training programs.

As material resources shrink, communities can and must begin to turn obstacles into assets. The foolhardiness of wasting natural resources has been widely recognized in this new era of ecological sensitivity, and yet in societies at all levels of development we continue to waste the most valuable resource of all: people. Teenagers, for example, in so many different places and circumstances, are regarded as a burden, if not as a threat. We allow them no useful role in society and then blame them for their alienation. Likewise, the increased longevity that is among the clear triumphs of postwar global development becomes a liability as the elderly are shunted aside into categories of dependence, their hard-won wisdom yet untapped. Thus an obvious first step in turning obstacles into assets would be to liberate the many categories of people who, for reasons of age, race, sex, or economic misfortune, have been prevented from fulfilling their potential and enable them to make the transition from alienation or dependence to being valued contributors to community well-being.

In fact, even as the relentless onslaught of modernization shrinks the global village, absorbing land and resources and threatening traditional livelihoods, one hardly finds a depressed area, rural or urban, where some vigorous collective self-help efforts are not under way. Casual surveys have identified hundreds of thousands of independent development groups in the Third World in the 1980s. And as U.S. government funding levels for development programs, as such, slip, other governments and nongovernmental organizations move into the breach. Moreover, increasingly organizations launched for other purposes assume developmental roles. By the late 1980s, for example, ninety U.S. cities had adopted sister cities in Nicaragua alone, and many were providing crucial development assistance.[4] In northern New Mexico, the prospect of assistance from the privately funded National Heritage Trust in renovating old churches has served to mobilize a number of Hispanic and Native American communities. The program provides resources for hiring technical expertise and assistance in bringing in volunteers from outside the community, but community members make all important decisions and supervise work in progress. In many instances, successes in these efforts have inspired communities to identify other needs and undertake, collectively, to meet them.[5]

Real development, of the sort we are calling empowerment, will never be neat and orderly and predictable. For better or worse, consequences do not derive directly from any identifiable constellation of motives. But the same uncertainty that makes development work so frustrating also makes it intriguing, challenging, and promising.

Likewise, such development cannot be unthreatening. No matter that change be sought by peaceful means or that initial goals be modest and nonpolitical. The empowerment of "have-nots" is by definition threatening to "haves." (The most insecure people and nations are those that have the most to lose.) Its very successes will continue to attract donors and agencies whose motives are hidden and less than benign. But poor people are often rich in ingenuity and spirit. Any program that pretends to promote organization and self-help on the part of the have-nots runs the risk of being successful.

NOTES

1. Frances Moore Lappé, Rachel Schurman, and Kevin Danaher, *Betraying the National Interest: A Food First Book* (New York: Grove Press, 1987), p. 15.

2. Ibid., pp. 84–115.

3. Mexican President Carlos Salinas de Gortari called attention to this pace of privatization during an official visit to the United States in October 1989. Among the most recent enterprises to be sold off were the two national airlines and the national telephone company.

4. The author became familiar with the extensive Sister City programs in Nicaragua in the course of leading a Sister City election observation delegation there in February 1990.

5. Participants in such programs, particularly in the U.S. Southwest, but from all parts of the world as well, congregate each fall at the Peter Van Dresser Workshop on Village Development, which takes place at the Ghost Ranch Conference Center in Abiquiu, New Mexico, to exchange ideas on development needs and approaches.

About the Book and Author

As wealthy countries focus more attention on the ravages of poverty and maldistribution of the world's resources, the rationales for what is or is not done in the name of "development" have become more elaborate and abstract. And as the literature has proliferated, communication among those who approach development from different perspectives, disciplines, and professions has become more strained. In this innovative text, Jan Black argues that what is missing is "appropriate theory" that can help place the findings of social scientists and seasoned development practitioners at the service of those who would promote a more equitable and empowering approach to development.

In the first section the author presents the differing and even contradictory definitions of development and the various explanatory models and means of measurement associated with them. This is followed by an analysis of the evolution of development strategies and programs both of the First World—donor countries and organizations—and of Third World leaders, movements, and regional organizations. The author highlights key issues in the development debate of the 1990s, including ecology, refugees, debt, the informal sector, and gender roles. In a final section she addresses the process of development and illustrates, through a number of vignettes and case studies, the sometimes illusory links between motives and consequences.

At a time when theoreticians and practitioners appear to occupy different worlds and speak different languages, and when a large number of developing countries seem to be falling into an irreversible cycle of debt and dependency, this book is particularly welcome and compelling.

Jan Knippers Black teaches at the Monterey Institute of International Studies and is research professor of sociology at the University of the Pacific. Previously she has taught and supervised research at the University of New Mexico and at American University in Washington, D.C. Her many publications include *United States Penetration of Brazil* (1977), *Sentinels of Empire: The U.S. and Latin American Militarism* (1986), *The Dominican Republic: Politics and Development in an Unsovereign State* (1986), and *Latin America, Its Problems and Its Promise*, second edition (Westview, 1991).

Index